VAMPIRE FORENSICS

VAMPIRE FORENSICS

UNCOVERING

THE ORIGINS OF AN

ENDURING LEGEND

MARK COLLINS JENKINS

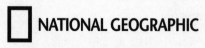

NATIONAL GEOGRAPHIC

WASHINGTON, D.C.

Published by the National Geographic Society
1145 17th Street N.W., Washington, D.C. 20036

Library of Congress Cataloging-in-Publication Data
Jenkins, Mark, 1960 July 12-
  Vampire forensics : uncovering the origins of an enduring legend / Mark Collins Jenkins.
     p. cm.
  Includes bibliographical references (p.   ).
  ISBN 978-1-4262-0607-8 (hardcover)
  1. Vampires. 2. Forensic sciences. I. Title.
  GR830.V3J44 2010
  398'.45--dc22

                        2009044631

The National Geographic Society is one of the world's largest nonprofit scientific and educational organizations. Founded in 1888 to "increase and diffuse geographic knowledge," the Society works to inspire people to care about the planet. It reaches more than 325 million people worldwide each month through its official journal, *National Geographic,* and other magazines; National Geographic Channel; television documentaries; music; radio; films; books; DVDs; maps; exhibitions; school publishing programs; interactive media; and merchandise. National Geographic has funded more than 9,000 scientific research, conservation and exploration projects and supports an education program combating geographic illiteracy.

For more information, please call 1-800-NGS LINE (647-5463) or write to the following address:

National Geographic Society
1145 17th Street N.W.
Washington, D.C. 20036-4688 U.S.A.

Visit us online at www.nationalgeographic.com

For information about special discounts for bulk purchases, please contact
National Geographic Books Special Sales: ngspecsales@ngs.org

For rights or permissions inquiries, please contact National Geographic Books
Subsidiary Rights: ngbookrights@ngs.org

Interior design: Cameron Zotter

09/WCPF/1

Contents

A Vampire in Venice, 2006

La Serenissima—"the Most Serene Republic"—is how we like to think of Venice, as she was during her golden age. The crumbling palaces, arched bridges, and exuberant churches topped by domes and campaniles all rise from that shimmering lagoon like mirages from the past. This is the Venice of our dreams.

And like all dreams, that Venice was an illusion. Today a World Heritage site, the Queen of the Adriatic attracts millions of tourists each year. Yet few of them cross the sparkling waters and visit Lazzaretto Nuovo Island, with its old quarantine station, high-walled hospital, and cemetery heaped with the bones of 16th- and 17th-century plague victims. Life had not always been serene in La Serenissima, as Dr. Matteo Borrini understood only too well. While directing an excavation of that cemetery in 2006, the forensic anthropologist had become puzzled by one broken skeleton in particular. Why, he wondered, had someone four centuries ago thrust a brick between its jaws? His quest for an answer, supported by a 2009 grant from the National Geographic Society, led him to uncover the legend of the "chewing dead," plague-causing vampires stopped only by ramming stones or bricks in their mouths.

They are but one of the many species that have arisen from the long, evolving history of vampires. Follow their wandering tracks, and you will wend ever deeper into the nightmarish mazes of our most remote past.

CHAPTER ONE

TWILIGHT ZONE

YOU OPEN THE DOOR. There in the gathering twilight he stands, caped and fanged and glowering. In the streets behind him, spectral legions are on the move. It's Halloween, and the visitor on your doorstep must be all of six years old.

Vampire chic—it's everywhere. It's cool to be one, and certainly cool to love one, judging from the popularity of a certain number-one best seller that ends with the heroine wishing to become a vampire like her boyfriend. Now that they've come out of the coffin, so to speak, vampires have never appeared more sensitive or romantic. They have never been more heroic. And they have never been portrayed more sympathetically. One is wickedly reminded of something Dr. Lewis Thomas once wrote about biological parasites: "[T]here is nothing to be gained, in an evolutionary sense, by the capacity to cause illness and death. Pathogenicity may be something . . . more frightening to them than us."

American popular culture is in the midst of a vampire epidemic that has sunk its fangs into fashion, film, television, and publishing. Vampire trappings—pallid complexions, eyeliner, dark clothing—have outgrown their origins in the Goth look and crossed into the mainstream. The vampire is the "new James Dean," no less a cultural arbiter than the *New York Times* pronounced on July 2, 2009. And on Sunday nights, admittedly after the family hour, millions of television viewers curl up for the latest installment of vampire mayhem set in the bayous of Louisiana as HBO broadcasts its decidedly Grand Guignol series, *True Blood*.

It's all irresistibly good fun. As folklorist Michael Bell once put it, "What better food for the imagination than a creature that incorporates sex, blood, violence, shapeshifting, superhuman power, and eternal life?"

Yet it is also a bewildering maze, a hall of mirrors in which—as, upon reflection, you'd expect—the original vampire is hard to see. Take Dracula: You can't find the porter for the baggage. As the *Irish Times* related when the novel of that name, written by its native son, was selected as the Dublin: One City, One Book choice for 2009:

> He's advertised throat lozenges, cat food, insecticide, pizza, security systems ("protects you against uninvited guests"), and many other products. He has been a breakfast cereal—Choculas. In the 170-odd

movies in which Dracula was featured as a main or lesser character, he has been black (*Blacula*, 1972), deaf (*Deafula*, 1975, the first-ever "signed" film), gay (*Dragula*, 1973), a porn star (*Spermula*, 1976), and senile (John Carradine keeping his teeth in a glass by the side of the bed in *Nocturna*, 1978). He has met Billy the Kid, Abbott and Costello, the Hardy Boys and Nancy Drew, and the Outer Space Chicks.

Nor can we forget Bunnicula, the vampire rabbit who sucks plant juices, and Vampirella, the redoubtable comic-book heroine of the planet Draculon, where all the rivers once ran with blood. Dracula himself, in altered form, has even had his own comic-book adventures: Marvel's *Tomb of Dracula* and *Dracula Lives* turned the Transylvanian count into a kind of reverse superhero, impossible to kill or to keep down; at one point in his Marvel-ous escapades, the cartoon Dracula marshals a vampire army on the moon and launches his minions like missiles at Earth—all the while sporting his trademark evening clothes and cape.

At least there he was recognizably evil. In Fred Saberhagen's novel *The Dracula Tape*, he is not only more sinned against than sinning; he's not even guilty. The death and damage the main character wreaks in the original novel is instead laid at Abraham Van Helsing's feet; in Saberhagen's sympathetic reimagining, the stubborn vampire slayer is so deluded by superstition that he, not Dracula, leaves a trail of disaster behind him.

The vampire also enjoys a special prestige in the pantheon of ghouls. Given the choice, says Peter Nicholls, editor of the *Encyclopedia of Science Fiction*, it's better to be a vampire than a werewolf or a zombie:

> Vampires are aristocratic, drinking only the most refined substances, usually blood. In the iconography of horror, the vampire stands for sex. The werewolf, who stands for instability, shapeshifting, lack of self-control, is middle-class and lives in a dog-eat-dog world. The zombie or ghoul, who shambles and rots, is working-class, inarticulate, dangerous, deprived, wishing only to feed on those who are better off; in the iconography of horror the zombie stands for the exploited worker.

The vampire, who started life like that shambling zombie, has climbed the social ladder. In fact, he has pulled a very neat switch. Once the epitome of corruptible death, he has become a symbol of life—of life lived more intensely, more glamorously, and more wantonly, with bites having become kisses, than what passes for life on this side of the curtain. Add to that a practical immortality if you behave yourself, and one can appreciate the temptation always dangling before the Sookies and the Bellas and the Buffys to cross the line. In Chelsea Quinn Yarbro's *Hotel Transylvania*, the very human Madelaine spells out the vampire appeal: "To know your freedom. To live in the blood that is taken with love ... I can hardly wait!"

Such characters are on the verge of deliberately choosing a fate their fictional ancestors would have considered abhorrent beyond all imagining. It's not just the old high-school romance given a new edge. It's not always rooted in the yearning to escape the strictures of society and convention. It also reflects a darker, more profound disenchantment, as Yarbro's Madelaine explains to her undead lover:

> In my reading of history there is war and ruin and pillage and lives snuffed out with such profligacy that my breath is stopped by the senselessness of it. One would think that all humanity had nothing better than to feed on its own carrion. I have thought as I read these books, how many worse things there are in this world than vampires.

It wasn't always that way. Vampires certainly have evolved—to the point where it is now difficult, but still tantalizingly possible, to catch a glimpse of their terrible origins.

NATURAL AND SUPERNATURAL

Dracula may still hold court as king of the undead, but his reign is nearing its end, thanks largely to the explosion of competing vampire epics since the 1970s. Those curious enough to trace the circuitous path by which the vampire arrived at his present mainstream status must survey these fictional worlds: By pushing the old fiend in new directions, they will reveal much about his origins.

Dozens of modern sagas are out there, each attractively packaged and each boasting its own ardent fan base. The offerings differ as radically from one another as Charlaine Harris's *Southern Vampire* series (aka *True Blood)* distinguishes itself from Stephenie Meyer's *Twilight* series, or as both of those are set apart from the 20 volumes (and counting) of Chelsea Quinn Yarbro's Saint-Germain epic, named for the enigmatic 18th-century French count and occultist who is her vampire hero. Comic book or novel, television spin-off or movie, most contemporary vampire tales honor the legend's supernatural grounding.

Rarely has the web of imagined vampire history been spun more intricately than in the ten novels, published from 1976 to 2003, that constitute Anne Rice's *Vampire Chronicles.* Embodying a night world of Dickensian proportions, its leading characters—and there are many, including Lestat, Louis, Armand, David, and the child vampire Claudia—represent an alternate society, riven by the same jealousies, angers, resentments, and affections, organized along the same hierarchical lines, as those of the day world. With each new title Rice unveiled, the history of her elaborate alternative universe grew ever more complex. Ultimately it would come to embrace both God and the devil.

And where did it begin? In ancient Egypt, circa 4000 B.C., when an evil spirit fused with the flesh of Queen Akasha, mutated her heart and brain, and made her the world's first vampire. Akasha then turned her husband, King Enkil, into the second one, and their predations gave rise to the whole dark brood to come. That creation myth typifies many found throughout the vampire's fictional universe—a remarkable number of which coalesce in ancient Egypt, traditionally viewed as the cradle of all black arts.

Although the vampire was busily accumulating this vast store of supernatural histories, might he have garnered some natural ones as well? Science fiction, in fact, has extended and elaborated the vampire myth for years. Shunning the supernatural, it has offered ingenious empirical explanations of the phenomenon, ranging from bizarre psychological conditions to alien species to literal vampire plagues.

The vampire as alien may first have appeared in two works by French science-fiction pioneer Gustave Le Rouge. In *Le prisonnier de la planète Mars* (1908), the thought power of Hindu Brahmans transports a young engineer to the fourth planet from the sun. There he discovers a fantastic biota that includes bat-winged, blood-drinking humanoid creatures. Some of them hitch a ride back to Earth, unleashing the epic battle that fills the pages of the sequel, *La guerre des vampires* (1909).

Miriam Blaylock, in Whitley Strieber's now-classic *The Hunger* (1981), is a vampire born in ancient Egypt several thousand years ago. As the daughter of Lamia, the child-devouring monster of myth, Blaylock suffers an eternal loneliness that has driven her to take a succession of mortal lovers as companions. Thanks to blood transfusions, she can keep each paramour alive for a few centuries, but then each withers away. The story pivots on the attempts of a human doctor to solve Blaylock's dilemma, with the result that her uniqueness is explained not thematically but hematically: Her blood evinces a unique biochemistry that identifies Blaylock as the sole representative of an entirely separate species.

No science-fiction tale of vampires, however, has exerted the influence of Richard Matheson's 1954 novel *I Am Legend*. After a virulent bacterial pandemic overwhelms the world and turns humans into cannibalistic vampires, the one man who remains immune—thanks to a previous inoculating bite from a vampire bat—struggles to comprehend the nature of the plague as he fends off vampire attacks all the while. Because it has been filmed three times—with Vincent Price in *The Last Man on Earth* (1964), with Charlton Heston in *The Omega Man* (1971), and with Will Smith in *I Am Legend* (2007)—the premise sounds familiar today. (It also inspired the *Night of the Living Dead* zombie movies.) But Matheson's was the first fictional depiction of vampirism as the result of physiological disease, not supernatural forces. It gave an ironic twist to an old pattern: Where vampires once were believed to cause epidemics, here epidemics spawn vampires.

Bram Stoker's *Dracula* (1897) first popularized the word *nosferatu* as a synonym for "vampire," supposedly gleaning it from Romanian folklore. Though linguists have been unable to trace the word's precise origins, popular etymology has sometimes ascribed it to the Greek *nosophorus,* or "plague carrier."

The one constant in the evolution of the vampire legend has been its close association with disease. Little surprise, then, that medicine in recent decades has stepped forward to offer its own explanations of vampiric origins.

One of the most frequently cited medical causes of vampirism is rabies. In 1998, for example, Spanish neurologist Dr. Juan Gomez-Alonso made a correlation between reports of rabies outbreaks in and around the Balkans—especially a devastating one in dogs, wolves, and other animals that plagued Hungary from 1721 to 1728—and the "vampire epidemics" that erupted shortly thereafter. Wolves and bats, if rabid, have the same snarling, slobbering look about them that folklore ascribed to vampires—as would a human being suffering from rabies.

Various other symptoms reinforce the rabies-vampire link: Dr. Gomez-Alonso found that nearly 25 percent of rabid men have a tendency to bite other people. That almost guarantees transmission, as the virus is carried in saliva. Rabies can even help explain the supposed aversion of vampires to garlic: Infected people display a hypersensitive response to any pronounced olfactory stimulation, which would naturally include the pungent smell of garlic.

Rabies may also harbor the roots of the vampiric fear of mirrors. Strong odors or visual stimuli trigger spasms of the face and vocal muscles of those with rabies, and this in turn induces hoarse groans, bared teeth, and a bloody frothing at the mouth. What rabies sufferer would not shrink from such a reflection? Indeed, Dr. Gomez-Alonso stated, in the past, "a man was not considered rabid if he was able to stand the sight of his own image in a mirror."

Rabies might furnish yet a third explanation—this one for the vampire's nocturnal habits and erotic predations. That's because the disease afflicts the centers of the brain that help regulate sleep cycles and the sex drive—keeping you up all night, quite literally, as some reports suggested that rabies victims had intercourse up to 30 times a night. Before French microbiologist Louis Pasteur discovered a vaccine for rabies in 1885, the ultimate outcome of the disease was mania, dementia, and death.

If rabies doesn't persuade you of vampirism's physiological underpinnings, there is always porphyria, a rare genetic disorder leading to a breakdown in the production of heme—the red pigment in blood. Dr. David Dolphin, a Canadian biochemist and expert in blood proteins, argued this case on talk shows and at scientific conclaves (including the annual convention of the American Association for the Advancement of Science) in the 1980s. Carried by one in about every 200,000 people, porphyria typically lies dormant in the bloodstream. Once it awakens, however, it makes the skin hypersensitive to sunlight, causing lesions so severe they may destroy the sufferer's nose or fingers. Gum tissue wastes away, making teeth appear more prominent—and therefore fanglike. Some porphyria victims may even grow hairier.

It is easy to imagine how such a victim, able to move about only at night, might be taken for a werewolf. Furthermore, whereas heme injections help alleviate symptoms today, Dr. Dolphin speculated that the afflicted individuals in times past might have been driven by instinct to drink blood. If they ingested enough of it, the heme might be absorbed directly into the bloodstream through the stomach wall. And porphyria as an epidemiological rationale for vampirism offers this bonus: Too much garlic is known to destroy the functioning of heme in the liver. So a porphyria victim, believing himself prey to a vampire and therefore moved to surround himself with garlic, might by that very action inadvertently trigger the latent porphyria in his own loved ones (the disease runs in families). Once he died, and his relatives sickened in turn, it might look to all the world like the handiwork of vampires—the latter being widely supposed to prey on their next of kin.

Porphyria had its day in the sun before giving way to pellagra. First recognized in 1735, pellagra results from a deficiency of niacin and tryptophan, usually caused by a diet overly dependent on maize, or corn. Corn was planted widely across southern and eastern Europe, where the climate was warm enough for it to flourish. And that's where pellagra became endemic.

One of the disease's early symptoms is hypersensitivity to sunlight. The skin becomes inflamed, then turns scaly and parchment-thin *(pelle agra* is Italian for "rough skin"). The breath turns foul, while the tongue thickens and blackens from bleeding sores. Brain neurons degenerate, leading to unpredictable behavior: insomnia, irritability, dementia, and violence. Diarrhea brings on weight loss, refusal of food, and anorexia. Left untreated, pellagra is invariably fatal—and in the few years before dementia leads to death, the anemia caused by gastrointestinal bleeding lends its sufferers an undeniable look of the "living dead."

Pellagra was thus a wasting disease, and the "main reason for identifying a person as a vampire," according to Drs. Jeffery and William Hampl, "was a wasting disease." In a 1997 issue of the *Journal of the Royal Society of Medicine*, the Hampls suggest a link between the incidence of pellagra in eastern Europe and the flourishing of the vampire legend there. Because most peasant families would likely suffer from similar nutritional deficiencies, at the moment one member died from pellagra, others would doubtless be sickening too. As the surviving relatives wasted away, this dynamic might be taken as evidence of the recently dead's having returned to prey on the living. When corpses were disinterred and examined for signs of vampirism, one telltale sign was said to be a ring of cornmeal around the mouth.

Insightful as they are, such white-jacketed explanations are ultimately unconvincing. Some element seems to have been left out—some aspect that, if not exactly supernatural, still partakes of the terrible.

A Strange, Batlike Figure

Despite the speculations of our scientifically inclined era, few nonfiction works on vampires have had the impact of those written in the 1920s by a medievally minded English reverend—Augustus Montague Summers. In his passages, one can almost hear the thundering cadences of the Inquisition itself:

> Throughout the whole vast shadowy world of ghosts and demons there is no figure so terrible, no figure so dreaded and abhorred, yet dight [adorned] with such fearful fascination, as the vampire, who is himself neither ghost nor demon, but yet who partakes the dark natures and possesses the mysterious and terrible qualities of both. . . . Foul are his ravages; gruesome and seemingly barbaric are the ancient and approved methods by which folk must rid themselves of this hideous pest. . . .

Summers (1880–1948) looked nowhere near as fierce as he sounded. Plump and pink, he sported gray curls resembling tresses and was not above applying a touch of makeup to accentuate his hazel eyes. Novelist Anthony Powell borrowed those eyes and lent them to his fictional Canon Paul Fenneau in *Hearing Secret Harmonies*: "They were unusual eyes, not only almost unnaturally small, but vague, moist, dreamy, the eyes of a medium. The cherubic side, increased by a long slightly uptilted nose, was a little too good to be true."

Perhaps so, for Summers was nothing if not a man of contradictions. Growing up in comfortable surroundings near Bristol, he was baptized in the Church of England but was already drifting toward Roman Catholicism by the time he graduated from Trinity College, Oxford. Yet, his earliest poetry was openly and very erotically gay. What's more, around the age of 20, he quite probably officiated at a black mass—a blasphemous ceremony mocking the Christian mass. He was a member of the British Society for the Study of Sex Psychology. And in 1920, Summers published the first treatise in English on the Marquis de Sade—noting, in his defense, that it was exclusively "for Adult Students of Social Questions."

Although Summers wore the attire of a Catholic priest, it is unlikely he was ever ordained one. While he was serving a curacy near Bristol, questions had arisen about inappropriate behavior with choirboys. But Summers *had* been ordained a deacon in the Church of England, giving him every right to be addressed as "Reverend"—however irreverent he usually chose to be.

Montague Summers made his first big literary contributions in the study of English Restoration drama—an irreverent corpus if ever there was one, given that late 17th-century plays abounded with naughty situations and double entendres. Summers was an outstanding editor, issuing multivolume editions replete with scholarly appurtenances. He also turned out to be a superb producer and a leading light of London's Phoenix Theatre. From 1918 to 1923, according to one friend, this "strange, bat-like figure," dressed like a medieval cleric, cloak and all, was the talk of the London theatergoing world.

Besides the stage, Summers cherished another love: the Gothic novel, that hoary 18th-century genre featuring brave young ladies, evil European noblemen, ghosts, and spooky old castles. He had even written about Jane Austen by the day in the mid-1920s when London publishing company Kegan Paul asked him to produce two volumes on witchcraft to round out its History of Civilization series. Summers quickly churned out *The History of Witchcraft and Demonology* (1926) and *The Geography of Witchcraft* (1928). "I have endeavoured to show the witch as she really was," he wrote in the first of those works, "an evil liver, a social pest and parasite; the devotee of a loathly and obscene creed; an adept at poisoning, blackmail, and other creeping crimes; a member of a powerful secret organization inimicable to Church and State; a blasphemer in word and deed . . . battening upon the filth and foulest passions of the age."

His juvenile dabblings in the occult may have rattled Summers, but here he found his voice. Soon he was translating the notorious *Malleus Maleficarum*, or the "Hammer of Witches"—the 15th-century witch hunters' handbook that was the bible of the Inquisition. When all these outpourings proved remarkably successful, his publisher approached him with another idea: Might he perform encores with tomes on vampires and werewolves? Summers accepted.

"During the year 1927," recalled his colleague, Father Brocard Sewell, "the striking and sombre figure of the Reverend Montague Summers, in black soutane and cloak, with buckled shoes—à la Louis Quatorze—and shovel hat, could often have been seen entering or leaving the reading room of the British Museum, carrying a large black portfolio bearing on its side a white label showing, in blood-red capitals, the legend, 'VAMPIRES.'"

The fruits of heaving his portly carcass up and down those august steps were *The Vampire: His Kith and Kin* (1928) and *The Vampire in Europe* (1929), two of the most frequently quoted and referenced books in the literature of vampire studies. Even a casual perusal of their pages exhibits the breadth of Summers's learning and the depth of his scholarship—that is, if paragraph after paragraph of untranslated Latin, German, or French does not prove too annoying. That might be Summers in a mischievous mood; quite likely, however, they betray his haste. Like many authors making a living from their pens, he was a tad overbooked in the 1920s. At times, his vampire chronicles have the feel of anthologies in the making, with his portentous pen bridging the gaps between great chunks of text plucked straight from his sources. And the reverend's professed antipathy to undue color in his narrative—"If a yarn is to be told for the shudder and the thrill, well and good; let the ruddle be thick and slab. But write the rubric without ambiguity that this is high romance to follow"—was a stricture honored more in the breach than in the observance.

What is the modern reader to make of the reverend's conclusion that such things not only *were* but still *are?* That vampires remain an incarnate evil, as real as the buckle on his shoe? "To the feather-fool and lobcock, the pseudo-scientist and materialist," he thundered, "these deeper and obscurer things must, of course, appear a grandam's tale." On the contrary, wrote Summers, they emblematize a "funda-mental truth, which, however exaggerated in expression and communication, essentially informs the vampire-tradition." Summers went so far as to suggest that vampires were as active in his day as they had been in the past, and that the public would have occasion to share his view had their attacks not been "carefully hushed up and stifled" by the authorities.

Many of the reverend's acquaintances dismissed this as all part of his act—the persona he adopted before the reading public. It is true that, after completing *The Were-wolf* (1933), Summers turned away from overtly supernatural topics and returned only to cobble together an anthology or two when he needed money. Instead, he concentrated his efforts on his two-volume history of the Gothic novel, *The Gothic Quest*, his last major literary contribution before his death a decade later.

It's possible that Summers genuinely believed his every claim about vampires. That might have been how he projected—or exorcised—his own forbidden impulses. We will never know, for he kept the veil tightly closed. As rare-book scholar Timothy d'Arch Smith once observed of Summers, "We are dealing very likely with a deeply divided personality."

HYSTERICAL HIGHGATE

The long shadow of Montague Summers falls squarely on the incredible story of London's Highgate Cemetery haunt-ings—a vivid example of the appeal that "true-life" vampire tales continued to exert on the human imagination in the late 20th century.

Once a favorite Victorian burial ground, Highgate Cemetery, which sprawls across a low rise overlooking north London, is a city of the dead that displays the marvelous funerary architecture of the 19th century: elaborate tombs, aspiring statues, pitying angels, pedimented mausoleums, and fantastic Egyptian avenues. By the 1960s, however, Highgate was ceding its dominion to forces both natural and preternatural. Ivy vines were creeping up the headstones, while foxes and badgers were found denning in the graves. Vandals had pushed over monuments, exposing coffins; coffins had lost their lids, exposing skeletons; weeds and wildflowers disguised dangerous sinkholes. So gloomily picturesque was the place that Hammer Studios used the cemetery as a setting for its *Taste the Blood of Dracula* in 1969.

This particular story, however, began two years earlier, in 1967, when two teenage girls were walking home one evening from their nearby convent school. Passing the entrance to Highgate, they saw what they afterward described as graves opening and the dead arising therefrom. One of the girls, Elizabeth Wojdyla, soon reported nightmares in which something evil, something with the snarling visage of a beast but the body of a man, was trying to get in through her bedroom window. Soon other people were spying ghostly figures in and around the cemetery: spectral cyclists, a classic woman in white, and a man in a hat. The most common sighting was a tall, floating figure with burning eyes.

Once the local paper got wind of this, all manner of ghost hunters and thrill seekers descended on Highgate. Among them was Seán Manchester, president of the British Occult Society. This self-styled psychic, an admirer of Montague Summers, eventually became the presiding bishop of something called the British Old Catholic Church. Manchester was convinced that a vampire lay behind the plethora of spectral sightings. Granted permission to examine Elizabeth Wojdyla, he detected symptoms of pernicious anemia—and what looked like two small puncture wounds in her neck. He sprinkled her room with holy water, salt, and garlic, after which her condition improved. Eventually—understandably—Wojdyla left the area.

Meanwhile, Manchester had begun talking to the press. He apparently told them his Vampire Research Society had found evidence that, back in the 18th century, one of the people who owned the house that once stood on Highgate's site was a mysterious gentleman of eastern European extraction who had arrived in London around the time a vampire craze was sweeping the Balkans. Well, perhaps the paper embroidered Manchester's account somewhat, for by the time it surfaced in the February 27, 1970, edition of the *Hampstead and Highgate Express,* that 18th-century immigrant had become a King Vampire—a medieval nobleman who once practiced black magic in Romania, was brought to London by coffin, and was buried somewhere in the neighborhood. The activities of modern Satanists, Manchester reportedly claimed, had unintentionally wakened the noble. He must therefore be hunted, staked, beheaded, and burned.

That was just what hip, youthful "swinging London" needed. On Friday the 13th of March 1970, Manchester told a television news team that he intended to perform an exorcism later that night in Highgate. Shortly thereafter, hundreds of revelers looking to make a night of it poured over the cemetery walls and swarmed among the darkened gravestones. Police officers were recalled from leave to stem the influx. Meanwhile, Manchester had managed to enter a tomb to which he had been led by "Lusia"—a sleepwalking young psychic with bite marks on her neck. There he found only empty coffins, which he seeded with garlic. No exorcism that night.

What we are told next comes entirely from Manchester. Later that summer, as Highgate hysteria reached a fever pitch, "Lusia" in a trance led him to one of the grand if crumbling mausoleums in the cemetery. Inside, he found a great coffin and, removing its heavy lid, discovered that it held a vampire, "gorged and stinking with the life blood of others," its "glazed eyes [staring] horribly, almost mocking me." A companion dissuaded Manchester from staking the corpse, however, so he contented himself with pronouncing an exorcism and resealing the vault with garlic-impregnated cement. But the vampire's sleep must have been disturbed, for it decamped for the basement of a nearby mansion—the "House of Dracula," the press gleefully nicknamed it—where, in 1977, the intrepid vampire hunter tracked it down and staked it, reducing it to slime.

This saga, believe it or not, continued until 1982, when Manchester claimed to have driven the final stake through the heart of the last remaining Highgate vampire. "Lusia," it seems, had died in the interim and was buried in a graveyard nearby. Encountering her in a dream, however, Manchester had realized that "Lusia," having been bitten by the vampire, was thereby infected herself—and destined to return from the dead. Visiting her grave site one autumn evening, Manchester was not at all surprised to confront what he described as a large, spiderlike creature about the size of a cat. After being dispatched in the time-honored fashion, the spider reverted to the form and figure of "Lusia." Manchester returned her to her grave.

What you make of this astonishing story may depend on how high your eyebrow is cocked. It has been recounted in numerous newspaper and magazine articles, providing grist for a shelf load of books. It has appeared regularly in television documentaries and soon will be dramatized in a feature film. And in a sign that even vampires are now online, the harrowing happenings of Highgate are frequently—and vigorously—debated on the Web.

The truly mind-boggling thing is that so many of the story's details could have been lifted straight from the pages of *Dracula*: the eastern European nobleman arriving in London by coffin, the vampire trying to enter the bedroom window, the sleepwalking "Lusia" (like the sleepwalking Lucy of the novel), and finally the vampire hunters breaking in to tombs (as Van Helsing did with his assistants).

Whatever else it might be, this is life imitating art on an epic scale.

PREY IS PREY

It's but a step from playing at vampires to believing you really are one. One night in 1959, when 16-year-old Salvatore Agron went on a killing spree while dressed like Béla Lugosi, he was actually the leader of a Hell's Kitchen, New York City, gang called the Vampires; the stabbings, though of innocent people, were motivated by gang warfare. In 1996, however, when 16-year-old Roderick Ferrell and four accomplices killed the parents of his girlfriend, it was a vampire fantasy run amok. These devotees of the role-playing game *Vampire: The Masquerade* had convened what the press later called a "cult," cemented by cutting themselves with razor blades and drinking one another's blood.

When Ferrell and his fellow "vampires" were arrested, a copy of Anne Rice's *Queen of the Damned* was found in their car. The film version of that book was later implicated in a murder in Scotland, where Allan Menzies, 22, so lost himself in its fictional world that he convinced himself he was a vampire. Menzies killed his best friend, ate part of his skull, and drank some of his blood. In 1998, Joshua Rudiger, 22, certain that he was a 2,000-year-old vampire, slashed the throats of homeless people in San Francisco because, he said, he needed a drink of blood. "Prey is prey," he supposedly told investigators.

Role-playing is one thing, compulsion something else. In 1886, German psychiatrist Dr. Richard von Krafft-Ebing published his pioneering *Psychopathia Sexualis*, the first compendium of case studies to illustrate the wide range of paraphilias, or what were once called sexual perversities. Case number 32 described a 26-year-old man who experienced an erotic charge from the taste of blood, stemming from a childhood incident in which he had impulsively sucked the blood from a housemaid's cut finger:

> From that time on, he sought, in every possible way to see and, where practicable, to taste the fresh blood of females. That of young girls was preferred by him. He spared no pain or expense to obtain this pleasure.

Case number 48 described a young man with scars covering his arms who had sought out Dr. von Krafft-Ebing. It turned out they were incidental to his wife's lovemaking technique: "[H]e first had to make a cut in his arm," Krafft-Ebing reported, and "she would suck the wound and during the act become violently excited sexually." In the good doctor's opinion, this case recalled the "widespread legend of the vampires, the origin of which may perhaps be referred to such sadistic facts."

Might "clinical vampirism," as the compulsion to drink another person's blood has been diagnosed, really explain the origin of the vampire legend? Certainly it describes a syndrome of pathological behaviors easily correlated to that legend. *Vampirism* was once rather widely used to describe activities ranging from the ingestion of blood to cannibalism. These would have to be irresistibly compulsive behaviors, almost ritualized, the discharge of which would afford only temporary relief. That spelled trouble if such compulsions manifested themselves in psychopathic personalities—especially in people who appeared to be functioning perfectly normally.

In 1931, as Americans packed movie palaces to watch Béla Lugosi play Dracula, German audiences were treated to a far darker tale. Fritz Lang's *M* is a film about a serial killer of children, purportedly inspired by a series of horrible crimes that had plagued the dark days of postwar Germany.

In the mid-1920s, after police in Hanover began dredging human bones from the nearby Leine River, a hunt was undertaken for what the press called the "Vampire of Hanover" or the "Werewolf of Hanover." Eventually police arrested a petty crook, stool pigeon, and sexual predator named Fritz Haarmann (1879–1925). Under the impulse of what his accomplice called his "wild, sick urges," Haarmann had picked up at least 27 young men—homosexual prostitutes, runaways, and street urchins—had taken them to his squalid room, and had gnawed through their throats during sex to kill them. He then butchered their remains, cast the offal and bones into the river, and sold the meat and clothes in the city's various markets. Not surprisingly, after a sensational two-week trial, Haarmann was beheaded in April 1925.

Five years later, it was the turn of the "Vampire of Düsseldorf" to make headlines. In late 1929, numerous bodies of women and girls—slashed and sometimes decapitated by knives and scissors, or bludgeoned by hammers—surfaced with sickening frequency in and around Düsseldorf. Eventually, a lifelong criminal named Peter Kürten (1883–1931) was arrested and charged with the murders. A neat man not devoid of feeling, he seemed unable to resist the compulsion toward sexual gratification that he found in the spurting blood of his victims. As he was led to the guillotine, Kürten supposedly asked the prison psychiatrist whether, "after my head has been chopped off, will I still be able to hear, at least for a moment, the sound of my own blood gushing from the stump of my neck?" He hoped that might be "the pleasure to end all pleasures."

On the other hand, the story of John Haigh (1909–1949), dubbed the "Acid Bath Murderer," is a bad B movie, complete with drums of sulfuric acid—Haigh's means of concealing the perfect crime. Haigh killed at least six people (he claimed nine) in or around London and dumped each body into an acid bath. After a day or two, the ghastly concoction had reduced each victim to a sludge that could easily be poured down a manhole. Eventually the police caught him, and found the remains of three human gall bladders and a partial set of dentures in one of the drums. At his trial, the nation was horrified to witness the offhand, even affable manner with which Haigh confessed to having cut his victims' throats in order to enjoy a revivifying glass of blood.

His testimony earned him the inevitable sobriquet of "Vampire of London." If it was an attempt to cop an insanity plea, the prosecutor saw through it: Haigh, whose primary motive seems to have been the petty one of theft, was hanged in August 1949.

Then there was a deaf-mute laborer named Kuno Hoffman who, in 1972, gained notoriety as the "Vampire of Nuremberg" after he shot a kissing couple one night and lapped up their blood—blood that was much fresher than the blend he habitually imbibed from buried corpses, several dozen of which he had disinterred expressly for that purpose.

An even more stomach-churning case was that of Richard Trenton Chase. The "Vampire of Sacramento," as he was branded, was a classic paranoid schizophrenic. He not only believed that his pulmonary artery had been stolen, but also was convinced that either UFOs or Nazis were poisoning his soap dish. Chase also showed a compulsion for drinking blood, which precipitated a killing spree. He murdered two infants and two adults—accompanied by disembowelments, the eating of brains, and the quaffing of blood from used yogurt cups—before the police finally caught up with him. Rather than face the electric chair, Chase poisoned himself.

This litany of latter-day vampirism seems inexhaustible indeed. But it may have reached its grisly apogee in 1980, when 23-year-old James Riva, using gold-plated bullets, shot and killed his 74-year-old disabled grandmother. Riva then drank her blood as it spurted from the wounds. He had attacked her, Riva later claimed, because the voice of a vampire had instructed him to do so. Riva further declared that he himself was a 700-year-old vampire who required his grandmother's blood to survive, only to discover that she was too old and dried up to serve that purpose. In 2009, he came up for parole. It was denied.

Such instances might be multiplied a hundredfold. Yet it is dangerous to ascribe too much to clinical vampirism, if only because the evidence for it gets flimsier the further back in history one searches. On a hilltop near Čachtice in Slovakia, for example, stand the moldering ruins of a castle. We shall never know exactly what happened there, for thick slabs of legend have accreted around an elusive core of fact. But this was once the home of Elizabeth Báthory (1560–1614), whom history has crowned the "Blood Countess."

The legend is well known: In 1600 or thereabouts, while having her hair combed, Báthory reacted violently to the clumsy brushwork of a maidservant and struck her, bloodying her nose. When a drop of the blood fell on the countess's hand, the skin beneath it soon turned magically younger. So the 40-year-old widow, anxious to maintain her fabled but fading youth and beauty, instigated a decade of butchery, arranging for upward of 650 virgin girls to be killed and drained to replenish her rejuvenating blood baths.

Much of that may be fabrication, of course. What's certain is that the King of Hungary presided over the trial of a Countess Báthory, who was convicted on 80 counts of murder. Seventeenth-century rules of evidence being less stringent than those in force today, many of the rumors—of

33

lesbian orgies, of torture, and even of cannibalism—are hard to prove. Crimes occurred, to be sure, yet it is difficult if not impossible to ascertain their true nature and extent (650 victims seems preposterous).

Accusations of witchcraft dominated Báthory's trial, leading two of her maidservants and her majordomo to be executed in horrific fashion. Báthory was spared their fate because she hailed from a noble family that had long produced rulers of Transylvania; but hers was a Protestant clan in a Catholic kingdom, and her sons-in-law—the ones who brought charges against her in the first place—stood to inherit her estates. Whatever the truth behind the gruesome tales, in 1611, the Blood Countess was walled into a suite of rooms in her castle, never to leave again. Her dark and solitary confinement ended only with her death four years later.

In far too many other instances, by contrast, the sad facts of clinical vampirism are undeniable. Its grisly catalogue of symptoms underscores a point made by Dr. Philip Jaffé, a psychiatrist, and Frank DiCataldo, an expert on juvenile delinquency, in 1994: Clinical vampirism brings together "some of the most shocking pathologic behaviors [ever] observed in humanity."

But does clinical vampirism help explain the historical origin of vampires, as Dr. von Krafft-Ebing suspected? Or might it be merely a convenient label to affix to the file drawer of case histories? Wherever the truth lies, the dramatic convergence of myth and reality contained in those histories is a sufficient goad to seek a better understanding of vampire origins.

BENEATH THE CLAY

"Everything must have a beginning," Mary Shelley writes in her foreword to *Frankenstein*, "and that beginning must be linked to something that went before." Anyone seeking the origins of the vampire legend must be prepared to uncover one beginning after another. Because the vampire is found mostly in story—perhaps *only* in story?—he must be tracked, as if down through the levels of an archaeological dig, from one layer of story to another. One must pass from the night world of the present, with its glittering abundance of images, and wend ever downward through the night worlds residing in printed books, or on incunabula, or inscribed on parchment and vellum, or dwelling in generations of folktales whispered in chimney corners, until only the tombs and the bones remain. That might be the ultimate level, the one—as the poet William Butler Yeats put it—where "under heavy loads of trampled clay / Lie bodies of the vampires full of blood; / Their shrouds are bloody and their lips are wet."

CHAPTER TWO

"The Very Best Story of Diablerie"

"It is a story of a vampire," begins the note accompanying the leather-bound presentation copy delivered to former prime minister William Gladstone on May 24, 1897:

> It is a story of a vampire—the old medieval vampire but recrudescent today. It has I think pretty well all the vampire legend as to limitations and these may in some way interest you. . . . The book is necessarily full of horrors and terrors but I trust that these are calculated to "cleanse the mind by pity & terror." At any rate there is nothing base in the book, and though superstition is [fought] with the weapons of superstition, I hope it is not irreverent.

Because Bram Stoker happily flogged his own books, many people in his wide circle of acquaintance received similar leather-bound volumes—and similar notes. The mystery was how the bluff, burly 50-year-old found time to write his stories and novels while working full-time as manager of the Lyceum Theatre, the toniest stage in London's West End. No doubt his friends were busy too, for they didn't acknowledge his gift. Arthur Conan Doyle, however, pulled out his pen and jotted a note: The 38-year-old creator of Sherlock Holmes, already one of Britain's most popular authors, declared *Dracula* the "very best story of diablerie that I have read in many years."

Late Victorian London, in the imagination's eye, is a sea of jostling hansom cabs, an ocean of bobbing bowler and top hats. It is the largest and most important city in the world, the seat of majesty and the pivot of empire. Yet it cloaks some very real horrors: Jack the Ripper—the midnight stalker who slashes the throats of women and occasionally eviscerates their bodies—is out there somewhere. Nevertheless, the figure standing near Hyde Park Corner one day in the early 1890s, watching the teeming millions passing by, will have a far greater impact on the world's apprehension of horror, despite the fact that he inhabits only the world of a novel. For Dracula is the original Undead—a name that Bram Stoker coined, and nearly used as the book's title—personifying the irruption of an archaic, supernatural terror in the complacent heart of civilization. His special diablerie is that, once loosed, he is not easily repressed:

My revenge is just begun. I spread it over centuries
and time is on my side.

If we are to understand the vampire, Dracula is the wolf
in the path. All roads lead to him.

LANDS OF SUPERSTITION

At the close of the 19th century, anyone in England who
aspired to write a vampire story could count on his readers to
know something about them, for books had made vampires
familiar figures. Hardly a literate household did not possess an old Gothic romance or two, whose stories were set
in gloomy castles and featured malevolent noblemen with
Italian-sounding names. Most homes would also have a copy
of John Keats's "Lamia" or Samuel Taylor Coleridge's *Chris-*
tabel, poems with ancient or medieval settings that featured
exotic, vampirelike beings.

Stoker's genius did not run to poetry; but for a grimly
realistic setting, he might have found inspiration in his own
heritage. Bram Stoker was born in Clontarf, Ireland, in 1847,
when the seven-year potato famine was at its worst. Eventually, it would kill nearly a million people and send a million
Irish emigrants to the New World on overcrowded "coffin ships." Stoker's mother could also recount the horrors of
the 1832 cholera epidemic, which had ravaged her native
Sligo; she recalled its victims' being buried in mass graves
while they were still alive. There were also Celtic tales of

bloodsucking *dearg-due*, and English tales (Stoker moved to London in 1879 to work for celebrated actor Henry Irving) such as that of the "vampire" of Croglin Grange in Cumberland: a brown, shriveled, mummified creature—discovered in a vault littered with overturned coffins and spilled corpses—that was said to have terrorized the neighborhood before being burned in the 17th century.

A vampire story, however, cried out for a central or eastern European setting, because that's where the legend had long been flourishing. That was also the region where four empires had long been grinding against one another. The Ottoman Empire, centered on modern Turkey, still embraced the Near East and most of the Balkans, as it had for four centuries—"the Balkans" being a case of geographic synecdoche, taking a part for the whole, for the Balkan Mountains in Bulgaria were just one in a series of ranges rising above the peninsula between the Adriatic and Aegean seas. The various nationalities that lived in this "Turkish Europe"—Romanians, Serbs, Bulgarians, Bosnians, Albanians, Macedonians, and Greeks—had been gradually winning their independence, though not without a fight. Hidden behind that Ottoman veil, however, was one of the most deeply rooted vampire folklores to be found anywhere.

The Russian Empire also harbored deep deposits of *upyr*, or "vampire," folklore, mined by such writers as Nikolai Gogol and Aleksey Tolstoy, uncle of another and more famous author of the same surname. Germany, too, would make a tempting choice for a vampire-story setting. When Jane Eyre, for instance, in Charlotte Brontë's 1847 novel of the same name, compared the madwoman in the attic to "that foul German spectre—the Vampyre," she was associating the monster with a tradition in German literature that had begun a century earlier, in 1748, when Heinrich August Ossenfelder wrote his poem "Der Vampir." The genre included such masterpieces as Johann Wolfgang von Goethe's "The Bride of Corinth," in which the eponymous heroine wanders from her grave to seek "the bridegroom I have lost / And the lifeblood of his heart to drink."

Stoker had certainly read Gottfried Bürger's *Lenore,* one of the most popular ballads of the late 18th century. It is the tale of a spectral soldier who returns from the wars one moonlit night to claim his bride. Spiriting her away by horseback, then galloping past the ghosts that haunt gallows and graveyards, he leads her to their marriage bed: his coffin, all "plank and bottom and lid" of it, in Hungary. That ballad's most quoted line, *"Die Toten reiten schnell"*—"The dead travel fast"—not only became proverbial, meaning that the dead are soon forgotten, but also appeared in a deleted early chapter of *Dracula*, where the four words were carved on Countess Dolingen's tombstone.

Nevertheless, Stoker chose to set his vampire story in the sprawling, polyglot Austro-Hungarian Empire, ruled by the Hapsburg dynasty from the fin de siècle Vienna of Strauss waltzes and Freudian psychoanalysis. He initially placed his castle in the mountainous Duchy of Styria, the setting for

Carmilla, an 1872 vampire story he admired whose author, Sheridan le Fanu, was a Dublin writer and newspaper editor who had once employed Stoker. In *Carmilla,* Styria was a Gothic landscape of limitless forests, lonely castles, and ruined chapels. And there Stoker's own fictitious castle might yet be standing had he not come across an article written by the English-born wife of an Austrian cavalry officer; her account described an even more remote corner of the empire, one tucked away in the isolation of the Carpathian Mountains: "Transylvania might well be termed the land of superstition," Emily Gerard had written in a July 1885 article for *The Nineteenth Century,* "for nowhere else does this curious crooked plant of delusion flourish as persistently and in such bewildering variety.

"It would almost seem," Gerard continued, "as though the whole species of demons, pixies, witches, and hobgoblins, driven from the rest of Europe by the wand of science, had taken refuge within this mountain rampart, well aware that here they would find secure lurking places, whence they might defy their persecutors yet awhile."

Bristling with caves and strange rock formations—Gregynia Drakuluj (Devil's Garden), Gania Drakuluj (Devil's Mountain), and Yadu Drakuluj (Devil's Abyss)—the landscape and superstitions that Gerard described must have appealed to Stoker, because he soon moved his castle to Transylvania. That decision would place the "land beyond the forest" (the literal translation of *Transylvania)* squarely on the imaginative map of Europe. Even though its paper position would change after World War I, when the Austro-Hungarian Empire was broken up and Transylvania was ceded to Romania, it was thanks to *Dracula* that Transylvania, not the Balkans, came to be identified in most people's minds as the vampire's true native land.

". . . THE MASTER İS AT HAND."

Dracula is an epistolary novel, told through letters, journal entries, and even telegrams—all of which should warn astute readers to be alert to the phenomenon of the unreliable narrator. It is also a sprawling novel, overflowing with characters and incidents. But we might glance anyway at how Count Dracula is portrayed throughout the course of the narrative.

The story opens with the journey of Jonathan Harker, a young English attorney, to Count Dracula's castle, situated in a remote reach of Transylvania. There, Harker is to help the count buy some property in London, where the nobleman hopes to move. As the castle door swings open, Harker beholds a seemingly courteous, if slightly creepy, figure:

> Within, stood a tall old man, clean shaven save for a long white moustache, and clad in black from head to foot, without a single speck of colour about him anywhere. He held in his hand an antique silver lamp, in which the flame burned without a chimney or globe of any kind, throwing long quivering

shadows as it flickered in the draught of the open door. The old man motioned me in with his right hand with a courtly gesture, saying in excellent English, but with a strange intonation, "Welcome to my house! Enter freely and of your own free will!" . . . I am Dracula, and I bid you welcome, Mr. Harker, to my house. Come in, the night air is chill, and you must need to eat and rest. . . .

His face was a strong—a very strong—aquiline, with high bridge of the thin nose and peculiarly arched nostrils; with lofty domed forehead, and hair growing scantily round the temples, but profusely elsewhere. His eyebrows were very massive, almost meeting over the nose, and with bushy hair that seemed to curl in its own profusion. The mouth, so far as I could see it under the heavy moustache, was fixed and rather cruel-looking, with peculiarly sharp white teeth; these protruded over the lips, whose remarkable ruddiness showed astonishing vitality in a man of his years. For the rest, his ears were pale, and at the tops extremely pointed; the chin was broad and strong, and the cheeks firm though thin. The general effect was one of extraordinary pallor.

Despite his unsettling appearance, Dracula seems at times almost cozily domestic—playing coachman and maid and cook, making the bed and setting the table, chatting all night about different subjects, eager to practice his English.

In his library—apparently the only cheery room in a long-disused castle—he reclines on a couch, studying English travel guides or the London Directory, *Whitaker's Almanack,* and other reference books that must have been hard to obtain in that faraway place. He is a proud old dragon, proud of his Szekely origins, believed at the time to be descendants of Attila the Hun:

> Ah, young sir, the Szekelys, and the Dracula as their heart's blood, their brains, and their swords—can boast a record that mushroom growths like the Hapsburgs and the Romanoffs can never reach. The warlike days are over. Blood is too precious a thing in these days of dishonourable peace, and the glories of the great races are as a tale that is told.

But this Transylvanian *Gemütlichkeit* doesn't last. Dracula, who has coarse hands with hairy palms and long nails "cut to a sharp point," is simply repulsive. "As the Count leaned over me and his hands touched me," Harker writes, "I could not repress a shudder. It may have been that his breath was rank, but a horrible feeling of nausea came over me, which, do what I would, I could not conceal." Harker is trapped in the castle.

One moonlit night Harker looks out the window and sees the count crawling down the castle wall like a human fly. On another night, wandering about in the warren of dust-shrouded rooms, he lapses into a trance and nearly falls prey to three horrifying female figures. Harker is saved by the timely entrance of Dracula, who tosses the harridans a sack containing a human infant for them to feed upon. Eventually, Harker finds his way into the crypt; it is daytime, and all the castle's vampires are at rest in their coffins:

> There lay the Count, but looking as if his youth had been half renewed, for the white hair and moustache were changed to iron-grey; the cheeks were fuller, and the white skin seemed ruby-red underneath; the mouth was redder than ever, for on the lips were gouts of fresh blood, which trickled from the corners of the mouth and ran over the chin and neck. Even the deep, burning eyes seemed set amongst swollen flesh, for the lids and pouches underneath were bloated. It seemed as if the whole awful creature were simply gorged with blood; he lay like a filthy leech, exhausted with his repletion.

Once Dracula arrives in England, the diablerie begins in earnest. Most of the action takes place in Whitby, a Yorkshire resort on the North Sea, and London, where it centers on a lunatic asylum that happens to be next door to the old abbey that Dracula has succeeded in purchasing. The count is rarely seen, and when Harker chances to glimpse him standing among the teeming crowds near Hyde Park Corner one day, seemingly unaffected by sunlight, he looks much younger.

For the most part, however, Count Dracula is an ominous, even insidious presence, taking the form of mist or a bat. Clearly, he has become demonic; to cover his arrival at Whitby by sea, for example, he raises a storm that hurls not only giant waves against the sands but also the Russian schooner on which he traveled—a derelict, because he left all the crew dead behind him.

Stoker must have read in the pages of Emily Gerard about the Scholomance—the iniquitous school, said to exist in the Carpathians, where the devil himself taught magic spells, the language of animals, and all the secrets of nature. One in ten students, Gerard had written, were "detained by the devil as payment, and mounted upon an *Ismeju* (dragon) he becomes henceforward the devil's aide-de-camp, and assists him in 'making the weather,' that is, in preparing the thunderbolts."

Dracula is even portrayed as a kind of infernal god. The demented Renfield, an inmate at the asylum who seeks eternal life by eating flies and spiders—"for the blood is the life," as the Old Testament puts it—can sense when "the Master is at hand," always referring to him (at least on the page) in the uppercase: "I am here to do your bidding, Master. I am Your slave, and You will reward me, for I shall be faithful...."

Alarmed by the gathering evil, a dedicated group of men—including Harker, the asylum director Dr. Seward, the nobleman Arthur Holmwood, and the American sportsman Quincey Morris—have gathered around Dr. Abraham Van Helsing, the canny Dutch prototype of the vampire slayer. Their mission is to protect two young ladies—Holmwood's fiancée, Lucy Westenra, and Harker's new bride, Mina—from Dracula's attacks, for the count is that most dangerous figure in Victorian England: the sexual predator.

"Your girls that you all love are mine already," Dracula gloats. "And through them you and others shall yet be mine, my creatures, do my bidding and to be my jackals when I want to feed." The most horrifying part of the novel might be the count's seduction and consequent killing of Lucy, followed by her return as the "Blooper lady," a monstrous vampire who preys on children. Holmwood, her ex-fiancé, is forced to drive a stake through her heart on what would have been their wedding night—a scene never overlooked by Freudians.

Dracula then directs his attention to Mina Harker. After one terrifying night when he fed upon her, Mina recalls that he "pulled open his shirt, and with his long sharp nails opened a vein in his breast. When the blood began to spurt out, he took my hands in one of his, holding them tight, and with the other seized my neck and pressed my mouth to the wound, so that I must either suffocate or swallow some to the—Oh, my God! My God! What have I done?"

Much has been read into this scene, too; but in the context of the story, the exchange of bodily fluids gives Dracula the power to control Mina's thoughts and actions. Yet, Mina can read Dracula's mind in return—a facility she uses to advantage, though it becomes a race to stop Dracula before he can completely subject Mina to his spell.

The hunters have a second mission, too: They must head off a vampire epidemic in London. When he was trapped in the count's Transylvanian castle, Harker unwittingly helped a monster escape to London; in that city for centuries to come, Harker agonizes, might this fiend "satiate his lust for blood, and create a new and ever-widening circle of semi-demons to batten on the helpless"? Dr. Van Helsing later underscores the point: "But to fail here, is not mere life or death. It is that we become as him; that we henceforward become foul things of the night like him, without heart or conscience, preying on the bodies and souls of those we love best."

As the race to save Mina and the city gets tighter, the suspense builds—and the story gains even more momentum. Autumn and the vampire hunters simultaneously close in and destroy one by one the coffins Dracula has scattered about the city. The count is forced to abandon London. While he boards the ship that will deliver him and his remaining coffin to a Romanian port, the hunters use the latest technology—trains, telegraphs, even a telephone—to monitor the vampire's movements.

As the sun sinks on a winter evening outside the gates of Castle Dracula, the hunters finally catch the hunted. A battle ensues with Dracula's gypsy carriers. With Mina looking on, Jonathan and the mortally wounded Quincey Morris attack the vampire king just as he is about to emerge from his coffin:

The sun was almost down on the mountain tops, and the shadows of the whole group fell upon the snow. I saw the Count lying within the box upon the earth, some of which the rude falling from the cart had scattered over him. He was deathly pale, just like a waxen image, and the red eyes glared with the horrible vindictive look which I knew so well. As I looked, the eyes saw the sinking sun, and the look of hate in them turned to triumph. But, on the instant, came the sweep and flash of Jonathan's great knife. I shrieked as I saw it shear through the throat. Whilst at the same moment Mr. Morris's bowie knife plunged into the heart. It was like a miracle, but before our very eyes, and almost in the drawing of a breath, the whole body crumbled into dust and passed from our sight. I shall be glad as long as I live that even in that moment of final dissolution, there was in the face a look of peace, such as I never could have imagined might have rested there.

The dragon is slain. Mina is restored to health and sanity. The community regroups, the fallen achieve heroic status, and the threat of a vampire epidemic vanishes.

CHILDREN OF THE NIGHT

Dracula, in his second death, had hardly vanished before his dust was fertilizing what would become, over time, a many-branched tree. It is not so much *Dracula* the novel as its progenies—the many stage and screen versions—that have had the greatest impact on the popular conception of the vampire.

Somehow the story is never quite the same, however. It has been dramatized, bowdlerized, and sensationalized, truncated here and expanded there. Characters have been dropped or conflated, while *Dracula*'s female leads have been interchanged with promiscuous abandon.

It all started within a few weeks of the novel's publication, when Bram Stoker—having written the book, no doubt, with one eye on a possible stage adaptation—gave it a shot himself. Actors from the Lyceum Theatre gave a public reading of Stoker's redacted play to secure its copyright for the future. But when stage star Henry Irving showed no interest, it was laid aside and never picked back up.

Ironically, the man who did more than anyone else to bring *Dracula* to the world had grown up just a few doors away from Stoker's childhood home. Hamilton Deane was a stagestruck youth who had joined Henry Irving's company in 1899, when he was only 19 years old. By his early 20s, Deane was brimming with ideas for bringing *Dracula* to the boards. It would take him nearly two decades to achieve his goal.

In 1922, German film director Friedrich Murnau made a film loosely based on *Dracula*. He called it *Nosferatu* (an old, folkloric name for the vampire), changed the main character to Count Orlock, shifted the location to Bremen, and brought in a chilling cast of rats to carry bubonic plague into the city.

Bram Stoker had died in 1912, but when his widow, Florence, got wind of Murnau's changes, she tried to shut the production down. Royalties from *Dracula* were her main income, and she found the German film a thinly disguised pirating of the novel. So she sued.

After spending the better part of a decade embroiled in legal wrangles, Florence came close to having the negative and all prints of the film destroyed. Much like its protagonist, however, *Nosferatu* proved exceedingly difficult to kill. One print of the film escaped destruction—much to the benefit of cinematic history, for *Nosferatu* ranks among the finest vampire films ever made: Max Shreck's creepy, cadaverous Orlock—all teeth and talons—sets a standard of excellence rarely matched by Dracula's later interpreters.

During this protracted legal battle, Hamilton Deane won permission from Florence Stoker to mount a stage adaptation of *Dracula*. Unable to find a competent playwright, Deane wrote it himself. He condensed the sprawling novel to fit within the limitations of a three-act play on a single set. This meant dropping the Transylvanian scenes; all the action would now take place in London.

Crucially, Deane made the count presentable for the drawing room. For the first time in his long career, Dracula donned evening clothes, underscoring his new identity as a suave eastern European nobleman. Because Dracula was only seen in the evening, he never appeared without sporting this garb—which thus became inextricably linked with his name.

Deane's most distinctive refinement of Dracula's image was the addition of an opera cloak with a high collar. This served a variety of purposes. Not least of them was providing cover for the vampire's vanishing act: With his back turned to the audience and cast members holding his cloak, Dracula could drop through a trap door in the stage and "disappear." That was only one of the special effects—which also included a trick coffin—that thrilled provincial audiences across England. Despite being scorned by West End critics at its 1927 London debut, *Dracula* would enjoy huge success for many years. It was among the last plays performed at Stoker's old Lyceum Theatre before it closed in 1939.

By then, *Dracula* had crossed the Atlantic. Rewritten once more to streamline the cast and plot even further, *Dracula* became a 1927 Broadway hit starring an immigrant Hungarian actor named Béla Lugosi. The tall, handsome, former Austro-Hungarian infantry officer with the mesmeric gaze had been born in 1882, near the border of Transylvania. Lugosi spoke barely a word of English upon his arrival in the United States after World War I, and he never lost his strong Hungarian accent. That seemed only to enhance his appeal as Count Dracula: The play ran for 261 performances in New York City before going out on tour. Then Universal Studios bought the movie rights.

The 1931 film version of *Dracula*, directed by silent-film veteran and former circus performer Tod Browning, is a curious movie to watch today. Though stagy and old-fashioned, its lack of musical accompaniment makes its long silent moments—when only the hiss and crackle of the soundtrack can be heard—chillingly effective.

And then there is Lugosi. His eyes burning, his dark hair slicked back, his attire immaculate, he stands in his cobweb-enshrouded castle and, as wolves howl outside, intones in that incomparable accent, *"Listen* to them, children of the night. What *music* they make."

For millions of people, this was their first encounter with a vampire, and audiences everywhere ate it up. Over the next 80 years or so, countless actors would play Count Dracula—Christopher Lee (who in the 1950s was the first to sport fangs), Jack Palance, Louis Jourdan, Frank Langella, Gary Oldman—but every portrayal invited comparisons with the image of Lugosi that was so deeply ingrained in the popular imagination. And most of them performed the role in evening clothes and cape.

The actor who forged the mold could never quite escape the clutches of the character he had fashioned. Béla Lugosi died in 1956. When he was buried in Hollywood's Holy Cross Cemetery, graveyard to the stars, he was wearing Dracula's cape.

Ravenous Harpies

That opera cloak had an additional critical function: When the actor lifted his arms, the cape spread out into the semblance of bat wings. Wolves may have been his familiars, but Dracula preferred to take the form of a bat.

When Lucy Westenra's increasingly anemic condition is linked to the presence of a giant bat outside her bedroom window, Morris (the American sportsman in the tale) recalls an experience on the South American pampas: "One of those big bats they call vampires had got at [the mare] in the night, and, what with his gorge and the vein left open, there wasn't enough blood left in her to let her stand up, and I had to put a bullet through her as she lay."

Bats have long been associated with the powers of darkness. Streaming out of their underworld caverns at twilight, their leathery wings and hideous faces have long been appropriated for depictions of devils.

A new twist was added to immemorial bat lore in the 16th century, when conquistadors returned from tropical America bearing lurid tales of bats "of such bigness," Pietro Martyre Anghiera wrote in 1510, that they "assaulted men in the night in their sleep, and so bitten them with their venomous teeth, that they have been . . . compelled to flee from such places, as from ravenous harpies."

These *vampiros,* as they came to be called, were accused of all kinds of predatory activities. By the time his *Explorations of the Highlands of Brazil* was published in the 1860s, Captain Richard Francis Burton could sum up in one sentence three centuries of loathing for vampiros: "It must be like a Vision of Judgement to awake suddenly and to find on the tip of one's nose, in the act of drawing one's life blood, that demonical face with deformed nose, satyrlike ears, and staring saucer eyes, backed by a body measuring two feet from wing-end to wing-end."

If anything, that was likely a case of mistaken identity. The vampiro was long assumed to be the large, fearsome-looking

monster that Swedish botanist Carolus Linnaeus had classi-
fied in 1758 as *Vampyrum spectrum*, or the spectral vampire
bat. Similar giant bats, in the Far East as well as in tropical
America, were also given names such as *Vampyrops, Vampy-
rodes,* or *Vampyressa.*

Because the activities of bats were cloaked by darkness, it was centuries before naturalists discovered the truth
about the creatures: Of the hundreds of bat species worldwide, ranging in size from the five-foot Malay kalang to the
tiny bumblebee bat of Thailand, only three were bloodsuckers, and they were all in the New World. Among the "false
vampires" and "ghost bats" spread from Africa to Austral-
asia, some are said to occasionally decapitate their victims.
But the primary culprit responsible for vampire-bat legends
is an unprepossessing little fellow called *Desmodus rotundus,*
found from Argentina to Mexico.

Measuring little more than a foot from wingtip to wingtip, *Desmodus* generally settles on the necks of livestock
for a midnight meal. But it is a stalker, too, quietly alighting near slumbering humans and stealing up to an exposed
toe or nose. Its bite, at most a slight tingle, rarely disturbs a
sleeper, and from the tiny puncture, a long tongue laps up the
blood. Although only rarely a killer, *Desmodus* can weaken
horses and cattle by repeated bloodlettings. It can also carry
rabies—though that would not be discovered until the 1920s.

What the bats lacked in size, however, they made up for
in conjured ferocity. Probing the same Brazilian highlands
that Burton had two decades earlier, British explorer James

W. Wells was warned by Indians in the 1880s that "vampire bats . . . were said to exist in such numbers in a part of the valley of the Sapão, about sixteen miles away, that it is there impossible for any animal to live through the night."

Those must have been the fearsome creatures Quincey Morris had in mind. The *Vampyrum spectrum* of the American tropics hunts only rodents, small birds, and insects. The spectral vampire bat, however, still haunts our nightmares, still beats at our bedroom windowpanes. Before Bram Stoker, cartoonists had occasionally used bats to depict political vampires, and as we shall see in the next chapter, sensationalistic "penny dreadful" novels had likewise employed them as vehicles. But not until *Dracula,* and that grimly flapping stage prop that dominated its 1931 incarnation in film, did the bat become the symbol it is today: the most widely recognized iconographical emblem of the vampire.

Dragon or Devil?

And finally there is the matter of that name.

Had Bram Stoker not come across a copy of William Wilkinson's *An Account of the Principalities of Wallachia and Moldavia,* in which he learned of a 15th-century Romanian prince named Dracula who fought the Ottoman Turks, we might today have a forgotten 19th-century novel about a Count Wampyr—the author's original choice for his main character's name. Happily for literary posterity, however, Stoker responded positively to the name Dracula: *Drakul* is

Romanian for "dragon," but it also means "devil," as in those distinctive Romanian landscape features Gregynia Drakuluj (Devil's Garden) and Gania Drakuluj (Devil's Mountain).

That may be all there is to it. Stoker might never have known about Dracula's other Romanian sobriquet, *Vlad Țepeș,* or "Vlad the Impaler."

A portrait of Vlad Țepeș hangs in Ambras Castle, Austria, alongside one of a man so hirsute he resembles a werewolf and another of a person who lived with a lance sticking through his head. Vlad won a place in this notorious "Chamber of Curiosities" because he was considered the archetype of the bloodthirsty ruler. This reputation had been fostered by a series of best-selling German pamphlets that depicted him, in one case, dining serenely while severed limbs covered the ground and all around him bodies hung from sharpened stakes.

Over the past several decades, a fierce debate has erupted about whether Stoker knew of Vlad's bloodthirsty reputation. If so, did he model his Dracula directly on that historical figure? The debate is not merely academic; many, if not most, tourists visiting Romania today equate Count Dracula with Vlad the Impaler. And many, if not most, Romanians object to this misconception, for Vlad is a national hero as the defender of their country. Celebrated in poems and ballads, his statue gazes over Romanian towns, and his visage has appeared on commemorative stamps. Under no circumstances, therefore, should Vlad be associated with the world's most famous vampire. Some locals, perceiving a business opportunity, shrug their shoulders and opt not to sweat the distinction; others justifiably resent the Vlad-vampire conflation as a myth imposed on them from outside.

No doubt both camps are correct. Whatever sins may be attributed to Vlad, however, vampirism cannot be counted among them. True, Vlad was accused in the old German pamphlets of dipping his bread in the blood of his victims. But it's unlikely that Bram Stoker knew much about him. The general traits of Stoker's vampire seem to have been settled when he was still known as Count Wampyr; from Vlad, Stoker borrowed only the more dramatic name—and perhaps the hint of a proud military past. Otherwise, the fictional Count Dracula owes more to the traditional villain of Gothic romance than he does to the historical prince of Wallachia.

That prince—he was actually a *voivode*, generally translated as "prince" or "duke"—was born in Transylvania in 1431. That was the year when Vlad's father, in charge of guarding the Carpathian passes against the Ottomans, was summoned to Nuremberg, Germany. There, the Holy Roman Emperor inducted Vlad's father into the Order of the Dragon, a military fraternity dedicated to defending Christendom against the Muslim Turks. As voivode of Wallachia, he became known as Vlad II Dracul, or "Vlad the Dragon." When his son eventually succeeded him as voivode, he naturally became Vlad III Dracula—"the Dragon's Son."

Part of southern Romania today, Wallachia is a grassy plain bordered on the east and south by the Danube River and on the north and west by the Carpathians. As the gateway to further Ottoman expansion in Europe, it lay fully exposed to the Turkish forces patrolling the river's south bank. Therefore, Vlad II, despite his oath to the Order of the Dragon, bought a tenuous security by paying annual tribute to the sultan. He also surrendered his two younger sons as hostages for good behavior.

By the time Vlad III Dracula became voivode in 1456, he was nursing two long-standing grievances: His years of captivity had imbued in him a deep hatred for the Turks, and the murder of his father and older brother (the brother had been buried alive) had induced a lasting enmity toward their killers, the Wallachian boyars, or nobles.

This is where the stories of Vlad's barbarism begin. In 1457, he invited the boyars to Tirgoviste, the Wallachian capital, for an Easter feast. There, Vlad sprang a trap: He impaled those complicit in the murders of his father and brother. The others he marched off to the mountains to build his castle, where he worked them until their clothes fell from their bodies in tatters and they were forced to slave away naked.

Emboldened by his coup, Vlad terrorized the Transylvanians between 1459 and 1460, impaling 10,000 in the city of Sibiu, and 30,000 boyars and merchants in Brasov—allegedly in a single day. In the midst of these killing fields, a table was laid so that boyars who escaped punishment might join Dracula for an alfresco feast. Unfortunately, one of his guests could not stomach the spectacle; the nauseating odors of the rotting corpses, the Impaler noticed, seemed to overcome the man. The sensitive noble was therefore impaled on a stake higher than all the rest, thus permitting him to die above the stench.

Two monks passing through Wallachia were accosted by Dracula, who asked them if his actions might be justified in the eyes of God. The first monk more or less told him what he wanted to hear. The second one, however, condemned his actions as reprehensible. In most German pamphlets depicting this episode, the honest monk is hoisted aloft while the cowardly one is rewarded. In most Russian pamphlets, by contrast, the honest monk is spared.

In another tale of savagery, two ambassadors arrive from a foreign court and decline to remove their hats in the presence of Dracula. Vlad thereupon orders that their hats be nailed to their heads.

There are dozens of such stories, and most of them are clearly exaggerated. This is not to suggest that executions did not take place—death by impalement was a custom in eastern Europe and among the Turks—but the numbers and incidents are almost certainly inflated. A typical impalement seems to have involved hitching a horse to each of a victim's legs and by those means pulling him slowly onto the point of a horizontal greased stake, driving it through the rectum and running it up through the bowels. The stake with its gory burden was then hoisted into a vertical position. Done correctly—if that is the word for it—the agony of death might be prolonged for hours. Whatever method was employed, impalement was unquestionably labor- and resource-intensive: It demanded time, men, horses, and wood. Vlad's forces were never very large, and although he had access to abundant timber in the Carpathians, most of Wallachia was steppe.

The Forest of the Slain

Menaced by the Turks to his front and by rebellious nobles to his rear, bled by German merchants in Transylvania monopolizing trade and ignoring his customs duties, Vlad, cruel though he might have been, had a motive for ruthlessness. On the other side, German pamphleteers, informed by refugees that German merchants were being persecuted, had every reason to depict Vlad as a bloodthirsty sadist. In any event, as owners of newly invented printing presses quickly discovered, sensationalism sold.

We are on firmer ground, thanks to Ottoman chronicles, when war between the Wallachians and the Turks resumed between 1461 and 1462. Here, Dracula proved himself an exceptionally able commander, raiding deep into Ottoman territory and waging daring attacks by night. But his forces were greatly outnumbered, and as he retreated deeper and deeper into Wallachia, he engaged in scorched-earth tactics: burning villages, poisoning wells, and sending plague victims in disguise to sow pestilence in the Turkish camps.

The harried Janissaries crumpled beneath their crescent banners. The final straw was apparently the sight of the "Forest of the Impaled"—the rotting corpses of thousands of Turkish prisoners that stood outside the city of Tirgoviste. Sultan Mehmed II, never one to quail easily, was so sickened by the sight of ravens nesting inside the putrid carcasses that he abandoned the campaign and returned to Constantinople.

Savior or psychopath, it seems unjust that Vlad would be arrested soon afterward by the Hungarian king. Preferring a policy of appeasement toward the Ottomans, the king schemed to replace Vlad with his younger, pro-Turkish brother. After that brother died in 1476, Vlad returned to Wallachia and resumed his campaign against the Turks. Forsaken by his allies, however, he was forced to march with fewer than 4,000 men against a far larger Ottoman army. It would be his last fight.

Yet, even Vlad's death and burial have their legendary elements. Dracula was most likely assassinated by a Turkish agent in the marshes of the Vlasia Forest near Bucharest in the last days of 1476. By all accounts, his severed head was then sent to the sultan. Whatever further indignities may have been inflicted on his body, it was said that monks eventually claimed it and ferried it across the deep waters of a lake to the island monastery of Snagov (reminiscent of the dying King Arthur's journey to the Isle of Avalon). There, Vlad was buried in the chapel, at the foot of the altar beneath a stone slab polished smooth by generations of piously shuffling feet.

Between 1931 and 1932, Romanian archaeologist Dinu Rosetti removed that slab and found a tomb containing nothing but scattered animal bones and a few bits of ceramic. Then another—and nearly identical—stone slab was discovered near the church doors. After removing it, Rosetti beheld a coffin covered by the remains of a gold-embroidered purple pall. Inside the coffin was a headless skeleton. It was clothed in disintegrating silk brocade, and in place of the missing skull were the remains of a crown, worked in cloisonné and studded with turquoise. There was also a ring such as the sort of token a 15th-century noblewoman might have bestowed upon her favorite knight—and indeed one did bestow such a prize on Vlad II Dracul, the father, on the night of his 1431 investiture in the Order of the Dragon, and he is believed to have passed it on to his son.

Rosetti, understandably, believed he had found Dracula's remains. Perhaps some abbot, discomfited by the notion of that man so near the altar, had moved the remains from their original crypt? However they got there, they were now transported to the Bucharest History Museum. From there, they disappeared during the chaos of World War II. They have not been seen since.

And the head? Reportedly, it was taken to Constantinople and displayed high atop a stake before the sultan's palace, where all might behold the Impaler impaled.

THE DEAD TRAVEL FAST

"There sleep the mighty dead as in life they slept," as James Joyce wickedly described the vaults of Dublin's St. Michan's Church, where for centuries the morbid and the curious have filed down the narrow corridors to gaze at the bodies. Sprawled and tumbled among the narrow arched galleries are coffins; here and there an arm or a leg protrudes, as if its owner were frozen in the very act of crawling out. Bodies dry and mummified, with taut skin and spidery hair, are everywhere on display. One is said to be a nun who died four centuries ago. Another, six and a half feet tall, is reputedly that of a crusader, cut in half to fit the coffin. Several—hanged, drawn, and quartered—belonged to leaders of the 1798 Irish Rebellion. One, no one knows why, had its hands and feet severed. Everywhere lies a deep and muffling dust—proof, if more were needed, that dust thou art, and to dust shalt thou return.

Legend has it that Bram Stoker visited these vaults as a child, or perhaps that his family had a crypt here, and that the vivid impression they made on the young boy found expression in the adult author's description of the vaults beneath Castle Dracula. Whether that connection is apocryphal or not, Stoker was not interested in letting his remains molder time out of mind in the sterile air of a magnesium limestone vault. When he died in 1912, he chose not dust to dust, but ashes to ashes.

Cremation had been a legal option for only ten years. Yet, public disgust with unhygienic graveyards had become a rising tide in the 19th century, culminating in 1884, when an eccentric physician named William Price, who strutted about from time to time in a druid's costume, was arrested for incinerating the body of his young son, Jesus Christ Price. His acquittal finally overturned the old Judeo-Christian abhorrence of cremation, and in 1902, it was legalized in Britain. Shortly thereafter, the Italianate doors of

Golders Green Crematorium, the first such establishment in London, opened for business. Bram Stoker was among its early customers.

That way, the dead travel fast indeed. Yet, Dracula went to dust, not ashes, even faster, in the twinkling of an eye—and with a sigh of relief, readers could close the book, the irruption of the supernatural healed over, the imagination cleansed by "pity & terror." After all, it was only a story of a vampire.

CHAPTER THREE

GATHERINGS FROM GRAVEYARDS

FOR DECADES TO COME, 1816 would be known as the Year Without a Summer. In the previous April, Mount Tambora had erupted on the Indonesian island of Sumbawa, filling the atmosphere with ash and blocking enough of the sun's rays to trigger temporary climate change around the world. In Boston some 15 months later, snow fell in July. In Europe, an incessant cold rain blanketed much of the Continent, confining a small circle of English poets and intellectuals inside the Villa Diodati, their rented lodgings on the shores of Lake Geneva.

Lord Byron, 28, and Dr. John Polidori, 20, Byron's personal physician and traveling companion, had been joined by Percy Bysshe Shelley and his lover, 18-year-old Mary Godwin, along with her half sister, Claire Claremont, who was secretly carrying Byron's child. Throughout the long, storm-swept June nights, they passed the time with conversation and books. By the glow of the hearth and the flicker of candlelight, Mary later recalled, the friends discussed ghosts and vampires and the "nature of the principle of life." "Perhaps a corpse would be reanimated," she remembered, for "galvanism had given token of such things." Recent Italian experiments in galvanism, or applied electricity, purportedly showed that supplying current to a corpse could prompt it to behave in strange ways: clenching its fists, for instance, blowing out candles, or sitting up in its coffin.

On the night of June 16, as violent thunderstorms cracked overhead, Byron read from a volume of ghost stories called *Fantasmagoria*. One tale in the collection told of a "reanimated" dead girl whose body, when her grave was opened a year after her death, showed no signs of corruption.

That spooky evening gave rise to the world's most famous ghost story contest. Perhaps the electricity in the air sparked to life the conceptions that eventually gave birth to the two most influential reanimated corpses in literature: Frankenstein's monster and the vampire.

ENTER THE VAMPYRE

Lord Byron drafted the original sketch for what became "The Vampyre." It would be the story of a mysterious nobleman who traveled to Greece, where his death would reveal, among other things, that he had been a vampire all along.

That was as far as the great poet progressed before setting the tale aside.

Doctor Polidori then picked it up. He discarded his original idea about a skull-headed lady peeping through a keyhole and fleshed out Byron's idea instead. As a writer, the doctor was not without talent; as a human being, he was touchy, petulant, envious, quick to take offense—and ultimately self-destructive. He and Lord Byron had quarreled endlessly, so as Polidori continued to create the vampire of his tale, Lord Ruthven, he modeled him on the now-hated figure of the poet. Thus did Polidori's jaundiced view of a former friend become the prototype of the literary vampire—which, in turn, has given rise to popular depictions of the vampire today.

The most lionized poet of his time, Lord Byron at first glance made a good model for a vampire. Dark and irresistibly handsome, he was, according to one former lover, "mad, bad, and dangerous to know." Even his friends, such as the dashing naval officer Edward John Trelawny, acknowledged he was "prouder than Lucifer" and flashed the "smile of a Mephistopheles." Byron stayed up all night, slept most of the day, and once used a human skull as a drinking bowl. He ate sparingly because he could not exercise; a lame leg, he said, made strenuous activity extremely painful. After Trelawny eventually saw the poet's corpse, he noticed that, beneath the magnificent torso, "both his feet were clubbed, and his legs withered to the knee—the form and features of an Apollo, with the feet and legs of a sylvan satyr."

But it was Byron's character that caused the most controversy. Much has been made of the Byronic hero—the man who lives by his own code outside the conventions of society, the figure that novelist Charlotte Brontë called the "corsair." But to Polidori, Lord Byron resembled nothing so much as Lord Ruthven in the opening scenes of "The Vampyre"; he may have been the talk of the ballrooms, but he was also cold, arrogant, haughty, cruel, and predacious—"a man entirely absorbed in himself."

Aubrey, the story's narrator, accompanies Ruthven on a tour of Europe but grows disenchanted with him after witnessing his voracious sexual appetites and his cruel treatment of women. Ruthven has a cold, gray eye, while his skin exhibits a hue "which never gained a warmer tint, either from the blush of modesty, or from the strong emotion of passion." Furthermore, all those to whom he gave money "inevitably found that there was a curse upon it, for they were all either led to the scaffold, or sunk to the lowest and most abject misery."

In Greece, Aubrey falls in love with Ianthe, a beautiful girl who is attacked in a remote place one night and killed by a vampire. Regaining consciousness after wrestling with the fiend, Aubrey beholds Ruthven sitting there. After further adventures in Greece, bandits ambush the two men, and Ruthven is killed—or perhaps not, for the moonlight seems to revive him.

Ruthven next appears in London at an engagement party for Aubrey's sister. Because he must feed at least once a year on the "life of a lovely female to prolong his existence for the ensuing months," Ruthven preys upon Aubrey's sister, which so enrages the young man that he dies of a stroke. In the closing line of the story, evil has emerged triumphant: "Lord Ruthven had disappeared, and Aubrey's sister had glutted the thirst of a VAMPYRE!"

Soon after being published—under Byron's name, which Polidori had not approved—in the April 1, 1819, issue of the *New Monthly Magazine,* "The Vampyre" was released as a book and became a best seller. Its initial connection with Byron was undoubtedly the reason; in Germany, for example, the poet Goethe supposedly pronounced it the greatest of all Byron's works.

Whether in England or on the Continent, the saga of the rapacious Ruthven was soon in readers' hands everywhere. Within a year, it had been mounted on the stage as well. French writer Cyprien Bérard churned out a sequel, *Lord Ruthwen ou les Vampires* (1820), which was attributed to the multitalented librarian and master of the literary fantasy, Charles Nodier. Though he had nothing to do with its genesis, Nodier proceeded to give Polidori's tale a second life as a play, *Le Vampire,* though he switched the locale from Greece to Scotland. The play's success incited a run on vampires in Paris, moving one critic to lament, "There is not a theatre in Paris without its Vampire!"

Several seasons later, the fad was still going strong: An English correspondent declared that the vampire was being received with "rapturous applause at almost all the spectacles from the Odeon to the Porte St. Martin. . . . Where are the descendants of the Encyclopedists and the worshippers of the goddess Reason," he asked, when Parisians were mad for *"apparitions nocturnes"* and *"cadavres mobiles?"*

A young theater innovator named James Planché brought a version of the French play back to London. *The Vampire, or the Bride of the Isles,* opened in August 1820 at the Lyceum; it was given an incongruous Scottish setting, Planché wrote despairingly, only because the producer had "set his heart on Scotch music and dresses—the latter, by the way, were in stock." Sensationalism, then as now, ruled the pens of copywriters; the playbill stated that vampires "are Spirits, deprived of all Hope of Futurity, by the Crimes committed in their Mortal State" but nevertheless are allowed to exert "Supernatural Powers of Fascination." They cannot be destroyed, it asserted, if they kill one female each year—"whom they are first compelled to marry." (That proviso clearly didn't stick.) Planché, who invented a "vampire trap" that allowed the fiend to vanish and reappear onstage in startling fashion, got it right on his second attempt a few years later, when he set a revised version of *The Vampire* in Wallachia, using Magyar costumes.

The literary vampire had been loosed upon the world, but Polidori did not live to see its success. He died in August 1821, only 26 years old, and was buried in the consecrated ground of London's St. Pancras churchyard. The truth of his demise—that he had poisoned himself in despair over gambling debts—was covered up, for in 1821, an Anglo-Saxon law grimly matching Polidori's fevered imagination still remained on the books: It stipulated that a suicide must be buried at a crossroads, with a stake through his heart. The law was repealed two years later.

Two others who shared those hours in the Villa Diodati that stormy summer of 1816 soon followed Polidori to the grave. In July 1822, Percy Shelley drowned in a sailing accident off the coast of Italy. His body was cremated on a makeshift pyre on the beach where it had washed up—a consummation common among the pagan Greeks the poet had so admired.

Not long after the torch was applied, eyewitness Trelawny recalled, the carcass cracked open; where the skull rested on the red-hot iron bars, the "brains literally seethed, bubbled, and boiled as in a cauldron, for a very long time." When the flames subsided, there remained only ashes, some bone fragments—and Shelley's heart, somehow undamaged. "In snatching this relic from the fiery furnace," Trelawny recalled, "my hand was severely burnt. . . ."

Less than two years later, in April 1824, Lord Byron died in Greece, where he had journeyed to fight in the Greek War of Independence from the Ottoman Turks. Byron apparently succumbed to a fever—if he wasn't in fact bled to death by overzealous physicians—in swampy Missolinghi, just south of the Albanian border.

Mary Shelley would die of a brain tumor in 1851, at the age of 53. As her son sifted through her effects, he found not only locks of her dead children's hair but also a copy of Percy Shelley's *Adonais*, an elegy for the poet John Keats, who had likewise died young (though of tuberculosis). One page of the elegy was folded around a silk bag, which, when opened, contained some ashes—and a desiccated human heart.

By Hook or by Crook

Such descriptions and mementos were not unusual in the 19th century, an era of fascination with death. People would hold picnics in such imposing cemeteries as Père Lachaise in Paris—*before* visiting the morgue, one hopes. Until a halt was put to the practice in 1905, thousands of people filed through the viewing gallery of that Paris morgue each year, gaping at the ever-changing display of corpses in much the same way they gazed into the new department-store windows a few blocks away. It was a social occasion, a place to take one's girl.

A deep tremor of unease, however, often rattled this apparent aplomb. Young David Copperfield senses it in Dickens's novel of that name: So frightened is David by the biblical story of Lazarus returning from the dead that the adults are "obliged to take me out of bed, and show me the quiet churchyard out of the bedroom window, with the dead all lying in their graves at rest, below the solemn moon."

Such a tranquil aspect, though, can mask a restless grave-yard. Horrible things might be going on down there. Stories of bodies found in their coffins arched, contorted, turned prone, their shrouds ripped, or otherwise wrenched into positions of inconceivable agony fed one of the morbid phobias of the age: the obsessive terror of premature burial.

By the 19th century, it was widely believed that many people fell into catalepsies or comas—one doctor posited a "death trance"—in which their vital functions were somehow suspended without incurring death. Such people appeared quite dead, of course—the ear could detect no heartbeat, the finger felt no pulse, the mirror held below their nostrils betrayed not a trace of breath—and so they were promptly buried. Yet, they still might revive in the grave, a thought so horrible that most people could not bear to imagine it.

So before being committed to the coffin, in an age before embalming was widespread, bodies were subjected to actual tortures—fingers were dislocated, feet were burned—to provoke a response. Sometimes they were just parked someplace and left—the Duke of Wellington remained unburied for two months—until the sure signs of decomposition began to show. Nevertheless, instances piled on instances of last-minute revivals at the graveyard gate, of corpses sitting up in their coffins and looking wonderingly about them. At a time when graves were often only 18 inches deep—and sometimes only six or eight—it was not hard to believe that someone might claw his way out and appear, like Madeline Usher in Edgar Allan Poe's "The Fall of the House of Usher," a bloody, haggard, shrouded figure returned from the dead.

Those with a morbid dread of premature burial could obtain all kinds of ingenious survival devices with which to outfit one's final home. Pipes leading aboveground might be fixed to the coffin so that its inmate would not suffocate should he awaken. Or "Bateson's Belfry"—a bell attached to the coffin—could be installed, with its cord thoughtfully placed in the corpse's hand so that he might give it a pull and ring for assistance. An inexpensive measure was to enclose a shovel and crowbar inside the coffin.

Some people opted to have their hearts cut out—the theory being that whatever can't revive you on the operating table certainly won't wake you in the grave. Chopin, for example, was so terrified of premature burial that he had his heart removed; it was preserved in alcohol (rumored to be cognac) and interred in the Holy Cross Church in Warsaw.

The idea of premature burial prefigured the larger idea of reanimated corpses, and for that reason, it was inevitably invoked as an explanation for vampirism. Premature burial was also seized upon as the rationale for why some bodies found in graves were better preserved than others: They had somehow remained *alive* down there. The atrocious concept also came in handy for explaining the blood found in coffins: The victim, buried alive, had understandably severed his veins and arteries in a frantic attempt to claw his way out, finally exsanguinating himself. Indeed, the whole vampire legend might be based on dim memories of living people who had actually returned from the grave. That seemed the rational explanation, for as an 1847 article in *Blackwoods* magazine put it, "no ghastlier terror can there be than the accredited apprehension of Vampirism."

It didn't help matters, though, if the bodies were missing altogether.

"As the dark nights of the late autumn came on," wrote Victorian author Thomas Frost of the early years of the 19th century, "the fears of the timid and nervous were doubled, and persons who lived in lonely places, or in the ill-lighted parts of towns, became afraid to leave their houses after nightfall." They were afraid not of goblins, but of body snatchers.

With the growth of medical schools, and in an era before refrigeration, came the need for a constant supply of fresh corpses for dissection. In England, the bodies of executed criminals had traditionally filled this need. After the British penal code was reformed at the turn of the 19th century, however, drastically curtailing capital punishment, that source effectively dried up. The anatomists then quietly circulated word that they would pay for fresh corpses, no questions asked. Body snatchers, known by the grimly ironic sobriquet of "resurrectionists," met the new demand.

Bribing cemetery watchmen and wielding quiet wooden spades, they worked in the dead of night. They dug only at the head of a grave and left most of the dirt intact. Using a crowbar, they would snap off the coffin lid, drag out the corpse by hook or rope, strip it of its cerements, sack it, carry it to a waiting hackney coach, and trundle it to the dissecting rooms. Ghoulish, yes, but the work was profitable: A leading resurrectionist once received £144 for 12 subjects in a single night. One body snatcher, when he in turn entered the graveyard (hopefully for good), left his family nearly £6,000.

The fresher the corpse, the better the pay. This led to burking—the murderous practice of clapping a pitch plaster over a victim's nose and mouth, ensuring a speedy death that left few or no signs of the violence responsible. It also produced the freshest corpse possible. Burking was named for William Burke, an Irish ne'er-do-well who, between 1827 and 1828, with his accomplice William Hare, murdered 16 people in Scotland and sold their bodies to an esteemed Edinburgh anatomist, Dr. Robert Knox. The doctor escaped prosecution, Hare turned King's evidence, and Burke was hanged for the crimes in 1829. In a pitiless twist of lex talionis, Burke's body was then dissected at the University of Edinburgh, and his skin was made into pocketbooks and other macabre trophies. His skeleton still hangs in the college's medical school today.

Horrors such as these led to the 1832 Anatomy Act, which expanded the legal options for obtaining cadavers. Body snatching remained a problem, though a lessening one, throughout the century.

In Canada, meanwhile, resurrectionists didn't even have to dirty their hands; they simply filched corpses from mausoleums in winter, where they had been stacked up to await the spring thaw. In the United States, body snatchers were equally contemptuous of propriety: After a corpse was stolen from the grave next to that of Ohio congressman John Scott Harrison in 1878—as the son of President William Henry Harrison and the father of President Benjamin Harrison, John lay in a sealed and guarded brick vault—a vigorous search was launched for the missing body. The seekers never found the ordinary citizen, but to their shock, they discovered a loftier cadaver instead: Congressman John Harrison's body had been suspended from a rope beneath a trap door inside the Medical College of Ohio. Soon afterward, a letter writer to the Zanesville (Ohio) *Daily Courier* opined:

> . . . our ghouls are no imaginary demons. They walk about among us in broadcloth and kid gloves; physicians and surgeons, with lawyers to defend them, when caught at their obscene work; nice young men, who clerk in stores during the day, take their girls to places of amusement in the evening, and then replenish their depleted pockets by invading the cemeteries, putting hooks through the jaws of our deceased friends, sacking and carting away the bodies, and selling them to Professors of Anatomy for $25.00 a piece!

Grave robbing, though, is as old as burial itself. Long before there were professors of anatomy, there were folk healers. In an 1880 issue of the London *Daily Mail,* there appeared a notice about a "strange and horrible Wendish superstition, which has been handed down from the Pagan ancestors of the Prussians." The Wends were Slavs living among the Germans of Thuringia, where grave robbing was punishable by life imprisonment:

> It is commonly believed among the poorer peasantry of Wendish extraction that several paramount medicinal virtues and magical charms are seated in the heart or liver of a dead maiden or infant of tender years, and that these organs, brewed with certain

herbs into a beverage, will cure diseases or inspire the passion of love in their consumers. The practical result of this barbarous belief is the constantly recurrent violation of the grave's sanctity, and the mutilation of the corpses secretly disinterred from the consecrated ground in which they have been laid to rest. Last week two graves in the new cemetery of Weissensee were broken open during the night, and the coffins contained in them forced, and the bodies of an unmarried girl and a male infant discovered next morning by the guardians of the burial-ground, mangled in the most revolting manner, the cavity of the chest in both cases having been completely emptied of its contents.

BURY ME DEEP

In the mid-1840s, those disinclined to pay 12 pence for each new installment of Charles Dickens's *Dombey and Son* could opt for a far cheaper (in all senses of that word) reading experience. The penny dreadful had arrived, and with it a series of luridly compelling titles: *Wagner the Were-Wolf*; *The Skeleton Clutch, or the Goblet of Gore*; *Sawney Bean, the Man-Eater of Midlothian*; *The Maniac Father, or the Victim of Seduction*; and so on, all vying to dethrone the penny-dreadful king: the 220 chapters on 868 double-columned pages of *Varney the Vampyre; or, The Feast of Blood*, once described by literary critic James Twitchell as among the "most redundant, exorbitant, digressive, thrilling, tedious, and fantastic works ever written."

From the outset, Varney is vampire-as-stage-villain. As he bends over the sleeping "fair Flora" Bannerworth, his face is "perfectly white—perfectly bloodless":

> The eyes look like polished tin; the lips are drawn back, and the principal feature next to those dreadful eyes is the teeth—the fearful looking teeth—projecting like those of some wild animal, hideously, glaringly white, and fang-like ... He drags her head to the bed's edge. He forces it back by the long hair still entwined in his grasp. With a plunge he seizes her neck in his fang-like teeth—a gush of blood, and a hideous sucking noise follows. *The girl has swooned, and the vampyre is at his hideous repast!*

On it goes like that—episode piled upon unbelievable episode—as the cadaverous, polite, and exceedingly well-spoken Sir Francis Varney preys on Sir Marmaduke Bannerworth's family at Bannerworth Hall or is chased over the countryside by enraged mobs. But Varney cannot be killed. Whenever he is cornered or on the verge of expiring, a few moonbeams suffice to revive him—leading to yet more hairbreadth escapes from other ravening mobs: "How frightful is the existence of Varney the Vampyre!"

How confusing, too: At one juncture, Varney is said to have lived in the reign of King Henry IV (1399–1413).

Another tale mentions that he died during the Common-wealth (1649–1660), having betrayed a royalist to Oliver Cromwell. Yet a third reveals that Varney was originally hanged as a felon, then revived by galvanism, like Franken-stein's monster. Or perhaps it was all of the above. From chapter to hastily penned chapter, the author or authors of the Varney yarns could not be troubled to get their story straight. And readers didn't seem to care.

Where Lord Ruthven had been entirely unsympathetic, Varney becomes the first literary vampire to betray the stir-rings of conscience. "I thought that I had steeled my heart against all gentle impulses," he laments after turning a young girl into a vampire, "that I had crushed—aye, completely crushed dove-eyed pity in my heart, but it is not so, and still sufficient of my once human feelings clings to me to make me grieve for thee, Clara Crofton, thou victim."

Finally—mercifully—Varney commits suicide. "You will say that you accompanied Varney the Vampyre to the cra-ter of Mount Vesuvius," he tells his Italian guide, "and that, tired and disgusted with a life of horror, he flung himself in to prevent the possibility of a reanimation of his remains."

At one point before his final immolation, the narrator muses on this "strange gift of renewable existence," fed by blood and moonlight (and food, for Varney can eat regu-lar meals, and sunlight, for he is often abroad by day). "Who shall say that, walking the streets of giant London at this day, there may not be some such existences? Horrible thought that ..."—and there we might have the seed of Dracula.

Bram Stoker clearly copied a thing or two from *Varney the Vampyre,* though in his hands, the story elements became less melodramatic and more chilling. Varney in *Feast of Blood* has fangs, crawls down castle walls, transforms himself into a bat, and possesses mesmerizing serpent eyes. He turns young Clara Crofton into a vampire, after which she must be staked and destroyed for preying on children. Unlike Béla Lugosi's Dracula, however, who claims, "I never drink—wine," Varney enjoys a good glass of claret, "for it looks like blood and may not be it."

Stoker, a man of the theater, glimpsed the dramatic potential in such details. But he probably never saw a performance of *The Vampire* (1852), yet another play loosely based on Polidori's work, because the production fared not so well with some highly placed critics: No less an arbiter than Queen Victoria described it in her diary as "very trashy."

Meanwhile, vampirism had been slipping its moorings in literature and drama. Friedrich Engels, in *The Condition of the Working Class in England* (1844), had described the "vampire middle classes" who bled the workers dry. In 1849, when Karl Marx moved to London, he began working on *Das Kapital,* in which he would proclaim that "capital is dead labor, that, vampire-like, only lives by sucking living labor, and lives the more, the more labor it sucks."

And then there was Emily Brontë's moody masterpiece, *Wuthering Heights,* published in 1847, while Varney was still on the lam from vindictive mobs. This tale of the tempestuous but doomed love affair between Catherine and Heathcliff, set against the wild, windy splendor of the Yorkshire moors, plays tantalizingly with the vampire motif. Is Catherine, who died of childbirth before the story opens, a ghost or a vampire? She apparently haunts Lockwood, the narrator, as he sleeps in her former bedroom. But when Lockwood rubs the specter's wrist against some broken window glass, he draws very real blood.

Or does Catherine turn Heathcliff into a vampire? At one point she tells him, "I'll not lie there by myself: they may bury me twelve feet deep, and throw the church down over me, but I won't rest till you are with me. I never will." And as he lies dying, Heathcliff turns a bloodless hue, "his teeth visible, now and then, in a kind of smile."

After Heathcliff's death, the nurse, Nelly Dean, speaks with Lockwood:

"Is he a ghoul, or a vampire?" I mused. I had read of such hideous, incarnate demons. And then I set myself to reflect how I had tended him in infancy; and watched him grow to youth; and followed him almost through his whole course; and what absurd nonsense it was to yield to that sense of horror.

The locals, for their part, *do* yield to that horror: "But the country folks, if you asked them, would swear on their Bible that he *walks*. There are those who speak to having met him near the church, and on the moor, and even within this house."

Emily Brontë knew about vampires, but in many ways, her tale is more effective for *not* being a vampire tale. What might have happened if Bram Stoker had not been a man of the theater, and had preferred the eerie figures of *Wuthering Heights* instead?

GATHERINGS FROM GRAVEYARDS

As the Victorians were reading their ghost and vampire stories, many doctors were convinced that the dead were literally killing the living.

In a scene from *Bleak House* by Charles Dickens, a burial takes place in an ancient London churchyard, one "pestiferous and obscene, whence malignant diseases are communicated to the bodies of our dear brothers and sisters who have not departed . . . here they lower our dear brother down a foot or two, here sow him in corruption, to be raised in corruption; an avenging ghost at many a sick-bedside, a shameful testimony to future ages how civilization and barbarism walked this boastful island together." Gazing at this cemetery, Lady Dedlock, a character in the story, can only exclaim, "Is this place of abomination consecrated ground?"

In the century from 1741 to 1839, when crusading doctor George Alfred Walker published his *Gatherings from Grave Yards,* more than two million people died and were buried in London alone. Walker's book is a compendium of mortuary horrors: The ancient graveyards were so saturated with the dead that coffins were piled on generations of coffins. In 1845, one gravedigger reported that he unavoidably "severed heads, arms, legs, or whatever came in my way" whenever he had to dig a new grave. "I have been up to my knees in human flesh by jumping on the bodies so as to cram them into the least possible space," he continued. He dug as many as 45 graves in one day, burying "2,017 bodies, besides stillborns" in a single year.

A visitor to another cemetery described its hideous "bone house," into which had been dumped the partially decayed remains from such smashed coffins:

> [Y]ou may see human heads, covered with hair; and here, in this "consecrated ground," are human bones with flesh still adhering to them. On the north side, a man was digging a grave; he was quite drunk, so indeed were all the grave diggers we saw. We looked into this grave, but the stench was abominable. We remained, however, long enough to see that a child's coffin, which had stopped the man's progress, had been cut, longitudinally, right in half; and there lay the child, which had been buried in it, wrapped in its shroud. . . .

Walker rightly calculated that such scenes would infuriate people, but he also insisted that they masked a serious menace to public health. It wasn't simply that graveyards fouled wells, or that rats dragged bones about, or that indescribable insects—"body bugs"—hatched in clouds and settled on passersby. No, graveyards were also "hot-beds of miasmata," sources of "mephitic vapors" widely believed to be extremely poisonous.

Official reports overflowed with accounts of gravediggers expiring on the spot after sinking their picks into some corrupted corpse and releasing its noxious gases. Such exhalations accumulated so thickly in the vaults of ancient churches that they extinguished lighted candles or, paradoxically, caught fire and burned for days. They were blamed for complaints ranging from headaches and convulsions to asphyxiation. "Although such remarkable effects are not produced upon people in general," wrote Walker, the same vapors, emanating from thousands of corpses, still mixed with the air and were breathed in by the city's inhabitants. "Thus the very putrefactions of the dead become part of the fluids of the living."

What was worse, those putrefactions were believed to carry the seeds of malignant disease. The opening of a single corpse, Walker claimed, had brought an epidemic to a vast area in France. When typhus, smallpox, or cholera struck, graveyards were blamed as the centers of infection. Typhus—actually carried by lice—was widely attributed to cadaverous vapors, while a French physician traced an outbreak of smallpox to emanations from dead bodies. In *Bleak House*, smallpox lurking in graveyard exhalations and deposited as "witch-ointment slimy to the touch" on cemetery gates and walls scars the once-beautiful Esther and kills Lady Dedlock.

As English readers were gulping down the adventures of *Varney the Vampyre* in 1848, a more dreaded monster was again stalking the land. In Dickens's day, no disease was quite so feared as cholera. "The speed with which cholera killed was profoundly alarming," declared historian William H. McNeill. A person might be hale and hearty at one moment, but then his bowels emptied without warning and never stopped—even as the diarrhea carried out pieces of intestinal lining.

"[R]adical dehydration," McNeill continued, "meant that a victim shrank into a wizened caricature of his former self within a few hours, while ruptured capillaries discolored the skin, turning it black and blue. The effect was to make mortality uniquely visible: patterns of bodily decay were exacerbated . . . as in a time-lapse motion picture. . . ." It was a startling and horrible transformation: You grew old in a day. Your eyes dulled, and you were forced into a fetal position, knees drawn up to your chin. If you died that way, you were buried that way, locked in rigor mortis.

Cholera ravaged town and country indiscriminately. At one point during the 1848–1849 outbreak, the disease was killing a thousand people a day in England. During an earlier outbreak, between 1831 and 1832, more than 50,000 people had died in the British Isles. In some places during that epidemic, cholera victims were buried so soon—sometimes within ten minutes of being declared dead—that premature burial was widely believed to be commonplace. These were the stories that Bram Stoker's mother had told him about her childhood in cholera-ravaged County Sligo. In his story "Some Terrible Letters from Scotland," Edinburgh writer James Hogg arranges for one character to escape being buried alive during the 1832 outbreak; another Hogg creation reports horrifying dreams of the cholera dead trailing about the kirkyard "wi' their white withered faces an' their glazed een [eyes]." That character's sisters then die of the illness after being infected by their mother. But they return from the grave to escort their mother on a vengeful "dance of death" back to the churchyard for good, for the "plague of Cholera was a breath of hell, they who died of it got no rest in their graves, so that it behoved all, but parents in particular, to keep out of its influences till the vapour of death passed over."

Indeed, it was widely assumed to be vapor until an 1854 outbreak in London, when Dr. John Snow proved that cholera came not from air but from water: Water contaminated by human waste carrying a toxic intestinal bacterium had leaked from a faulty cesspool, infecting a Soho water pump.

In some places, however, graveyard effluvium—Dickens's "witch-ointment slimy to the touch"—might be seen as having curative properties. If there were ever such a thing as grave mold coating the grass and trees in cemeteries, folklore would give it a ritual value. In the north of England, it so happens, a young tuberculosis patient "was at last restored to health by eating butter made from the milk of cows fed in kirkyards, a sovereign remedy for consumption brought on through being witch-ridden."

Consumption, aka tuberculosis, didn't kill quickly, as did cholera or bubonic plague. Instead, it was the archetypal "wasting disease," steadily and remorselessly consuming its victims, draining them of vitality and life. If it was "galloping consumption," this happened in a matter of months; more often, it was a question of years. Yet, by the time the first rattling coughs appeared, accompanied by bloody sputum, it was almost too late. You lost flesh. You bled energy. You were being eaten from within by an invisible demon, or you were being hag-ridden at night—that is, you had become the prey of witches or vampires. No other explanation sprang readily to hand, especially when a bloody froth might bubble from your lips as you slept.

"The emaciated figure strikes one with terror," states a 1799 description of a tuberculosis patient, "the forehead covered with drops of sweat; the cheeks painted with a livid crimson, the eyes sunk; the little fat that raised them in their orbits entirely wasted; the pulse quick and tremulous; the nails long, bending over the ends of the fingers; the palms of the hand dry and painfully hot to the touch; the breath offensive, quick and laborious, and the cough so incessant as to scarce allow the wretched sufferer time to tell his complaints."

The stubbornly rational blamed tuberculosis on bad air—*mal aria*—or cold, damp climates. Those consumptives who could afford it decamped to the magic mountains, with their thin air, or to the warm south—the Mediterranean, say, or the American Southwest desert, with its dry climate. But among the poor, forced to share beds in stifling rooms in unsanitary houses, tuberculosis—already frightfully contagious—reached epidemic proportions.

Yet, as Dickens noted in *Nicholas Nickleby,* tuberculosis was also a disease "in which the struggle between soul and body is so gradual, quiet, and solemn, and the result so sure, that day by day, and grain by grain, the mortal part wastes and withers away, so that the spirit grows light and sanguine with its lightening load." Languid periods might be followed by an upsurge in energy, a sharpening of appetite, or even an unparalleled sexual ardor. And because consumption was believed to fuel the fire of creativity, making it burn brightest just before the dark, it became the Romantic death par excellence, and spirited away innumerable poets, painters, and musicians—among them Balzac, Keats, Chopin, Elizabeth Barrett Browning, and the Brontë sisters. As they were "consumed," they grew emaciated, their cheeks hollowed, their skin turned pallid and translucent, and their eyes appeared luminous—the "consumptive look" that so impressed itself on the literature of the age.

Bram Stoker's depiction of the fading Lucy Westenra in *Dracula* has often been diagnosed as a description of anemia, but it might also depict a case of tuberculosis: "I do not understand Lucy's fading away as she is doing," the character Mina notes. "She eats well and sleeps well, and enjoys fresh air; but all the time the roses in her cheeks are fading, and she gets weaker and more languid day by day; at night I hear her gasping as if for air." Dr. Seward gazes upon her with equal futility: "There on the bed . . . lay poor Lucy, more horribly white and wan-looking than ever. Even the lips were white, and the gums seemed to have shrunken back from the teeth, as we sometimes see in a corpse after a prolonged illness."

The title character of Edgar Allan Poe's "Ligeia," to take another example, is described as slender, "even emaciated," with skin like the "purest ivory," a sensual mouth, raven-black hair, and eyes so extraordinary they were "large and luminous orbs." She suffers from a wasting disease and broods continually on death and dissolution. She pens a poem, "The Conqueror Worm," in which even ". . . the seraphs sob at vermin fangs / In human gore imbued." After her death, the narrator again marries, only to find that his light-haired, blue-eyed bride also sickens and dies—and is resurrected as the very same emaciated, raven-haired Ligeia he once loved.

For eons, the affliction was inexplicable. Consumption was contagious, clearly, and it had something to do with the air—that much was known. But not until 1882, when Robert Koch discovered *Tuberculosis bacillus* (he ultimately won a Nobel Prize for his work), did people recognize that the culprit wasn't the air but rather the suspended droplets it carried—the effluvia of coughs and sneezes.

ONE FOREVER

In Dublin, he became known as the "Invisible Prince," a glitteringly handsome writer who had once moved through society with such quiet assurance that he nearly stood for Parliament. But that was before his wife's death under mysterious circumstances, and his virtual disappearance. After that, recalled the poet Alfred Perceval Graves, Sheridan Le Fanu could be glimpsed only "at odd hours of the evening,

when he might occasionally be seen stealing, like the ghost
of his former self, between his newspaper office and his home
in Merrion Square; sometimes, too, he was to be encountered in an old out-of-the-way bookshop poring over some
rare black letter [tome in] Astrology or Demonology."

Le Fanu is remembered today as one of the supreme masters of the ghost story. Even the noted M. R. James, his peer
in that uncanny art, admired the way the brilliant if reclusive Irishman handled his material. James admitted, however,
that if Le Fanu had one flaw, it lay in his predilection for "the
Vampire-idea." Certainly *Carmilla*, published in 1872, the
year before Le Fanu died at 58, is among the most exquisitely
rendered—and influential—vampire stories ever written.

Laura, its narrator, is a child living with her father in a
lonely castle buried deep in the forests of Styria, a province
of southern Austria. One night a beautiful lady visits her in
her bedroom and seems to bite her on the chest, but this is
dismissed as a dream. Years later, however, a carriage full of
strange people overturns in the moonlight nearby and leaves
one of its occupants, an injured young woman, in the care of
the castle. Her name is Carmilla, and Laura recognizes her
as the toothsome visitor from her childhood dream.

The two are about the same age, so they become—seemingly—the best of friends. Yet in breathless, erotically charged
passages, Carmilla is clearly making more than a pass at Laura:

Sometimes after an hour of apathy, my strange and
beautiful companion would take my hand and hold it

93

with a fond pressure, renewed again and again; blushing softly, gazing in my face with languid and burning eyes, and breathing so fast that her dress rose and fell with the tumultuous respiration. It was like the ardour of a lover; it embarrassed me; it was hateful and yet overpowering; and with gloating eyes she drew me to her, and her hot lips travelled along my cheek in kisses; and she would whisper, almost in sobs, "You're mine, you *shall* be mine, and you and I are one forever."

Carmilla sleeps most of the day, never needs to eat, and is absent much of the night. Odder still, Laura and her father discover an old family portrait from her Hungarian mother's side of one "Mircalla, Countess Karnstein," dated 1698. The woman in the painting is a dead ringer for their guest, down to the mole on her neck.

Meanwhile, Laura's midnight visitor has resumed her predations, thus leaving the girl wasting dangerously away. Young ladies everywhere in the forest are falling prey to "the malady," and the story of one of them, who dies from the disease, bears an eerie resemblance to Laura's: This girl lives in a distant castle, which likewise has an eldritch visitor, "perfidious and beautiful," named Millarca. Both Millarca and Mircalla are discovered to be anagrams of Carmilla, now clearly understood to be a vampire. Carmilla disappears but is eventually traced to a ruined crypt in a ruined chapel in the ruined village of Karnstein. When the crypt is opened, there the countess lies:

Her eyes were open; no cadaverous smell exhaled from the coffin. The two medical men, one officially present . . . [detected] a faint but appreciable respiration, and a corresponding action of the heart. The limbs were perfectly flexible, the flesh elastic; and the leaden coffin floated with blood, in which to a depth of seven inches, the body lay immersed.

These are damning proofs of vampirism. Carmilla/Mircalla/Millarca is staked—not without a bloodcurdling scream—and then decapitated.

In its mastery of tone and suspense, *Carmilla* couldn't be more different from *Varney the Vampyre*. Its influence has been subtler but no less enduring. More 20th-century vampire films, for example, owe something to *Carmilla* than to any other story besides *Dracula*. Bram Stoker, as we have seen, held *Carmilla* in such high regard that he initially planned to set his novel, too, in the forests of Styria—an homage to his fellow countryman.

BALKAN DREAMS

Only a mountain range away from those forests is what was once called Carniola but is today known as Slovenia. There, in 1734, three Englishmen journeyed through the wintry forest on very bad roads. An hour before sunset they rode into Ljubljana, where at the Black Horse, a garrulous innkeeper regaled them through the long winter's night with tales of bears and stags and wild boars—and other creatures as well:

> We must not omit observing here, that our landlord seemed to pay some regard to what Baron Valvasor has related of the Vampyres, said to infest some parts of this country. These Vampyres are supposed to be the bodies of deceased persons, animated by evil spirits, which come out of the graves, in the night time, suck the blood of many of the living, and thereby destroy them. Such a notion will, probably, be looked upon as fabulous and exploded, by many people in England; however, it is not only countenanced by Baron Valvasor, and many Carnioleze noblemen, gentlemen, &c. as we were informed, but likewise actually embraced by some writers of good authority. . . .

It might be a comparatively crude account, but it typified many similar ones that came from travelers to eastern Europe and the Balkans. The Romantic writers fed off such depictions, because so few had ever been there. Lord Byron was an exception, having visited Albania in October 1809. The first two cantos of his 1812 piece, *Childe Harold's Pilgrimage*, helped fix the Balkans as a place of rugged and primitive isolation in western Europeans' minds. Shortly before returning there to die, Byron remarked that "I have . . . a personal dislike to 'Vampires,' and the little acquaintance I have with them would by no means induce me to divulge their secrets."

Those secrets are carried on a buried stream of peasant superstition flowing out of eastern Europe. The vampires there, however, never would have been admitted to a drawing room. They would not have been caught dead in the crypts of castles. English and Irish writers, in creating the literary vampire, had tidied them up a bit.

CHAPTER FOUR

THE VAMPIRE EPIDEMICS

IN 1685, THE TRAVELER who left the gates of Vienna and turned east "seems to take leave of our World," as the English writer Edward Browne reported, "and before he cometh to Buda, seems to enter upon a new stage of world, quite different from that of the western countrys."

This was Hungary, final port on the great sea of grass that, stretching ever eastward, ended only on the borders of China. Out of these prairielands had swept the mounted archers of Attila the Hun, of the Avars, of the Mongols, and finally of the Ottoman Turks. East of Vienna, even the natural world seemed imbued with the oriental: The oaks had a different cut to their leaves and bore acorns capped, like Turkic tribesmen, with a wild fringe of pendant and tassel.

Rimmed by hills and mountains, the sea of grass that was the Hungarian plain was also a Hapsburg lake. An imperial dynasty, stolidly German, devoutly Catholic, the Hapsburgs ruled from Vienna's Hofburg Palace a polyglot empire that embraced not only the Magyars, or Hungarians, but also those subject peoples who dwelt in the surrounding hills: Bohemians, Moravians, Czechs, Slovaks, and Romanians. Each could be told by their distinctive dress. The Hapsburgs even ruled Poles, whose natural affinities—like the course of Poland's rivers—ran toward Prussia and the Baltic, and Ruthenians, who looked toward Russia and "Little Tartary," the nomad-swept grasslands north of the Black Sea.

In the south, the Hapsburgs would come to absorb Slovenes, Croats, and Bosnians as well. Greeks, Bulgars, Turks, and Jews swarmed the cities and towns. Gypsies wandered everywhere, especially in Transylvania, where they had long been famed as musicians and great dancers—whirling, stomping, hand-clapping dancers. Though the hills and orchards, wheat fields and vineyards of Bohemia and Moravia, Slovakia and Slavonia, were all classically European, the presence of these colorful peoples lent those lands an air of exoticism to the Hapsburgs and their fellow elites. Wolfgang Amadeus Mozart regarded his visits to Prague, more than 150 miles northwest of Vienna, as "excursions into a culturally different world."

Armies had long fought for those hills and grasslands. Vlad the Impaler had battled the invading Ottomans on the plains of Wallachia in the 15th century, and the Turks had surrounded the gates of Vienna on more than one occasion. Few travelers had willingly ventured into such a dangerous region, and when they finally did begin to arrive, they found, anthropologist Edith Durham discovered in 1906, that its inhabitants "live in the past to an extent which it is hard for us in the West to realize."

Harvests in Hungary, Slovakia, or Romania had on occasion been so abundant that grain was left to rot in the fields. As late as the eve of World War I, agriculture in the region was not merely unmechanized but practically medieval: Oxen still pulled wooden plows and harrows, while reaping and haying were done by sickle and scythe.

These crude conditions were even more pronounced in lands long subjected to Ottoman rule. The ebbing of the Turkish tide took centuries: Greece freed itself in 1830, but Romania and parts of Serbia and Bulgaria did not break free until 1878. Lines of castles edged the former tidemarks, as did a shifting zone of desolate countryside, abandoned and wild. The few border crossings were not just Austrian military posts but *lazzaretti,* or quarantine stations. These had been compulsory stops for all travelers coming from the east since at least the mid-18th century, and they had been erected out of fear of a new invader, or rather an old one: the plague.

Seen from a distance, looming over the confluence of the Sava and the Danube, was the dazzling white fortress of Belgrade—*Beo-grad,* the "white city," gateway to the maze of mountains that were the Balkans (*balkan* is Turkish for "mountain"). From Serbia and Bulgaria down through

Macedonia, Albania, and northern Greece, men might be garbed in sheepskin and clad in knee-high sandals reminiscent of Alexander the Great. Women might be decked in colorful embroidery and half-hidden behind scarves and kerchiefs. These were lands of vendetta, but of hospitality, too: the fiery plum wine called slivovitz, the spitted lamb, the Turkish coffee, and the music of horsehair-stringed instruments and goatskin bagpipes.

Although the Ottomans still dominated here, their mosques were squat and uninspiring. Ottoman graveyards, by contrast, were picturesque in the extreme, the tombstones raked at every conceivable angle by the passage of time. Islam had won only Albania and parts of Bosnia; elsewhere, the censer of Eastern Orthodoxy held sway. No organs sounded in those churches, however—only chants that seemed to issue from smoke-blackened icons with large, expressive eyes. Outside its doors might stand an ancient tree, emblazoned with a cross that barely disguised its origins as an object of pagan devotions.

Before the 20th century, travelers had to rough it in the Balkans. Roman roads had degenerated into mere cart tracks, and even four-wheeled carts were rare for years; you went by foot or on horseback. The endless oak forests were haunted by bear, wolf, and the lean, rakish pig that saddled Serbia with the label of "a nation of swineherds." Higher on the hillsides stretched somber beech woods. "Those of us who have ridden for hours through what is left of the Balkan primeval forests . . . ," wrote Edith Durham nearly a century ago, "know the awe inspired by the silence, the gold green light, and the endless army of mighty grey trunks towering erect from the soil that is muffled and bedded with the dead leafage of a thousand years and echoes no tread. The horse sinks knee-deep. You dismount and plunge through it with difficulty."

Those were the forests travelers once had to cross on their way from Belgrade to Nis, where stood the notorious Skull Tower, made from the severed heads of Serbian rebels. There they crossed the mountains to Sofia and rode down the via militaris, the old imperial road that once echoed to the tramp of the legions, to Constantinople. From the 1880s on, they could follow that route in relative comfort by riding the *Orient Express*.

By that time, a visitor could stand on the ramparts of the old fortress at Belgrade and gaze out over the rippling Hungarian plain at its famous sunsets. With the fall of night, he might turn away, call for a fiacre, and head for a delicious dinner at the Crown of Servia, never suspecting that his perch of the past half hour had once been an execution ground where the reigning pasha displayed the blackened corpses of impaled Christians as a warning to the infidels.

Nightfall, however, brought enormous isolation deep in the interior of the Balkans. There, the traveler caught far from a village had better check his pistols. Bandits and smugglers were rumored to be at large—but were they the sole reason his driver, before snapping the reins in the gathering gloom, had so tremulously crossed himself?

Deep in the Forest

In 1717, when Lady Mary Wortley Montagu passed through Belgrade, it was still a Turkish frontier fortress garrisoned by elite Janissaries, and she was accompanying her husband, the newly appointed British minister to the Ottoman Empire, on his way across the Balkans to Constantinople. For seven days, they and a company of these Janissaries wound their way up the Morava River valley, traversing what Lady Montagu described as the "deserts of Servia." Others knew it less poetically as the great Serbian forest—a primeval place of giant oaks and beeches, its dread reinforced by the beatings the Janissaries inflicted on the inhabitants of each village they passed through. The abuse brought tears to Lady Montagu's eyes.

Fifteen years later, much had changed yet little had changed. Having been on the losing side of the 1718 Treaty of Passarowitz, the Turks had withdrawn from Belgrade and most of the Morava River valley. Austrians were now the overseers of that demoralized, undernourished population. Yet, the forest was still there, and quite likely it was up that same road that an Austrian military detachment rode in January 1732. Regimental Field Surgeon Johannes Flückinger, accompanied by two medical examiners and two regular army officers, had departed Belgrade, bound for the village of Medvegia.

Several weeks earlier, an Austrian officer who was a contagious disease specialist had visited Medvegia to investigate the unusually high mortality rate reported there. In three

months, 17 people—a large number for a small village—had died, many after an illness of two or three days. The officer had found no evidence of pestilence—only chronic malnutrition. He was urged, however, to examine some of the recent dead—the inhabitants were blaming the deaths on the dead—and probably blanched at what he saw, for he recommended that the villagers be indulged in their desire to destroy the bodies of their former neighbors.

But Belgrade was not yet prepared to go that far. Instead Flückinger and his retinue were dispatched to make a thorough investigation. Medvegia stood near the new border with Turkey, so the Austrians had settled there a company of hajduks—Serbian guerrillas who had once fought the Ottoman occupiers. Upon arriving in the village, Flückinger met with the leading hajduks and the hadnack, or village elder. From them, he heard the story firsthand—or as much of it as could be interpreted, as the villagers surely did not speak German.

Five years earlier, it seemed, a hajduk named Arnold Paole had lived in Medvegia. Paole had served as a Turkish conscript in Kosovo—where, he believed, he had fallen prey to a vampire. At the direction of some folkloric remedy, he had eaten dirt from his assailant's grave and somehow had smeared himself with its blood. Yet around Medvegia, it seems, such actions were deemed only to deepen, not to remove, the taint. Several weeks after Paole was killed in a fall from a hay wagon, his neighbors began complaining that he had returned as a vampire and was throttling them at night. Soon four of them died, as did some of the village livestock.

Forty days after being buried, therefore, Paole was exhumed and staked through the heart. The villagers then burned his carcass and tossed its ashes back into the grave. And because his four supposed victims would certainly become vampires, too, their bodies were likewise dug up and subjected to similar treatment. Yet, all that had occurred five years earlier, and Medvegia had since returned to normal. Then came this new round of deaths, which the villagers believed to be a fresh outbreak of vampirism.

Perhaps it was the hadnack's description of the exhumed Paole that intrigued Field Surgeon Flückinger; he emphasized it in his subsequent report. After 40 days in the grave, the village elder related, the dead man had shown no signs of decay. Quite the contrary: Not only had he sloughed off his old skin and nails, but new ones were apparently growing in their places. Though blood was widely supposed to coagulate after death, Paole was said to be wallowing in a coffin full of liquid blood. Blood also flowed from his mouth, his nose, his ears, and even his eyes. When a wooden stake was driven through Paole's heart, the hadnack asserted, he had emitted an audible groan.

Perhaps Flückinger had read about a similar case in the *Wienerisches Diarium* back in the summer of 1725. This case had taken place in Kisilova, a Serbian village on the Danube east of Belgrade. Villagers there had demanded that an Austrian official be present at an exhumation, else the hamlet might be destroyed—not an uncommon occurrence "in Turkish times," they claimed. After a peasant named Peter

Plogojowitz had died, nine other people had followed him to the grave in the space of just eight days. All had complained of being throttled at night by the resurrected Plogojowitz, who was also said to have visited his wife and asked for his shoes; trusting her own heels instead, the sensible woman had promptly fled the village. By the time an Austrian official arrived, Plogojowitz had already been exhumed.

Though he had been ten weeks in the grave, the Austrian official noted, Plogojowitz's body was apparently ruddy and plump, its eyes still open. The nose had collapsed, but otherwise the corpse seemed completely fresh. There was not the slightest whiff of odor. Hair, beard, and nails had apparently grown. Old skin was giving way to new. Moreover, the mouth was full of "fresh" (liquid) blood—which, to hear the villagers tell it, belonged to his victims. As the official looked on in horror, a sharpened stake was pounded into the chest of the corpse, whereupon more blood gushed from its mouth and ears, accompanied by certain "wild signs" (customarily interpreted as an erection). The villagers then burned the body—an act that the official insisted had not been his fault: The "rabble . . . were beside themselves with fear."

Whether or not Field Surgeon Flückinger had read the official's report, he probably entered the Medvegia graveyard that January afternoon knowing what to expect. Even so, it must have taken a cold few hours to perform field autopsies on 17 corpses.

The renewed vampirism, the villagers concluded, must have been occasioned by two women: Stana, who had admitted to once painting herself with vampire blood, and Miliza, who had eaten part of a sheep Paole had supposedly killed. These actions had guaranteed that the pair of women would become vampires at death—and their deaths had come just before those of the 15 others.

Stana, 20, had died in childbirth three months earlier. The baby had died, too—but, being unbaptized, it had been carelessly buried behind a garden fence and half eaten by dogs. With the exception of her ravaged womb, Flückinger noticed, Stana—like Paole and Plogojowitz—was remarkably undecayed. Her old skin and nails had given way to new, and her arteries and veins were full of fresh, not coagulated, blood, which was also pooling in her chest cavity. Her lungs, liver, stomach, spleen, and intestines appeared quite fresh, too.

Miliza, 60, had been dead even longer. Her chest, too, was full of liquid blood, Flückinger discovered, while her viscera—like Stana's—appeared fresh and normal. Most remarkable, however, was the hajduks' reaction upon viewing the bloated figure stretched out before them; Miliza had been very lean when she was alive, they asserted, and therefore she must have "come to this surprising plumpness in the grave."

The same thing was observed, with sickening regularity, in one corpse after another. Flückinger described it as *das Vampyrenstande*—the "vampiric condition." An eight-day-old child, also dead for three months, was in that state. A ten-year-old girl, two months in the grave, was similarly undecayed, and fresh blood pooled in her chest. Sixteen-year-old Milloe, nine weeks under the earth, "was found like the other vampires," as was 17-year-old Joachim, "buried eight weeks and four days."

A 60-year-old man who had been dead for 6 weeks; a girl named Ruscha, prey to a 10-day illness; an 18-day-old child; a 25-year-old man—all exhibited profuse liquid blood and a puzzling lack of decay. Stanoika, 20, was quite vividly ruddy. Her viscera appeared healthy, her skin and nails were fresh, and her blood flowed freely. Before she had died, Flückinger learned, Stanoika had complained of being throttled by the dead teenaged Milloe at night. On the right side of her throat beneath the ear was the evidence, a "bloodshot blue mark, the length of a finger."

None of these bodies had been in the ground longer than three months. That meant most of them had been buried in October or November. The onset of winter might have slowed their decomposition—yet how to account for the corpses that did *not* display "vampirism"? The hadnack's own wife had been dead for seven weeks, and her newborn child had not survived her for long. Yet, both mother and child were completely decomposed, although their grave lay in ground no different than that of the apparent vampires nearby. A servant named Rhade, 21, had died following a three-month's illness. After five weeks in the ground, his remains, too, were completely decomposed. So were those of yet another mother and child, who had been laid in their joint grave more than a month earlier.

The hajduks would have had an explanation: The five decomposed bodies were the result of natural death, while the dozen others had been victims of vampire attacks—and were becoming vampires in turn. Unless these vampires were destroyed quickly, the rest of the village was doomed. Flückinger must have given them permission: "After the examination had taken place," he reported, "the heads of the vampires were cut off by the local gypsies and burned along with the bodies, and then the ashes were thrown into the river Morava. The decomposed bodies, however, were laid back into their own graves."

It is debatable how much of this Flückinger and the four other members of the Austrian military detachment actually witnessed. They did not enter the graveyard until at least midday, which would have left them only five hours or so to examine 17 corpses. Not only that, but human remains do not burn easily. The cremation of a single body (much less a dozen) would have been a daunting task, even if some were newborns. Then the pyres would have to cool before the ashes could be gathered. Darkness was surely falling, and the gypsies may already have begun their gruesome work.

Having just sanctioned this mass desecration, the Austrians were doubtless eager to depart. Perhaps they would find an old Ottoman caravanserai somewhere along their return route to Belgrade. Or perhaps they stayed in the village instead, watching the massive pyres roar throughout the night, the severed heads rolling about as the burning wood shifted and settled. After what they had just seen and heard, it would be understandable if they chose not to return through that dark forest by night.

FALLACIOUS FICTIONS OF HUMAN FANTASY

Back in Belgrade, Flückinger dutifully prepared his report. "Visum et Repertum"—"Seen and Discovered"—was sealed and notarized by the surgeon, his two medical associates, and the two regular officers. They further attested that all that had been observed "in the matter of vampires . . . is in every way truthful and has been undertaken, observed, and examined in our own presence." It was dated January 26, 1732, and dispatched to Hapsburg emperor Charles VI.

Within weeks of being reprinted in a Nuremberg scientific journal, "Visum et Repertum" became a surprise best seller at the 1732 Leipzig Book Fair.

Not that stories about *revenants*—those returned from the dead—were new; reports of vampire eruptions had been regular features of central and eastern European life for years. But "Visum et Repertum" was not just another compendium of fantastic tales; there was no fiendish corpse in it. Rather, as a report of scientific observations, it appealed to Enlightenment scholars precisely because Flückinger's conclusions amounted to a medical acknowledgment that a phenomenon called vampirism might exist. It thus kindled a fierce debate throughout the German academic and medical establishment.

Suddenly Arnold Paole and Stanoika were on lips from Leipzig to London. Newsstands carried copies of "Dissertatio de Vampyris Serviensibus" ("On the Serbian Vampires"), "Dissertationes de Masticatione Mortuorum" ("On the Chewing Dead"), "Dissertatio de Cadauveribus Sanguisugis" ("On the Bloodsucking Dead"), and so on. At least 14 treatises and 4 dissertations on the subject were published within a year or two of "Visum et Repertum."

Smelling sensational copy, journalists quickly picked up on the trend as well, and the word *vampire* began to infiltrate western European languages. It appeared in Britain, for example, in the March 11, 1732, *London Journal*—mere weeks after Flückinger returned to Belgrade. Two months later, the May 20 issue of *The Craftsman* described a dispute "between a grave *Doctor of Physick* and a beautiful young *Lady*, an Admirer of strange Occurrences. The Doctor ridicul'd such romantick Stories, as common Artifices of Newswriters to fill up their Papers; The Lady insisted on the Truth of this Relation; which stood attested by unexceptionable Witnesses...."

That typified the public reaction to the vampire madness: It was either peasant superstition, or it was chillingly true. According to English novelist Horace Walpole, King George II was a confirmed believer, while in 1750, one Constantino Grimaldi of Italy claimed that no vampires were found where peasants drank wine; according to him, they existed only in countries "where beer, this unhealthy drink, is widespread."

To the Marquis D'Argens of France, however, it was all hysterical self-fulfilling prophecy. "In examining the Story of the Death of these pretended Martyrs to Vampirism," he wrote in the 1737 edition of his celebrated *Lettres Juives*, "I discover all the Marks of an epidemick Fanaticism, and I see clearly that the Impressions of their own Fears was the true Cause of their Destruction." Thanks to D'Argens's influence, incidents like the Serbian ones came to be called vampire epidemics wherever they cropped up.

Of all those who weighed in on the vampire question, perhaps no one had a greater impact than Dom Augustin Calmet, abbot of the Benedictine Abbey at Senones in France's forested Vosges Mountains. A biblical exegete of unimpeachable authority, Calmet was probably the Catholic church's leading intellectual when he published his mammoth *Traité sur les Apparitions des Esprits, et sur les Vampires* in 1746. A treasury of tales of angels and demons, specters and apparitions, ghosts and resurrections and revivals, the *Traité* was one of the first works to apply rudimentary rules of evidence to folklore. "Every age, every nation, every country has its prejudices, its maladies, its customs," the abbot observed. Then, warming to his subject, he continued in the most vivid terms:

> In this age, a new scene presents itself to our eyes, and has done for about sixty years in Hungary, Moravia, Silesia, and Poland; men, it is said, who have been dead for several months, come back to earth, talk, walk, infest villages, ill use both men and beasts, suck the blood of their near relations, destroy their health, and finally cause their death; so that people can only save themselves from their dangerous visits and their hauntings, by exhuming them, impaling them, cutting off their heads, tearing out their hearts, or burning them. These are called by the name of oupires

or vampires, that is to say, leeches; and such particulars are related of them, so singular, so detailed, and attended by such probable circumstances, and such judicial information, that one can hardly refuse to credit the belief which is held in those countries, that they come out of their tombs, and produce those effects which are proclaimed of them. . . .

Leery of charges of frivolity, Calmet emphasized that his examination was important from a religious point of view: "For, if the return of vampires is real, it is of import to defend it, and prove it; and if it is illusory, it is of consequence to the interests of religion to undeceive those who believe in its truth, and destroy an error which may produce dangerous effects. . . ."

At times, the abbot's view of the undead seemed positively cavalier. Not only did Calmet believe medieval tales of the sinful dead trudging out of their churchyard graves during divine services and then dutifully filing back, but also he was not overly concerned with the condition of the corpses found in the Medvegia graveyard:

That bodies which have died of violent maladies, or which have been executed when full of health, or have simply swooned, should vegetate underground in their graves; that their beards, hair, and nails should grow; that they should emit blood, be supple and pliant; that they should have no bad smell, &c.,—all

these things do not embarrass us: the vegetation of the human body may produce all these effects.

For Calmet, the "grand difficulty," not surprisingly, lay in explaining how vampires could emerge from the grave in the first place. That would be the "most interesting part of the narrative":

> How a body covered with four or five feet of earth, having no room to move about and disengage itself, wrapped up in linen, covered with pitch, can make its way out, and come back upon the earth, and there occasion such effects as are related of it; and how after that it returns to its former state, and re-enters underground, where it is found sound, whole, and full of blood, and in the same condition as a living body? This is the question. Will it be said that these bodies evaporate through the ground without opening it, like the water and vapours which enter into the earth, or proceed from it, without sensibly deranging its particles? It were to be wished that the accounts which have been given us concerning the return of the vampires had been more minute in their explanations of this subject.

It was this habit of conditional conclusions, not without art—"If these *revenants* are really dead, whatever state they may be in in the other world, they play a very bad part here"—that hinted at the very real possibility of vampires for many readers. And the prestigious Calmet had many readers, as his book went through numerous reprintings.

A more clear-cut, ringing denial was needed, according to Monsignor Giuseppe Davanzati, the archbishop of Trani in southern Italy. As early as 1738, he began writing the dissertation eventually called *I Vampiri*, or *The Vampires*. Fierce and uncompromising, Davanzati deplored the vampire hysteria primarily because the desecration of corpses mocked and undermined the doctrine of the resurrection. By 1744, a manuscript copy of his work had found its way to the Vatican, where some very sympathetic eyes indeed fell upon it.

Pope Benedict XIV, a man of sunny temperament, had risen to the papacy despite having declared himself neither a saint nor a statesman but simply a stubbornly honest man. He was also a distinguished scholar, having steeped himself in the lore of bodies corruptible and incorruptible while writing his treatise on the beatification of saints, *De servorum Dei beatificatione et Beatorum canonizatione*. When published in 1734, it studiously ignored the vampire craze in full swing at the time. In the book's second edition, however, published 15 years later, Pope Benedict addressed the undead issue head-on, branding vampires the "fallacious fictions of human fantasy."

Roma locuta; causa finita—"Rome has spoken; the case is closed." Dom Calmet duly fell in line. In 1751, in the final edition of his work, the old abbot penned a new conclusion: "I doubt that there is another stand to take on this question other than to deny absolutely that vampires return from the dead." Then, in 1774, the imprimatur was bestowed on Monsignor Davanzati's *I Vampiri*. The gates to the tomb were sealed shut. For Roman Catholics, there were no such things as vampires.

The temporal powers also obeyed. The devout Maria Theresa now sat on the Hapsburg throne, and in 1755, she moved to halt any further exhumations in her realm. After her personal physician, the eminently rational Gerard van Swieten, had investigated vampire hysteria and called it all a "vain fear," she issued a resolution condemning belief in vampires as "superstition and fraud." The resolution likewise criminalized the staking or burning of corpses. In August 1756, the empress further strengthened her hand by transferring responsibility for witchcraft, vampire, or any other cases "not readily explainable in natural terms" from the priests to the Conciliar Appellate Court. Her mortal enemy, Frederick the Great of Prussia, with whom she was already again at war, quickly followed suit.

THE MORE THEY ARE BURNED . . .

The "vampire epidemics" seemed contained. Church and state had closed ranks. It remained only for the Enlightenment to administer the *coup de grâce*. And who better for that task than François-Marie Arouet, better known as Voltaire?

A man of many interests, ranging from the nature of fire to biblical criticism, Voltaire possessed a scathing wit. By the

1750s, he was holding court in Ferney, his chateau outside Geneva, because his satire had won him too many enemies in France. At Ferney, he finished his masterpiece, *Candide* (1759), and completed his *Dictionnaire philosophique*, fruit of a lifetime's musings on God, metaphysics, immortality, the soul, ethics, and any number of other topics—all turned to so many arrows fired at his favorite targets: the Catholic Church, fanaticism, and political or religious persecution. Published anonymously in 1764, the *Dictionnaire* was punchy rather than lengthy—the better to hide in one's pocket.

Under *V*, of course, was an article on vampires. "What!" mocked Voltaire. "Is it in our eighteenth century that vampires exist? We never heard speak of vampires in London, nor even at Paris. I confess, that in both these cities there were stock-jobbers, brokers, and men of business, who sucked the blood of the people in broad daylight; but they were not dead, though corrupted. These true suckers lived not in cemeteries, but in very agreeable palaces. . . ."

As for the vampire epidemics:

After slander, nothing is communicated more promptly than superstition, fanaticism, sorcery, and tales of those raised from the dead. There were [vampires] in Wallachia, Moldavia, and some among the Polanders, who are of the Romish church. This superstition being absent, they acquired it, and it went through all the east of Germany. Nothing was spoken of but vampires, from 1730 to 1735; they were laid in wait for, their hearts torn out and burnt. They resembled the ancient martyrs—the more they were burnt, the more they abounded.

Nor did Voltaire spare his friend Dom Augustin Calmet: "Calmet became their historian," he concluded, "and treated vampires as he treated the Old and New Testament, by relating faithfully all that has been said before him."

If he intended to instruct and amuse in portable format, Voltaire was vindicated: The *Dictionnaire philosophique* sold out its first edition, brought down the wrath of the Catholic Church, and was banned and burned in France and Geneva.

Meanwhile, that other lion of the Enlightenment, Jean-Jacques Rousseau, was likewise invoking vampires. In 1762, the apostle of the "natural man" had been called upon to defend himself against ecclesiastical attacks, too. The archbishop of Paris had taken great offense at *Émile*, Rousseau's antiestablishment treatise promoting educational reform and "natural religion." Both author and book were banned from France; there, thankfully, only the book could be burned, for the author took to his heels. Protesting this treatment, Rousseau wrote an open letter to the archbishop in which he sought to drive home a point about the interpretation of evidence:

> If there is in this world a well-attested account, it is that of the vampires. Nothing is lacking: official reports, affidavits of well-known people, of surgeons,

of priests, of magistrates; the judicial proof is most complete. And with all that, who is there who believes in vampires?

The answer was seemingly no one—at least no one in Enlightenment France.

Voltaire and Rousseau died within weeks of each other in the summer of 1778. Because Voltaire was an excommunicate and Rousseau was rumored to have shot himself, they should both, by the rules of folklore, have risked becoming vampires. But during the French Revolution, their bodies—or at least their coffins—were removed from their lonely graves and installed in the Panthéon in Paris, the former church that was supposed to become the sacred space for a new secular state.

By the 1830s, the Panthéon had become a church again, and it was whispered that the remains of Voltaire and Rousseau had been clandestinely dumped in a sewer. As one newspaper reporter put it, the "faithful and pious couldn't worship over the heads of two such infidels." Or was it the other way around? As a waggish King Louis XVIII was said to have put it, had those two heads simply grown annoyed at having Mass celebrated above them? Perhaps they had risen from the crypt and trooped out of the church, like Dom Calmet's excommunicates in the Middle Ages.

In December 1897, an official delegation tiptoed down into the vaults of the Panthéon and had the tombs opened. The great men were indeed still there, although no signs of vampirism despoiled their bodies. A *New York Times* article reported that "A viscous matter, apparently coagulated saw-dust" coated Voltaire's remains. Although his skull had been sawed in half when his brain was removed soon after death, he was still eerily recognizable. Voltaire, who had looked mummified even in life, was now a dead ringer for the famous bust of him by the sculptor Pigalle: "... even the sardonic smirk was recognizable in the thin skin drawn tightly over the cheek bones and frontal."

Rousseau's hands were still clasped over his chest, and though the "thread of the shroud enveloped the skeleton; the body had evidently been imperfectly embalmed." A few teeth were still visible, as were a few hairs on the skull—a skull, it was observed, that showed no signs of a self-inflicted gunshot wound: Jean-Jacques Rousseau had died of a cerebral hemorrhage.

THE DEATH VINE

Though far removed from the European world of Medvegia, New England, with its rock-ribbed hills and once-dense forests of chestnut and white pine, originally bore a striking resemblance to parts of the Balkans.

Among headstones carved with skulls and destroying angels in the Old Burying Point in Salem, Massachusetts, lie the graves of the judges who presided over the notorious witchcraft trials of 1692. Nearby is Concord's Sleepy Hollow Cemetery, the final resting place of Emerson, Thoreau, and other leaders of 19th-century transcendentalism.

New England would seem to have come a long way between those two milestones.

Or maybe not. On September 29, 1859, three years before he died of tuberculosis, Thoreau noted in his journal, "I have just read of a family in Vermont who, several of the members having died of consumption, just burned the lungs, heart and liver of the last deceased, in order to prevent any more from having it."

Thoreau was still alive and writing when a small family graveyard, set on a sandy knoll outside Griswold, Connecticut, was abandoned. Gradually it was overgrown, then forgotten—until November 1990, that is, when a sand- and gravel-mining operation began biting into it. As three boys played among the fresh cuts one day, they rolled down the hill and discovered two human skulls bouncing after them.

By the time Connecticut State archaeologist Nick Bellantoni arrived, any headstones that might have remained had been lost to mining machinery. So a grid was set up, and the site was mapped, photographed, and excavated. Like so many others, the site was small—about 17 yards by 25 yards—and apparently marked out by stakes surrounded by heaps of stones. That was not much to go on, but some determined sleuthing uncovered the site's history: In 1757, a farmer named Walton had purchased the knoll from his sea-captain neighbor for 12 shillings. It was used as a cemetery by several generations—and by several families—until about 1840. Then it was abandoned to the rhythms of seedtime and harvest, summer and winter.

In the end, Bellantoni recovered from the Walton Cemetery the remains of 27 individuals: 5 adult males, 8 adult females, and, in a touching reminder of the appalling rate of infant mortality in previous eras, 14 children and adolescents.

Each corpse was carefully removed from what remained of its pine or oak coffin and was wrapped in acid-free paper. Bits of debris—artifacts, hair, wood, soil samples, or straight pins that once held a shroud in place—were painstakingly plotted, labeled, and collected. The site's lack of machine-cut nails suggested that most burials predated the 1830s. Two of the bodies had been laid in crypts of stone and unmortared brick; spelled out in brass tacks on their coffins were the designations "NB-13" and "JB-55." We may never know what names those initials stand for, but the numerals suggest their age at death.

All in all, it seemed to be a representative graveyard for its time and place, distressingly full of infants, perhaps—a quarter of the burials were infants under two years old—but otherwise indicative of a typically hardscrabble, physically demanding rural life. That was the story that Paul Sledzik was reading in the bones. As curator of the anatomical collections at the National Museum of Health and Medicine in Washington, D.C., Sledzik knew his bones, having the better part of 2,000 Civil War soldiers under his supervision.

It had seemed like just another day among the skeletons when Sledzik's telephone rang. It was an old classmate of his, Nick Bellantoni, saying he had found something that Sledzik might find interesting.

Back on the knoll near Griswold, when the archaeologists had opened the coffin labeled "JB-55," Bellantoni was momentarily taken aback. The skeleton looked like no other he had seen: These bones had been rearranged in a classic skull-and-crossbones pattern. This grave had been desecrated, apparently many decades earlier.

Though the University of Connecticut initially processed the remains from the Walton Cemetery, they were then sent to Sledzik and his colleagues for more extensive analysis. As soon as Sledzik received the bones, he laid them out and ran his trained eyes over them. JB-55, a male, showed signs of chronic dental disease, as did most of the adults from the graveyard. Its owner also showed signs of arthritis, especially in the left knee, which meant he had almost certainly limped at times. He had signs of healed fractures, too, especially on the right clavicle, or collarbone, which must have been "insulted"—broken—by some kind of direct blow. It had never been properly set.

What's more, JB-55 had probably been coughing up blood, if the lesions on the upper left ribs told Sledzik anything. Scattered across the visceral rib surface adjacent to the lung, the pitted, whitish-gray lesions were telltale signs of primary pulmonary tuberculosis. They might have been the residue of typhoid, syphilis, or pleuritis, but tuberculosis was the logical candidate. In any event, they marked a chronic pulmonary infection that would have produced the coughing and expectoration others regarded as tuberculosis, or consumption.

Though not widely known in New England, vampire epidemics are not exactly unknown there, either. Indeed, they have provided consistent fodder for local news stories over the years. Around a dozen incidents have now been documented—mostly from rural Rhode Island, Connecticut, Massachusetts, and Vermont—from the late 18th century until the 1890s. Eleven of them involved tuberculosis.

In Foster, Rhode Island, for example, Captain Levi Young and his family settled on a farm—and all too soon provided an occupant for the plot of land they had set aside as a burial ground. Young's daughter Nancy, 19, succumbed to consumption in April 1827. Then Nancy's younger sister, Almira, started showing symptoms—as, inevitably, did the other children in the neighborhood. Those neighbors apparently persuaded Captain Young to dig up Nancy's casket. As the story goes, her disinterred coffin was placed on a funeral pyre and the villagers gathered around it, inhaling the fumes in the belief that this "sympathetic magic" would not only cure those infected with the disease, but also confer immunity on everyone else.

The most sorrowful tale of all, however, is that of Mercy Brown. In the late 19th century, George and Mary Eliza Brown and their seven children lived in Exeter, Rhode Island—"Deserted Exeter," as it came to be called. In December 1883, Mary Eliza died of consumption and was buried in Chestnut Hill Cemetery. But the chain of contagion had already set in: Mary Olive followed her mother six months later. Several years passed before son Edwin fell ill as well. Edwin fled west to the dry mountain air of the Rockies, widely believed to be curative. It seemed to work.

Then, on a cold January day in 1892, Edwin's sister Mercy Lenna died of tuberculosis. But the ground was frozen, so her coffin was laid in a mausoleum to await the spring thaw. Meanwhile, Edwin had returned home, but he immediately fell ill again. Apparently he was told—by whom we do not know—that one of his deceased relatives must be preying upon him. The only remedy anyone could suggest was to exhume his mother and sisters; if any of the bodies was still undecomposed, Edwin was to rip out the heart and burn it.

Mary Eliza and Mary Olive were exhumed and found to have decomposed into skeletons. But Mercy, her body preserved by the freezing cold of the mausoleum, was found to be in something approaching Flückinger's "vampiric state." Blood was in her heart, and blood was at her mouth. A victim rather than a fiend, Mercy was ripped apart so that her heart and liver could be removed and burned on a nearby rock. Edwin apparently mixed the ashes into a potion and quaffed the grisly antidote. "Not surprisingly," reported a subsequent newspaper article, "he died four months later."

Might the tragedies of the Young and Brown families be correlated with a forgotten cemetery near Griswold, Connecticut? Surprisingly, yes, in Griswold itself, only two miles from the cemetery and only a few years after JB-55 was likely buried.

The May 20, 1854, issue of the *Norwich Courier* tells the story of Griswold's Ray family. Horace Ray died of tuberculosis around 1846. Within the next eight years, two of his sons likewise succumbed. After a third one fell ill, the now-familiar remedy was invoked: In early May, the dead brothers were exhumed and burned.

That tale had been told in books, but Sledzik's lab contained a version of it written on bones. We may never learn anything more about JB-55, but his skeleton tells us that he probably limped about with a hacking, rattling cough that produced bloody sputum. When consumption flared up again in the community after JB-55 died, did someone remember—and blame—his limping figure? Somebody desecrated JB-55's grave only a few years after he was laid to rest inside it. The evidence tells us, however, that whoever defiled his grave would have found only a skeleton there, with no heart left to burn. Did the invaders then improvise on the spot and rearrange the bones in a time-honored symbol of death? Were they, in effect, using the dead to ward off death itself?

Griswold had been settled just after 1812 by farmers—probably uneducated, and almost certainly considered crude. Life was hard, and the threat of starvation was a wolf at the door. Several generations of a single family often lived together in crowded, unsanitary conditions—perfect breeding grounds for such epidemic diseases as smallpox, measles, and tuberculosis. This family dynamic, writ large, was projected into the grave.

With justifiable exaggeration, the tuberculosis bacillum might be said to consume the life force of its victim, thus overwhelming the victim's will to live. Yet the pathogen has also evolved to spread via contagion, feeding off a new host before its old one dies, and so on down the line. Take away the understanding of microscopic pathogens, however, and what is left? A mysterious life force consuming one person after another, and believed powerful enough to act from afar—even from the grave.

The evil agent must still lurk in the heart of the recently deceased, where it continues to exhale and to seed itself into the blood and heart of the next person in the house. Burning the dead, infected heart then becomes the only way to root out the malady and destroy it. That belief might underlie this account of an unnamed Connecticut writer in 1888:

> The old superstition in such cases is that the vital organs of the dead still retain a certain flicker of vitality and by some strange process absorb the vital forces of the living, and they quote in evidence apocryphal instances wherein exhumation has revealed a heart and lungs still fresh and living, encased in rottening and slimy integuments, and in which, after burning these portions of the defunct, a living relative, else doomed and hastening to the grave, has suddenly and miraculously recovered.

A more picturesque way of saying the same thing had appeared just a few years earlier, in an 1884 magazine article, whose author speculated about how galloping consumption could so quickly fell, one after another, the apparently hale and hearty members of a single family:

> Among the superstitions of those days, we find it was said that a vine or root of some kind grew from coffin to coffin, of those of one family, who died of consumption, and were buried side by side; and when the growing vine had reached the coffin of the last one buried, another one of the family would die; the only way to destroy the influence or effect, was to break the vine; take up the body of the last one buried and burn the vitals, which would be an effectual remedy....

The word *remedy* might be the crucial clue here. As folklorist Michael Bell has surmised, these gruesome rituals constituted more an experiment in folk medicine than a belief in supernatural horrors. The word *vampire,* in fact, was never used—if indeed it was even known.

Yet, as forensic anthropologist Paul Sledzik and his museum colleagues concluded, the role of tuberculosis is key to understanding these folktales of New England "vampires." Might epidemiology be fundamental to understanding the vampire wherever he has appeared?

CHAPTER FIVE

CORPI MORTI

SKELETONS AND GRINNING SKULLS in niches and church windows; "Dances of Death" woodcuts in which cadavers take people by the hand and lead them to the grave; *transi* tombs bearing the effigies of their occupants, who—being in transition between body and skeleton—are shown as festering corpses; a church banner depicting a spear-wielding angel fighting a winged demon clad in putrescent flesh.

Images such as these flowered, if that word can be applied to such a ghastly phenomenon, during the late 14th century—a response, some scholars believe, to the greatest pandemic of them all, the Black Death, which swept into Europe and peaked somewhere between 1348 and 1350, killing perhaps half the Continent's population.

The plague had come from the east and had left 25 million dead in China and Mongolia, where it erupted around 1320. By 1347, it had reached the Crimean Peninsula, where Khan Jani Beg of the Golden Horde—the Mongol conquerors of Central Asia—was laying siege to the Genoese trading city of Kaffa. When the infection descended upon the encircling army, however, the besiegers became the beset. Jani Beg was forced to decamp, but not before he flung a few pestilential souvenirs at his triumphant enemy: He ordered his army to catapult plague-ridden corpses over the walls and into the streets of Kaffa. Many residents died as a result, but some escaped in ships to the west—and carried the epidemic with them.

Once those ships arrived in European ports, the infection metastasized throughout the populace. People broke out in dark spots and swollen lymph glands. They coughed up blood, vomited, writhed in agony, slipped into comas, and died. *La peste* was all they could call it: the plague.

Physicians of the time were baffled. Those at the University of Paris advised consuming no meat, fat, fish, or olive oil; vegetables, they decreed, were to be cooked in rainwater. Others suspected that wool, fabrics, or pelts harbored the source of the strange new scourge. Convinced that the pestilence resided in pets, some authorities killed and skinned domestic cats and dogs.

They were aiming way too high on the food chain. Instead, they should have targeted the grain sitting in the holds of ships, for grain, it seems, was a primary communicator of the plague; where grain resides, there dwell rats as well. And indeed, rats were everywhere in the medieval world: They lived inside thatch roofs and walls, in barns and in markets. Rats battened on filth. In some places, the plague was known as the "Viennese death" because, lacking sewers, that city was a byword for garbage and offal.

The real culprit was not the rat but the rat flea, whose bite might be laced with a virulently toxic bacterium, *Yersinia pestis* (though that crucial fact would not be discovered for another 500 years). Rat fleas can live for months inside clothes and straw mattresses. A bite from an infected flea usually transferred the bacillus to the human lymph system, where it flourished, causing the classic bubonic plague (named for the buboes, or painfully swollen lymph nodes, that erupted on victims). About half its victims died. That percentage soared, however, if the parasite entered the blood, in which case it caused septicemic plague, or the lungs, in which case the result was pneumonic plague. The latter could then be spread by the simple but brutally efficient contagion mechanism of infected droplets expelled by a cough. Both septicemic plague and pneumonic plague were generally death sentences.

People fled, sequestered themselves, or abandoned themselves to the pursuit of lust and hedonism. In Pistoia, Italy, travel was prohibited and guards were posted throughout the town. Coffins became a precious commodity; as fast as carpenters could turn a new one out, a body was placed inside and the lid nailed shut to contain the stench and contagion. Mourners were forbidden any contact with the dead. Traditional burial customs lapsed—a trend accelerated by municipal officials, who mandated, in historian Mary Ellen Snodgrass's words, "an end to wailing for the dead and the ringing of the cathedral's bells as a means of avoiding panic in the living when they realized how many had died."

"It is impossible for the human tongue to recount the awful truth," scrawled one Sienese chronicler, who had buried his five children and feared the end of the world was nigh. "Father abandoned child, wife husband, one brother another. . . . And in many places in Siena great pits were dug . . . with the multitude of dead." In Paris, 500 corpses a day were stacked awaiting burial at Les Innocents Cemetery. In Vienna, one mass grave was said to hold as many as 40,000 corpses. And in Avignon—seat of the papacy from 1305 to 1378—it took only six weeks to bury 11,000 people in a single cemetery. As graveyards overflowed, Pope Clement VI consecrated the Rhone River so that the bodies of Christians might be dumped into its waters.

Whereas the plague ravaged lands from Armenia to India—it is known as "the Great Destruction in the Year of Annihilation" in Muslim annals—it utterly desolated Europe. Abandoned ships drifted at their moorings. Farm animals became feral, while people died in droves in the fields. Nearly 200,000 villages are said to have disappeared from the medieval map. In Scotland, a standing stone commemorates a hamlet where everyone but an older woman perished; she collected the corpses on a donkey cart and buried them herself in a nearby field. Near Ragusa (today's Dubrovnik, in Croatia), weakened plague victims were eaten alive by wolves.

Ragusa at that time belonged to the Venetian empire. Venice itself, despite stringent health measures—vessel quarantines, the use of barren islands as burial grounds, and the enforcement of burials at five feet deep—suffered one of the worst outbreaks, with close to 75 percent fatalities. Entire noble families vanished, while every morning, cries of *"Corpi morti!"* ("Dead bodies! [Bring out your] Dead bodies!") echoed from the building fronts and along the canals.

Eventually, the plague dissipated. Venice not only recovered but also entered its golden age. "Once did she hold the gorgeous East in fee / And was the safeguard of the West," wrote Wordsworth in a panegyric to Venetian glories. At the city's height in the 15th and 16th centuries, much of the commerce of central Europe flowed across the Alps to Venice—whence, transferred to galleys, it was carried down the Adriatic to far-off Constantinople and the Levant.

As a maritime empire trading with lands to the east, where plague always smoldered, Venice may have been the European city best prepared to fight its eventual return. Venetian public health measures became second to none. The first lazaretto in the lagoon had been established as early as 1423; the second one, Lazzaretto Nuovo, or "new lazaretto," came into operation in 1468, primarily as a quarantine station. Its hospital, surrounded by high walls, ensured its being used during times of pandemic as a place where people went to die.

These and other bulwarks were breached all too often, but at least they helped confine outbreaks to flare-ups. An example of how seriously the plague was taken can be found today in the sacristy of Santa Maria della Salute on the Grand Canal: There, Titian's *St. Mark Triumphant*, probably painted during or after a plague outbreak in 1510, depicts an enthroned St. Mark, the patron saint of Venice, flanked by Cosmas, Damian, Roch, and Sebastian—the saintly foursome traditionally invoked to ward off the affliction.

Despite such prophylaxis, la peste returned to Venice with a vengeance in the autumn of 1576. The usual strict ordinances were imposed, with severe penalties for breaking them: New cases should be promptly reported, the sick immediately isolated, the clothes and bedding of the dead swiftly burned. The contagion only spread. Officials imposed a weeklong quarantine on the entire city. It had no effect.

On the Rialto, life came to a standstill. The Piazza San Marco stood empty. Innkeepers locked their doors, and shopkeepers shuttered their stalls. Those who could afford it headed for the hills inland. Too often, though, they were felled before they could flee. Most senators departed, but not the Republic's courageous leader, Doge Alvise Mocenigo I, who steadfastly remained in office as the epidemic burned through his city month after month, eventually infecting half of its 180,000 citizens.

Anyone who fell sick or showed even the slightest symptom was exiled to the lazarettos until they recovered or died.

When those outposts reached (and exceeded) capacity, two ancient galleons were towed into the lagoon and used as isolation wards. Even that did not suffice. Soon both Lazzaretto Vecchio and Lazzaretto Nuovo were ringed with ships, giving them the appearance of beleaguered island fortresses.

Within the walls and aboard the vessels, doctors sheathed in protective garments, their face masks packed with aromatic herbs, used hooked sticks to examine patients from a safe remove. With thousands of people falling sick, however, hundreds died each day. "It looked like hell. . . . The sick lay three or four in a bed," wrote the 16th-century Venetian chronicler Rocco Benedetti. "Workers collected the dead and threw them in the graves all day without a break. Often the dying ones and the ones too sick to move or talk were taken for dead and thrown on the piled corpses."

Thus did the burial grounds quickly fill up, becoming so saturated that gravediggers had to lay each new shrouded corpse on top of the one below. Constantly being opened and reopened, the cemeteries took on the appearance of festering mass graves.

DR. BORRÌNÌ DÌGS BONES

Nearly 400 years later, the Archaeological Superintendence of Veneto decided to excavate the remains. Across the sparkling waters of the lagoon from the old city, members of La Spezia Archaeological Group assembled to undertake a dig on Lazzaretto Nuovo.

In August 2006, with Venice given over to tourists for the summer season, this small band of archaeologists was carefully spading away under the watchful eye of their supervisor, Dr. Matteo Borrini. A forensic anthropologist associated with the University of Florence, Dr. Borrini had logged countless hours helping the Italian police investigate various crime scenes. He was using this dig, in fact, as an opportunity to refine some old methods—and to test out some promising new ones on how best to recover bodies from clandestine graves.

The plot they were excavating, though only 17 yards (16 meters) square, abounded with skeletons. Borrini was using what he called "taphonomic know-how" (from Greek *taphos*, "grave") to make sense of this jumble of bones by tracing their layers of deposition. Because this was not a conventional cemetery—rather a burial ground crammed with bodies every which way—the anthropologist's task was a little trickier. It soon became clear, however, that Borrini was dealing with at least two "stratigraphic macro-units," or two layers of bodies buried at different times. The topmost layer showed no postburial disturbance. Judging from medallions found among these remains from the Venice Jubilee of 1600, it represented the dead of the 1630–1631 plague epidemic, which had killed some 40,000 people.

Underlying and interpenetrating that layer of dead, however, was an older one composed of more fragmented skeletons, broken and shattered as if by the spades of gravediggers. The bodies in this layer had been skeletons for several decades when the victims of the 1630–1631 plague were laid on top of them. Borrini's team was able to establish that they almost certainly represented the dead from an earlier outbreak, this one the 1576–1577 plague.

August 11, 2006, promised to be as tediously exacting as any other day at the site. Borrini was making his usual rounds when a voice summoned him to a corner of the site where his sister had begun coaxing yet another skull from the dirt.

But not just any skull.

As was his habit when it came to unusual finds, the director took over and painstakingly removed the accretion from around the skull. It seemed that a brick, lodged between its jaws, was propping its mandible wide open.

That was odd. No other bricks or stones had been found in the backfill of that grave. Otherwise, the skeleton—or what was left of it, for the only portion not shattered by later gravediggers extended from the rib cage to the skull—seemed normal enough. It had been interred supine (on its back), its arms apparently at its sides, although the left clavicle, or collarbone, was pushed up at an angle—probably the result of a shroud wound too tightly about it. Quite likely from the older, or 1576, layer, it was catalogued as "ID6."

That brick bedeviled Borrini. He had enough experience as a forensic anthropologist to recognize an artifact of intentional action when he saw it. His first thought, in fact, was that this signaled some kind of bizarre, ritualized murder carried out at the height of a raging epidemic. Because there was no damage to the teeth, however, and because the jawbones were still perfectly aligned, the brick had probably not been rammed into the mouth of a violently struggling person. Instead, it had been inserted between the jaws of a corpse, when soft tissue was still present.

So far, so good. But *why?*

Throughout that autumn and into the winter, Borrini—now back at his academic office in Florence—puzzled over the find. Eventually, he was drawn to the university library, where he read up on the history of the plague and researched funerary practices common during pandemics. One book led to another, until finally Borrini came across a tract published in 1679 by Philip Rohr, a Protestant theologian at the University of Leipzig. It was called "De Masticatione Mortuorum": "On the Chewing Dead."

This volume described the *Nachzehrer*—German for "after-devourer"—a kind of mindless, vampirelike corpse that chews its shroud in the grave before consuming its own fingers. As it nibbles away, by some occult process, it also slowly kills the surviving members of its family. It may then begin gobbling corpses in neighboring graves.

As if all that were not grisly enough, the Nachzehrer's appalling dietary habits can be heard aboveground, where they come through loud and clear as a grunting, smacking sound like that of a pig snarfing garbage (dignified in Latin as *sonus porcinus*).

Born somewhere on the north German and Polish plains, this horrible figure made his appearance all over central

Europe during the 17th and 18th centuries. In "De Mastica-tione Mortuorum," Rohr culled examples from several even more obscure German dissertations, emphasizing that the grunting noise in particular was heard mostly, if not exclu-sively, during eruptions of the plague. One of his sources, in fact, had concluded that "corpses eat only during the time of plague." Rohr went on to cite a certain Adam Rother, who claimed that, as pestilence ravaged the German university town of Marburg in 1581, the dead in their graves could be heard uttering ominous noises from all over the town and surrounding countryside.

The same thing happened in Schisselbein, according to another little-known chronicler named Ignatius Hanielus. "Although both the corpses of men and of women are known to have grunted, gibbered, and squeaked," Rohr reported, for some inexplicable reason "it is more often the bodies of the weaker sex who have thus uttered curious voices."

Ever the inquiring theologian, Rohr offered an explana-tion for this postmortem mastication: The devil was using corpses to induce epidemics of plague by the mere act of their chewing. Why? For one thing, the very monstrousness of such an act was guaranteed to sow terror and confusion among the living. For another, every time a body had to be exhumed to stop its gnawing, the unearthed corpse would broadcast its infection and pestilence even farther afield.

Yet, unearthing a Nachzehrer was apparently the only way to stop the damned thing from grinding its teeth during the night: One had to seal its mouth with a handful of soil.

Denied the ability to chew, it would then die of starvation. "Some deeming this not altogether sufficient," Rohr wrote, "before they close the lips of the dead place a stone and a coin in the cold mouth, so that in his grave he may bite on these and refrain from gnawing further."

When Matteo Borrini read that, he understood why the brick had been thrust into the mouth of ID6: This person was suspected of being a vampire.

To Scapegoat Is Human?

For centuries, epidemics had been viewed not in natural terms but rather in supernatural ones, as by-products of the struggle between God and Satan. As late as 1692, in Salem, Massachusetts, a desperately cold winter had been followed by a smallpox outbreak; the deadly confluence was viewed as evidence that witches, allied with Satan, were at work. The stage was set for the Salem witchcraft trials.

The Old Testament attributed visitations of pestilence to God. In 1679, the same year that Rohr published "De Masticatione Mortuorum," an outbreak of plague in Vienna was blamed on a kind of supernatural visitant called a *Pest Jungfrau*, or "Plague Maiden."

Other scapegoats, tragically, were all too human.

In 1321, Philip V of France made leprosy a treasonable offense. Lepers, it seems, were supposed to be in league with Muslim Moors in Spain and Jews in Europe to poison the wells of Christendom. Lepers were burned at the stake—or locked in their houses while the houses burned down around their ears. Their property confiscated, they were interred without religious blessing. Soon leprosaria were in flames from southern France to Switzerland. Jacques Fournier, bishop of Mirepoix, oversaw the execution of thousands of lepers—shortly before he became Pope. Such was the mentality that reigned over Europe on the eve of the Black Death.

Once that epidemic hit, the scapegoating turned to even older targets. Anti-Jewish pogroms flared in cities all over Europe. In Basel, more than 600 Jews were burned at the stake, and their remains were deliberately left unburied. In Frankfurt, Jews were incinerated in their own houses. In Speyer, the burghers sealed Jewish corpses in wine casks and tossed them into the Rhine River, while Jewish mothers threw their babies into the fires and leaped in after them. And in Strasbourg, 2,000 Jews were rounded up, corralled on a wooden scaffold in the Jewish cemetery, and burned. Finally, in 1348, Pope Clement VI issued two papal bulls condemning such actions and declaring that the perpetrators had been "seduced by that liar, the Devil."

Witches were also to blame. In the 15th century, Sisteron in France was so beset by plague that its citizens executed suspected witches—a bid to perform a sort of communal pestilential exorcism. In 1545, judges in Geneva accused 62 people, 49 of them women, of being *engraisseurs,* or "plague spreaders"; 32 of them were burned at the stake. As the plague devastated Milan as well as Venice in 1576, Jews, beggars, and gypsies were victimized once again, being hunted down and killed. When that failed to end the pestilence, health workers were targeted instead.

Or might the fault lie in the stars? During the Black Death, King Philip VI of France convened the medical faculty at the University of Paris to explain what was happening. Following Hippocrates and the Arab physician Avicenna, they ascribed the plague to an evil conjunction of the planets Jupiter, Mars, and Saturn in the sign of Aquarius that had occurred on the afternoon of March 20, 1345, generating noxious fumes and a putrefaction that rotted the heart.

So, two centuries later, it might not have seemed so improbable to attribute the plague to corpses gnawing away in their graves at the goading of the devil.

HARD DAYS' LIFE

Back at the University of Florence, as winter turned to spring in 2009, Matteo Borrini was launching an intensive study of that brick-in-mouth skeleton, ID6. It would amount to a literal odyssey, with Borrini driving his suspected vampire from one high-tech lab to another all over Italy. Though he had only a partial skeleton to work with, he was going to subject it to a battery of tests to better understand who this person once was.

Might ID6 have been a Jew? A Levantine merchant? A North African Moor, like Othello? To find out, Borrini sought out any vestiges of hair, fiber, or other materials that might still be clinging to ID6's bones. Using powerful forensic light source lamps, he fired beams of multispectral light onto the traces of dirt adhering to the skull—and discovered two rosary beads. That was a key clue, for it meant that ID6 had almost certainly been Roman Catholic—as were most Venetians. And its skull fit known European profiles.

Determining its sex was a bit trickier. Judging from what was left of the skeleton, ID6 had once belonged to a small person—someone, Borrini estimated, who stood about one and a half meters tall, or a little over five feet. Yet it was missing the telltale hip bones, which usually revealed gender at a glance. He therefore turned to the skull. The mastoid process—a spurlike projection just behind the ears, where the neck muscles attach—is generally larger in men than in women. On ID6, it seemed quite small. Furthermore, the chin seemed demurely pointed. So this was most likely a woman.

If so, how old was she? Calcification of the ribs is one way to judge age. But the condition of ID6's skeleton was too fragmented to reveal anything more precise than that it belonged to somebody probably older than 50. High-tech X-ray imaging of the canine teeth (of all things) is notably more precise because their internal cavities age at a known rate. Those tests indicated that ID6 was a chronological standout for her era. She had reached the remarkably advanced age of 61 to 71 years old.

This vampire, if such it was, had been a little old lady—and a not particularly bloodthirsty one at that. Trace element testing of her bones had turned up a high sodium reading, consistent with a largely vegetarian diet, perhaps supplemented with a little fish from time to time. She had also lived a physically demanding life, judging from a ridge that had formed around the head of her right humerus, or upper arm bone, where it fits into the shoulder socket. This indicated constant and repetitive lifting; from this, Borrini deduced that the shoulder might have been causing her pain.

ID6 was an ordinary, working-class Venetian woman —neither poor nor rich, but most decidedly a survivor. Though Borrini divined that she had suffered a skull injury as a young girl, evidently she had recovered from that and had managed to live past 60—no mean feat at the time. A century later in London, an examination of the Bills of Mortality from 1629 to 1660 revealed that "of 100 quick Conceptions about 36 of them die before they be six years old, and that perhaps but one surviveth 76."

In between those two ends of the age spectrum lay some even more sobering actuarial details: Only one-fourth of all those born were still alive by the age of 26, and only 6 out of every 100 lived to see 56. The main killers were infectious diseases—the grim gauntlet through which the race of life was run. ID6 had gotten pretty far down the course before being tripped up by tiny *Yersinia pestis*. The bacillus landed her in a quarantine hospital, where she may have spent her final few days in agony.

She was just one of the tens of thousands the plague swept away. Borrini had seen it in the cemetery: Plague was the great leveler, and in those layers, he could glimpse a cross section of the human condition on a fine day in the Piazza San Marco circa 1575, just before the invader struck. Rich and poor, soldier and diplomat, merchant and laborer, servant and beggar, ladies in oriental silks and gallants in brightly colored hose—all soon to be mowed down by death's scythe and deposited equally in the boneyard.

"An old woman who lived a long, hard life," Borrini reflected about ID6, "and was falsely accused after her death of being a vampire."

As a forensic anthropologist, Borrini knew the reason why. It all had to do with the state of her corpse.

Death Be Not Proud

In the 1980s, the forensic approach to the study of vampires was pioneered not by a pathologist but rather by a folklorist. Paul Barber took the widely accepted notion that a vampire was a reanimated corpse and pursued it to its logical conclusion: "[A] vampire," wrote Barber in his now-classic *Vampires, Burial, and Death* (1988), "is a body that in all respects appears to be dead except that it does not decay as we expect, its blood does not coagulate, and it may show changes in dimension and in color."

Barber's contention was that nearly all the traits associated with the folkloric vampire originated in misunderstandings about decaying bodies. Blood sucking? Just a "folkloric means [for clarifying] two unrelated phenomena: unexplained deaths and the appearance of blood at the mouth of a corpse." Before the late 19th century, when embalming started to become standard practice in Western nations, dead bodies did strange but perfectly natural things in their graves. The course of physical corruption—and this is not for the weak of stomach—does not always run true.

Bodies exposed to summer heat and air, for instance, tend to decay quickly. At the end of the battle of Gettysburg, fought from July 1 to 3, 1863, a 27-year-old Confederate artilleryman named Robert Stiles encountered the carcasses of those who had been slain only two or three days previously:

> The sights and smells that assailed us were simply indescribable—corpses swollen to twice their original size, some of them actually burst asunder with the pressure of foul gases and vapors. I recall one feature never before noted, the shocking distention and protension of the eyeballs of dead men and dead horses. Several human or unhuman corpses sat upright against a fence, with arms extended in the air and faces hideous with something very like a fixed leer, as if taking a fiendish pleasure in showing us what we essentially were and might at any moment become. The odors were nauseating, and so deadly that in a short time we all sickened and were lying with our mouths close to the ground, most of us vomiting profusely.

The same processes so horribly apparent in those summer fields were equally present in the grave, although burial—again, depending on the circumstances of deposition—might slow them considerably. Bodies decompose most rapidly when exposed to air, most slowly deep in the earth. The more air, insects, moisture, bacteria, and other microorganisms that are present, generally speaking, the faster it happens. The slain soldiers were decomposing before the eyes of stunned survivors; by contrast, the dead in their wintry graves in Medvegia, as we saw in the last chapter, were just getting under way—this despite the fact that some of them had been underground a full three months.

And then there is the mindset of those forced to gaze upon such spectacles: If people are determined to find a vampire, they will find one. Writer Elwood B. Trigg, in *Gypsy Demons and Divinities,* neatly sums up the double bind: "If, after a period of time, [the corpse] remains incorrupt, exactly as it was buried, or if it appears to be swollen and black in color, having undergone some dreadful change in appearance, suspicions of vampirism are confirmed."

Nevertheless, some telltale signs of bodily decomposition that have often been mistaken as evidence of vampirism include bloodstained liquid flowing from nose or mouth, bloating, changes in skin color, enlargement of the genitals (in both sexes), and the shedding of nails or hair. (With other signs—the liquefaction of eyeballs, the conversion of tissues into a semifluid guck or the presence of maggots—even the hardened vampire hunter must admit defeat.)

The appearance on a corpse of growing hair, nails, or teeth is illusory. They do not grow. Instead, the surrounding skin and gums contract, making them look longer or more prominent. By the same token, reports that a vampire has sloughed off its old skin like a snake, revealing a grisly new reddish one beneath, represent what forensic pathologists call skin slippage, or the loosening of the epidermis from the underlying dermis—again, all perfectly normal.

A body long buried in a deep, cool, moist environment is often subject to saponification, another natural process in which fats are rendered into adipocere—a waxy, soapy substance, sometimes called corpse wax or grave wax, that sheathes the entire carcass like some gruesome body cast. Although rarely correlated with supposed vampirism, saponification may explain why some corpses were seen as being incorruptible. Barber even quotes a former lecturer in "Morbid Anatomy" at the University of London, W. E. D. Evans, as claiming that the reddish color of saponified muscles can "give the impression of muscle freshly dead, even though the death occurred more than 100 years previously."

Another charge hurled at the coffined vampire is its lack of rigor mortis (the stiffening of the body after death). True, rigor mortis follows swiftly on the heels of death as chemical changes start to stiffen the muscles—producing those upthrown arms and fiendish grins of the Gettysburg slain—but it starts fading as early as 40 hours after death. In the old days, the corpse would likely be in its grave by the time its limbs settled and flopped into whatever position gravity dictated. That, combined with the shifts occasioned by internal pressures and bloating, might contort the body into a position different from the one in which it was originally buried—with all the alarums that development might engender were it to become known.

The exhumed vampire is often described as ruddy in appearance. Yet, color changes in corpses are transitory—and contingent on innumerable variables. Not long after death, for instance, the settling of blood lends the human face the bluish cast that has become familiar as livor mortis, or death blue. Usually there follows a sequence of changes known as the chromatic stages of decomposition, running from red to green to purple and then to brown. Furthermore, a corpse may actually grow warmer as serious decomposition sets in—heat being a natural by-product of microorganisms hard at work.

And then there were the bloated bodies: Dracula in his coffin swollen "like a filthy leech," the once-lean Miliza in Medvegia astonishing her former neighbors by the "surprising plumpness" she had gained in the grave. All that, of course, is the result of gas, mostly methane, that accumulates in the body's tissues as those same microorganisms metabolize a corpse. Though postmortem swelling is most pronounced in the abdomen—home to legions of intestinal bacteria—every part of a corpse may puff up to two or three times its natural size, rendering its features unrecognizable. This ghastly appearance was a familiar enough encounter in war zones. Just a few days before they were discovered on the killing fields of Gettysburg, for example, those bloated and blackened bodies had been lean and hungry young men.

Given the right circumstances, this gas might erupt—often with explosive force. "It is well known to those engaged in burying the dead," Dr. George Walker writes in his *Gatherings from Grave Yards*, "that when leaden coffins are employed, the expansive force of the gas, and the consequent bulging out of the coffin, compels the workmen frequently to 'tap' it, that the gas may escape." This demanded some skill. After boring a hole with a gimlet—a handheld auger that resembles nothing so much as a corkscrew—a "jet of gas instantly passes through the aperture, and this, when ignited, produces a flame, that lasts from ten minutes to half an hour. The men who perform this operation are perfectly aware of the risk they encounter, and they are extremely careful how they execute it."

And then there is the disturbing matter of "corpse light." At Gettysburg, the layer of dirt covering the mass graves was so thin that a strange phosphorescence emanated from the ground at night. For years, understandably, locals shunned such places as haunted. Eerie glows reported near cemeteries, will-o'-the-wisp phenomena, even the blue flames that Slavic folktales describe as appearing over the sites of buried treasure on St. George's Eve (and used to such chilling effect in the opening pages of *Dracula*) are typically written off as cases of hyperimagination. Yet, they might be actual instances of bioluminescence:

Photobacterium fischeri, forensic pathologists will tell you, is but one of many luminous bacteria known to settle on a shallowly buried body.

Don't Mock Your Own Grinning

Certainly the most dramatic manifestation of suspected vampirism is blood at the mouth. Surely that was the vampire's most recent meal, now trickling down its chin? Horrifying as they appear, bloody lips on the dead are nothing out of the ordinary. "Decay of the internal organs," Borrini points out, "creates a dark fluid sometimes known as 'purge fluid': it can flow freely from the nose and mouth (or from the corpse, if it is staked) and could easily be confused with the blood sucked by the vampire."

Exhumed cadavers are likewise frequently reported as wallowing in blood-filled coffins. That was an unfailing sign of vampirism because blood was known to coagulate after death. Well, yes and no: Under certain circumstances—especially if death was abrupt—blood might reliquefy. But though blood will out, as the proverb has it, the liquid that seeps out of a corpse's orifices into the coffin is almost certainly, Borrini says, purge fluid.

Bodies can also literally return from the grave. If not buried deep enough, their natural buoyancy might propel them to the surface. This may explain why archaeologists have found so many skeletons deliberately weighted down by rocks or timbers.

And then there is the groaning—sometimes, in literature or cinema, the screaming—of the vampire as it is staked through the heart. One could easily, and justifiably, pass this off as a folkloric embellishment. On the other hand, it might be a legitimate physiological reflex. "Indeed, it would have been odd if his body had *not* let out a sound when a stake was driven into it," Barber remarked of Arnold Paole, staked in 1725 in Medvegia. Hammering a piece of wood into a chest cavity violently compresses the lungs and forces air past the glottis as if expelled through the pipe of an organ.

That the dead grow slack of jaw is familiar enough through literature. "Not one now, to mock your own grinning?" asks Hamlet of poor Yorick, "quite chap-fallen?" Scrooge gazes in horror when Marley's ghost loosens its head bandage and "its lower jaw dropped down upon its breast." As the jaw muscles relax with the dissipation of rigor mortis, the mouth predictably falls open. But if a body is wrapped too tightly in its shroud—as ID6 was, for it bent her left clavicle upward—the shroud will collapse into the gaping cavity. Then, as Borrini puts it, "cadaveric gases and purge fluid flowing from the mouth can moisten the shroud" and rot it as it dries. To the unenlightened observer, the resulting gap in the fabric may suggest the corpse has chewed right through it. If that cadaver also shows fingers lacerated by decomposition or the action of maggots, it can be taken for a Nachzehrer.

In view of all this, we may now at long last be able to glimpse what happened to ID6 in her cemetery at Lazzaretto

Nuovo. Imagine the loathsome scene: Its overhanging stench, the pockmarked ground suppurating with putrescent bodies hidden by the barest covering of dirt. Flies swarm over the exposed bodies, which are soon crawling with maggots.

The pit is a fearsome place. Daniel Defoe, describing the Great Plague that punished London in 1665, reconstructed its burial pits in his *Journal of the Plague Year* (1722):

> I went all the first part of the time freely about the streets, tho' not so freely as to run my self into apparent danger, except when they dug the great pit in the church-yard of our parish of 'Aldgate'; a terrible pit it was, and I could not resist my curiosity to go and see it; as near as I may judge, it was about 40 foot in length, and about 15 or 16 foot broad; and at the time I first looked at it, about nine foot deep; but it was said, they dug it near 20 foot deep afterwards, in one part of it, till they could go no deeper for the water. . . . The pit being finished the 4th of September, I think, they began to bury in it the 6th, and by the 20th, which was just two weeks, they had thrown into it 1114 bodies, when they were obliged to fill it up, the bodies being then come to lie within six foot of the surface.

There was also the grimly ironic Holywell Pit, or "Black Ditch," and the one in Finsbury Fields. "People that were infected, and near their end, and delirious also," Defoe wrote, "would run to those pits wrapt in blankets, or rugs, and throw themselves in, and as they said, bury themselves. . . . I have heard, that in a great pit in 'Finsbury,' in the parish of 'Cripplegate,' it lying open then to the fields; for it was not then wall'd about, [they] came and threw themselves in, and expired there, before they threw any earth upon them; and that when they came to bury others, and found them there, they were quite dead, tho' not cold."

The cemetery at Lazzaretto Nuovo surely had its visible horrors. It may have had audible ones as well. The waxing and waning of chewing sounds said to reflect the coming and going of epidemics might arise in the documentable fact that, during such times, hundreds of hastily buried and rapidly decomposing bodies were generating their own horrid symphony. As Barber memorably captured it, the "disruption of large numbers of bodies bloating and bursting caus[ed] a sound rather like an epidemic stomach-rumbling."

At some point—perhaps months but probably scant weeks after ID6 had died and been buried—a burial detail, having no choice, opened her grave to add yet another occupant to it. At that point, quite likely, they saw that she had "chewed" a hole in her shroud. Someone, likely one of the gravediggers, knew the superstition associated with this, and knew how to stop it—literally, with a brick. Whether they recoiled in horror at the sight, whether they concluded that this particular corpse was responsible for all the suffering of the plague, or whether that brick was placed in the cadaver's mouth as a precautionary measure, we will never know. But this much is clear: Utterly unfairly, ID6 was treated as if she were a vampire.

Requiescant in Pace

During the year and a half that it ravaged Venice, la peste carried off 46,000 people—nearly one-third of the city's population. In due course, however, it abated, and an official proclamation of health was announced on July 21, 1577. In gratitude for the deliverance, the doge and the senate erected the basilica of Il Redentore (The Redeemer) on the island of Giudecca. Over the years since then, every third Sunday in July, bells announce the Feast of the Redeemer with the joy that life has been restored.

The deliverance was short-lived, as we have seen, and when the plague returned between 1630 and 1631, it laid another 40,000 bodies on top of ID6 and her fellow victims in cemeteries scattered throughout Venice. That visitation, many historians believe, spelled the beginning of the end for the Queen of the Adriatic. The city slowly declined until 1797, when Napoleon ended its existence as an independent republic.

If ID6 was a vampire, it is only in the sense that Paul Barber defined the term: "a corpse that comes to the attention of the populace in times of crisis and is taken for the cause of that crisis." According to anthropologist Edward B. Tylor, writing in 1871, "Vampires are not mere creations of groundless fancy, but causes conceived in spiritual form to account for specific facts of wasting disease." More than a century later, folklorist Michael Bell refined Tylor's point: "Reduced to its common denominator, the vampire is a classic scapegoat."

We have now arrived at one very compelling explanation for vampiric origins: The whole mythology grew out of observations of corpses—superstition wrapped around forensic fact. As Barber puts it, "Our descriptions of revenants and vampires match up, detail by detail, with what we know about dead bodies that have been buried for a time."

"In the end, from a forensic point of view," Borrini muses, "we can accept the reports about the 'vampire corpses' as real descriptions, but we can also realize why those legends spread especially during plagues." After all, during pandemics, it was standard practice to reopen tombs and mass graves so as to add more victims. "In this way, it was easier to find bodies that were not completely decomposed, thus increasing dread and superstition among people who were already suffering pestilence and massive deaths."

Nevertheless, stories about vampires have been evolving for centuries, and we must follow that trail. As we close the case of ID6, however, we leave her—and all other "vampires" whose only crime was to die and be buried—with a heartfelt *"Requiescant in pace"* ("May they rest in peace") on our lips.

CHAPTER SIX

TERRA DAMNATA

WHEN SHAKESPEARE'S HAMLET encounters the ghost of his father on the battlements of Denmark's Elsinore Castle, he cannot believe his eyes: "Let me not burst in ignorance," he begs, "but tell why thy canonized bones, hearsed in death, have burst their cerements." A moment later he asks why his father's "dead corse" is making the night hideous.

Bones? Corpse? Is it a ghost or a corpse that Hamlet sees? Today we make a distinction between a ghost, which is an incarnate spirit, and a vampire, which is a walking corpse. But in Shakespeare's day, that separation wasn't quite so pronounced. Even Englishman Henry More (1614–1687), a leading authority on the world of spirits, chose to call walking corpses specters.

More had recoiled from the "too sterile" Puritanism of his Lincolnshire youth, embracing instead the Neoplatonist philosophy he had discovered as a Cambridge undergraduate. His lifelong fascination with spirits was said to have led him into many a ruined vault echoing with dismal sighs and groanings and heaped with skulls and bones. His collected ghost stories—"stories sufficiently fresh and very well attested and certain," he claimed—were published in *An Antidote Against Atheism* (1653), which More offered as an attempt to prove the metaphysical priority of spirit, and thus the primacy of God.

Two of those tales have since become touchstones in the literature of vampirism. In More's retelling of the first story, on September 20, 1591, in the Polish city of Breslau (today Wroclaw), a prosperous shoemaker slipped into his back garden and, for reasons unknown, slit his own throat. For more than a thousand years, Christians have viewed suicide as a sin against God and man, so according to doctrine, this unnamed shoemaker never should have been buried in consecrated ground. Yet his family successfully concealed his crime. He had died of disease, they maintained, so as a stalwart member of the community he was interred in terra sancta: the churchyard.

Soon, however, the good burghers of Breslau began to whisper. Rumors of suicide spread. The town council launched an investigation, and the widow confessed the truth.

But by then, in More's words, the shoemaker had reappeared:

Those that were asleep it terrified with horrible visions,
those that were waking it would strike, pull or press,

lying heavily upon them like an ephialtes [night-mare] so that there were perpetuall complaints every morning of their last nights rest, through the whole town. . . . For this terrible apparition would some-times cast itself upon the midst of their beds, would lie close to them, would miserably suffocate them and would so strike them and pinch them that not only blue marks but plain impressions of his fingers would be upon sundry parts of their bodies in the mornings.

As more and more people reported such visitations, hysteria spread. Soon the authorities, as More continued his tale, had no choice but to disinter the corpse:

He had lain in the ground near eight months, viz. from Sept. 22, 1591 to April 18, 1592, when he was digged up which was in the presence of the magistracy of the town, his body was found entire, not at all putrid, no ill smell about him, save the mustiness of his grave clothes, his joints limber and flexible, as those that are alive, his skin only flaccid but a more fresh grown in the room of it, the wound of his throat gaping but no gear [pus] nor corruption in it. . . .

Nearly a week passed before the shoemaker was reburied—this time in terra damnata, beneath the gallows. Yet the "spectrum," as More called the apparition, raged all the worse until the widow gave in, and once again the body was unearthed. Now even more swollen and repulsive, it was decapitated and its limbs were cut off. The heart, still appearing fresh and whole, was ripped out and burned to a cinder, whereupon its ashes were cast into the Oder River. The spectrum was never seen again.

More's second iconic ghost story related the eerie tale of Johannes Cuntius, a wealthy alderman of Pentsch in Poland, who died after being kicked by a horse. Soon, rumors circulated that, on his deathbed, Alderman Cuntius had admitted forging a pact with Satan to gain his riches. That had led to stories that a tempest had arisen at the moment of his death, and that a black cat had rushed into the room and scratched his face. One sighting triggered another, and soon a revivified Cuntius was being spotted all over town. In More's recapturing of the sinister events that followed, Cuntius shook houses, turned milk to blood, and defiled the altar cloth with blood stains. He sucked cows dry; he violently assaulted former friends; he ravished his widow. At one time Cuntius was a mere phantom, disappearing when a candle was lit; at other times, he was only too corporeal, with a fetid stink and a touch as cold as ice.

Not surprisingly, Cuntius, too, was evicted from his grave:

. . . they dig up Cuntius his body with several others buried both before and after him. But those both after and before were so putrefied and rotten, their skulls broken, and the sutures of them gaping, that they were not to be known by their shape at all, having become in a manner but a rude mass of earth and dirt; but it was quite otherwise in Cuntius. His skin was tender and florid, his joints not at all stiff but limber and moveable, and a staff being put in his hand, he grasped it with his fingers very fast. His eyes also of themselves would be one time open and another time shut; they opened a vein in his leg and the blood sprang out as fresh as in the living. His nose was entire and full, not sharp as in those that are ghastly sick or quite dead. And yet Cuntius his body had lain in the grave from Feb. 8 to July 20, which is almost half a year.

The corpse was burned but even that brought no relief, for the carcass seemingly refused to be cremated; only after it was hacked to bits did the flames finally consume it.

To a modern reader, these stories are all too predictable. A prosperous citizen dies. Rumors of suicide or secret sin begin to circulate and ignite mass hysteria. Finally, the corpse is dug up and discovered to be undecomposed, seeming to substantiate the tittle-tattle. No blood has been sucked; nobody has died.

Henry More, however, saw it otherwise:

I look upon it as a special piece of Providence that there are ever and Anon such fresh examples of Apparitions and Witchcraft as may rub up and awaken [the atheists'] benumbed and lethargic Minds into a suspicion at least, if not assurance that there are other intelligent beings besides those that are clad in heavy Earth or Clay.

More's ultimate inspiration may have been Plato, but Christianity had long offered a rival vision of a fundamentally spiritual universe. Although the Christian world was fragmenting—Roman Catholics and Eastern Orthodoxy had split in 1054, the Protestant Reformation was well under way, and the English had recently beheaded their king, the Anointed of God—that vision would linger well into the 18th century. And the impression of its saints and angels, its miracles and monsters, and above all its witches and demons can be traced in the features of the vampire today.

The Art of Dying

Ars moriendi—the art of dying—and its popular woodblock illustrations brought that spiritual universe into sharp focus. On a bed lies the dying person, attended on one side by haloed angels and saints, and on the other by a gang of leering, impish demons, all horns and tails. The clear implication is that the forces of heaven and hell have gathered to battle for the soul at the moment of death.

Those demons were but foot soldiers in the vast hierarchy of hell. With its dominions, principalities, and powers, its thrones and choirs and seraphim, hell was the infernal parody of heaven. Satan was its god, Beelzebub its lord, Carreau its prince of powers, and so on down through all those unpronounceable names: Anticif, Arfaxat, Astaroth, Asmodeus, Behemoth, Calconix, Enepsigos, Grongade, Leontophone, Leviathan, Saphathorael, Sphendonael, and even Shakespeare's "foul fiend Flibbertigibit," to name only a demon's dozen. No complete roster of their legions was ever compiled, and no wonder: If a single satanic prince was said to have 60 billion dukes in his retinue, the foot soldiers of the vasty deep—horned, spiked, scaled, ass-eared, and cloven-footed—must have been numberless indeed.

That's why last rites were administered to that person expiring on his deathbed: They helped purify his soul so that it might be received by the hands of ministering angels, not lurking demons. Confession, absolution, extreme unction, and the final Eucharist, or viaticum, was the prescribed order for Roman Catholics, but Eastern Orthodoxy observed a similar ritual. Then, as now, Catholics dreaded the prospect of sudden death because no one wanted to die without benefit of confession and absolution. Life had to be ebbing rapidly before the oil of extreme unction could be applied; those lucky enough to return from the brink after that potent touch were dismayed to find themselves deemed ritually dead—living corpses on the order of "stinking Lazarus," whom Christ had brought back from the tomb. There was also the option of exorcism, the expelling of "evil" or "unclean" spirits from diseased bodies. Finally, there was viaticum, or "provision for the journey"; this last Eucharist or communion might be the final experience the flickering consciousness perceived before departing.

That was about all that could be done for the soul. The body, still supernaturally charged, had to be attended to soon thereafter. Funeral and burial rites were performed so that the body might be wrapped, not merely in its shroud, but also in a protective cocoon of sanctity, within which it might await the last trump and the resurrection. That's why cremation was so abhorrent to the medieval Christian: It not only smacked of paganism but also destroyed the "temple of the Holy Ghost," denying the soul any vehicle for restoration. (Despite Saint Paul's pronouncement that we are sown a natural body but raised a spiritual one, most people in the Middle Ages believed that resurrection meant a reawakening in their familiar flesh.)

By the time the corpse arrived at the graveyard—whether borne in a closed coffin by bearers, as in England, or carried in an open casket trailing long black streamers, as in Greece—it had already been washed, sprinkled, censed, purified, enshrouded, prayed for, chanted over, and blessed for days, almost without surcease. Although the grave site already lay in consecrated ground, the priest would sanctify it again by making the sign of the cross over it and sprinkling it with holy water. The body, too, would be blessed, censed, and sprinkled one final time—and, once the appropriate words had been read over it, lowered into the grave. Finally, before the grave was closed, a handful of dirt would be strewn over the coffin in the shape of a cross.

Yet, even then, the ritual wasn't over: Obsequies would be made at certain times—typically the 3rd, 9th, and 40th days after burial, as in the Orthodox Church, and then yearly on the anniversary of the death.

If all went well, the decedent—both body and soul—would be not just protected but integrated into the larger community of the faithful existing in eternity. The Catholic notion of purgatory, with its cult of intercession—well-paid priests in chantry chapels praying to saints to speed a given soul's progress through the purging fires—greatly enriched this overall sense of community. So much money flowed into the upkeep and beautification of churches in order to propitiate the saints that purgatory wound up having a positive economic impact, making medieval Catholicism, as one historian put it, a "cult of the living in the service of the dead."

In Eastern Orthodoxy, by contrast, there was no purgatory; the 40-day period after burial was its rough equivalent. By the end of that period, the soul should have completed its journey, and the physical decomposition of the body would be under way. Occasionally, the dead were exhumed at that time to allow the priests a peek. Apparently they didn't always relish what they saw, for three years became the standard in most places. The grave was then opened and the body examined. If the priest seemed relieved, all was well; the bones would be collected and, after due observances, either reinterred or sent to the charnel house.

But if doubt flickered over the pastor's features, things might be looking ominous. An undecomposed body, as we have seen, was typically interpreted as a sign of vampirism. In the absence of any vampire complaints, however, the priest might simply seal the grave. The ritual might be repeated three years later—by that time, surely, the worms would have done their work.

Vampire symptoms were often attributed to mishaps along the ritual trail. A cat jumping over the corpse, to cite a well-known folklore example, might allow a demon to exploit an opportunity. It was much easier to suspect demonic possession, however, if the corpse was that of an excommunicate. There were many reasons for excommunication—heresy, chiefly, but also smaller infractions such as a refusal to confess—and to die in an excommunicated state meant, quite literally, permanent exile from the community of the faithful. Buried in unconsecrated ground, the bodies of excommunicates—as well as those of witches, sorcerers, suicides, criminals, or any other anathematized people— were bereft of God's holy protection. Demons could then possess their corpses, using them as instruments to sow evil and destruction. The unmistakable sign that demonic possession had occurred, to many village priests in the Slavic world, was a corpse found bloated, ruddy, and undecomposed in its grave.

So often and so insistently was demonic possession used as an explanation for vampirism that the vampire came to be seen as the typological inverse of the saint: One was a blessed soul with the power to heal and protect, while the other was a wandering corpse strewing death, disease, and pestilence in its wake. The vampire's very existence was an infernal parody of the resurrection, and its chief means of sustenance was a diabolical twist on Christ's words: "Whoso eateth my flesh and drinketh my blood hath eternal life."

WITCHES AND WEREWOLVES

In 1484, Pope Innocent VIII issued a papal bull making witch-craft a heresy in Catholic Europe. Yet, the hysteria that over-took Europe in the 16th and 17th centuries, when 30,000 to 60,000 people were burned at the stake, never really ignited in the Slavic east. There the witch was, more often than not, the village "wise woman." The horseshoes, hares' heads, and boars' tusks nailed on walls and barns, or the garlic cloves, blue beads, and bloodstones that decorated houses, horses, and caps were as much a defense against the evil eye—the intense gaze, the unblinking stare, the envious glance—as they were charms against witches or vampires. Anyhow, in folklore, witches and vampires were often the same thing.

In Romania, *strigoi* are vampires, while *strigele* are the spir-its of witches. In Italy, *strega* are witches or vampires, as the occasion demands. Both shared the same attributes: Witches were said to have long teeth, their bodies might be possessed by demons, and they could leave the grave to eat people. Witches could enter a house through a keyhole; many had to disappear by cockcrow. The hexing action of a witch could dry up cattle's milk, blast the crops, and unleash the plague among people. All of these activities are likewise imputed to vampires. Little wonder, then, that a Slavic proverb holds that the "vampire and the devil are blood relatives of all witches."

Many folklorists would include the werewolf in that list. The Serbs, for instance, conflate vampire and werewolf in a single word—*vukodlak*—as do the Greeks in *vrykolakas*. Ukrainians believe a vampire to be the offspring of a witch who mated with either a werewolf or a demon. And in Russia, all three became one: According to 19th-century dictionaries, a vampire was "a sorcerer who turns into a wolf." You could tell one by its tail.

Werewolves were depicted as particularly savage. Werewolf madness existed alongside witchcraft hysteria. From 1520 to 1630, there were 30,000 reported cases of lycanthropy—men becoming wolves—in central France alone.

The most notorious werewolf, however, was German. Under torture in 1589, a Westphalian farmer named Peter Stubbe, or Stumpf, confessed to having made a pact with Satan. In return, Stubbe claimed, he had received a magical wolfskin belt that allowed him to rampage in the guise of a wolf for the next 25 years. According to Stubbe's confession, he had indulged in every act of bestiality that the depraved imaginations of his inquisitors could dream up. This included killing and eating children, pregnant women, and even his own son. Rounding out this litany of horrors was incest with his daughter.

Or so Stubbe said—as might anyone who had been broken on the wheel. His demise was especially grisly. First, Stubbe was flayed alive, his skin peeled off with red-hot pincers. Next, all of his bones were broken with the blunt end of an axe. Finally, he was decapitated. As Stubbe's carcass went up in flames (alongside those of his daughter and mistress), his severed head was placed on a spike and mounted atop the ghastly agent of his martyrdom, the wheel.

DISENCHANTMENT BY DECAPITATION

Medieval Christendom may have envisioned the world as a spiritual battleground, but it inflicted horribly real outrages on earthly tabernacles as well. The desecration of dead bodies—the beheading, the dismembering, the burning of them—was a recapitulation of the capital punishments inflicted on living ones. Such abominations were rooted in a primitive desire to destroy the corpse—an action that in turn was designed to deprive the malefactor of the blessings of resurrection, or to deny a vengeful ghost any instrument for retaliation.

"Disenchantment by decapitation" is a phrase that folk-lorists have coined to describe those actions in fairy tales where the hero, by cutting off a monster's head, releases a soul trapped in the fiend's body by evil enchantment. That motif has deep roots in global culture: The severed head has traditionally constituted the ultimate gory trophy.

Beheading, in fact, was the execution method of choice for kings and aristocrats of old. Of the many heads lost in England, only one had been crowned, anointed, and hedged about with all the supernatural protection that ritual and ceremony could provide. Yet none of that could shield its owner from his own disenchantment by decapitation. "I go from a corruptible to an incorruptible crown," declared deposed King Charles I as he stepped out of London's Banqueting House and onto the scaffold on a dark January day in 1649, when he lost his head in a terrible culmination to the English civil wars. Though Charles I was hastily buried in Windsor Castle's St. George's Chapel, it was soon bruited about that he had been denied the burial rites in the *Book of Common Prayer*. Eleven years later, the son of Charles I was restored to the English throne, and he went looking for his father's remains. Neither head nor body could be found.

A century and a half later, in 1813, workmen in the vaults of St. George's Chapel accidentally broke in to the crypt of King Henry VIII. Although the crypt was supposed to contain just two coffins—King Henry's and Queen Jane Seymour's—the workmen found three. The prince regent assembled a small party, which included Sir Henry Halford, future president of the Royal College of Surgeons, and together they climbed into the dark, musty vault to investigate.

They couldn't resist peering into the leaden coffin supposed to contain King Henry VIII's remains. They spied the skeleton within—"some beard remained upon the chin"—but nothing else of note. They chose, however, to leave inviolate the sepulcher containing the queen, as they deemed "mere curiosity" an insufficient motive for disturbing her remains.

The investigators then turned to the third coffin, likewise made of lead. First they discovered an inscription bearing the name of King Charles. Then, prying the lead back, they peered inside.

If the martyred king had indeed been refused burial rites, his body would have been vulnerable to demonic possession. And they did see inside a figure, wrapped in cerecloth, "into the folds of which," Halford later reported, "a quantity of unctuous or greasy matter, mixed with resin, as it seemed, had been melted, so as to exclude, as effectually as possible, the external air." Carefully removing these cerements, they beheld a remarkably well-preserved face. This was no skeleton; clearly, Charles I had been embalmed. The cartilage of the nose was gone, "but the left eye, in the first moment of exposure, was open and full. . . ."

A transfixing eye in that dismal place—but instantly it turned to dust. Then, carefully lifting the severed head, the party gazed at the long-dead monarch: The familiar Vandyke beard was perfect, many teeth were still in place, and the left ear was likewise intact. The fourth cervical vertebra had been cleaved in half, "an appearance which could have been produced only by a heavy blow," Halford continued, "inflicted by a very sharp instrument. . . ." Before laying the head back in its coffin, where presumably it remains to this day, the men noticed—the passage of 164 years notwithstanding—that it was "quite wet" with what everyone present, including the surgeon, believed to be blood.

Severed heads. The sultan in his palace supposedly greeted Vlad Dracula's impaled head with delight. The severed heads of malefactors—especially bandits and rebels—adorned city gates, bridges, and public squares all over the ancient and medieval worlds, and could be found in China as late as the 20th century. Such gruesome mementos made the most explicit of warnings. They were bloody cousins of the "hanging" executions, which encompassed crucifixion and impalement in addition to the rope and gallows commonly denoted by the term. All were abominably exemplary: Corpses were often left to rot where they dangled. Little wonder that gallows and execution grounds were seen as polluted, demon-haunted places—every bit the terra damnata of any heretic's grave.

To be hanged, drawn, and quartered was the particularly barbaric punishment reserved for high treason in England. The condemned man (women convicted of treason were burned at the stake) would be carted to the place of execution, hanged until near the point of death, then cut down, castrated, and disemboweled, his entrails and genitals burned before his dying eyes. His carcass was then decapitated and cut (or often pulled by horses) into four quarters, with the gory head propped atop a pike for all to see.

Such was the punishment meted out to many of the men who had signed the death warrant of King Charles I. The diarist Samuel Pepys watched one of those regicides, Thomas Harrison, get ripped apart in October 1660. Looking "as cheerful as any man could do in that condition," Pepys recorded, Harrison was hanged, drawn, and quartered. His "head and heart [were] shown to the people, at which there was great shouts of joy." Tearing him asunder might not stop his returning, however; "he said that he was sure to come shortly at the right hand of Christ to judge them that now had judged him; and that his wife do expect his coming again."

Even the dead were not immune from this long arm of the law, for traitors could be hanged, drawn, and quartered posthumously. Three months after Harrison's demise, for example, his fellow regicide, Oliver Cromwell—the lord protector who had ruled the Commonwealth of England with an iron fist—was removed from his tomb in Westminster Abbey. On January 30, 1661, what was left of his putrefying cadaver was ceremonially hanged, drawn, and quartered before being tossed, it seems, into a pit (although his family was rumored to have spirited it away). Cromwell's severed head, however, was impaled before Westminster Hall, where it stood in the sun, wind, and rain for nearly 15 years before finally being blown to the ground by a storm. Passed from one collector to another, it became one of the most grotesque objects in any cabinet of curiosities—brown and wizened and repulsive. Mercifully and at long last, Cromwell's head was interred in the gardens of Sidney Sussex College in Cambridge—in 1960.

And then there was burning. As an explicit punishment for heresy, burning is at least as old as the reign of the Byzantine emperor Justinian in the sixth century. Upon spreading to Catholic Europe, this most dreadful of all methods for sundering body from soul was employed with appalling frequency during the witchcraft hysteria of the 16th and 17th centuries. Death by flame, though agonizing, was swift; the corpse itself, however, seemed to almost actively resist incineration—as we saw in the case of Johannes Cuntius. When St. Joan of Arc, the soldierly Maid of Orleans, was convicted of witchcraft by an opposing English army and put to the torch in 1431, she had to be burned three times; some of her organs, it was said, were impervious to the flames. This was interpreted as a miracle, leading to her canonization 500 years later.

Intriguingly, in 1867, a jar was discovered in the attic of a Paris pharmacy bearing the label "Remains found under the stake of Joan of Arc, virgin of Orleans." Inside was a paltry set of objects: a charred human rib, some carbonized wood, a fragment of linen, and what turned out to be a cat femur, probably the result of tossing black cats—witches' familiars—onto the pyres. Yet, all of the items quickly achieved the status of relics.

In 2006, a French forensics team gained permission to examine the articles. Applying cutting-edge spectrometry alongside such traditional techniques as pollen analysis, the team also engaged the noses of celebrated perfumers, who detected traces of "burnt plaster" and "vanilla" in the remains—yet vanillin is the product of decomposition, not cremation. The black crust on the rib bone, long assumed to have resulted from charring, instead turned out to be a mixture of resin, bitumen, and malachite—a mixture akin to that used in primitive embalming. The linen fragment, for its part, matched similar ones from ancient Egypt. Finally, carbon-14 dating fixed the origin of the remains between the third and sixth centuries B.C. Far from being saintly relics, these were pieces of an ancient mummy.

Perhaps the dead feed off the living, perhaps not; but in the cultural cannibalism that was the medieval mummy trade, the living were feeding off the dead.

Mummy, or *mumia,* comes from the Arabic word *mumiya,* which originally meant "bitumen"—the sticky, tarlike petroleum derivative that was once spread abundantly over the sands of Mesopotamia. Its use as an embalming agent in ancient Egypt gave the word its modern meaning; it also encouraged the belief that bits of a cadaver treated with bitumen, once swallowed, would have a strangely powerful preservative effect on the eater.

This is why, by the 12th century, pulverized Egyptian mummies, mixed with bitumen, pitch, tar, and spices, were being imported into Europe in astonishing numbers, there to be consumed as a tonic, a panacea, and a preservative. "Mummie is become Merchandise," mused Sir Thomas Browne, "Mizraim [ancient Egypt] cures wounds, and Pharaoh is sold for Balsoms."

These nostrums didn't always come from Mizraim, and they certainly weren't always pharaoh. Unscrupulous middlemen, it appears, made substitutions. The corpses of suicides were passed off as mummies, as were those of executed criminals who had hung in the sun too long, and even bodies discovered in bogs by Danish peat cutters. In 1645, a Dutch apothecary scolded his colleagues for labeling certain concoctions "mummy" when what they were really offering was an "arm or a leg of a decaying or hanged leper or of some whorehopper suffering from syphilis."

WARNINGS FOR POSTERITY

Twelfth-century England, in our imaginations, is the green and pleasant land of Ivanhoe, Robin Hood, and Richard the Lionhearted. We do not normally associate it with pestilence, much less with *sanguisuga*, or "bloodsuckers."

Yet, such creatures were apparently plentiful, at least in the imaginations of the ecclesiastical chroniclers who, by guttering candles in cold abbeys, penned their tales of prodigies "as a warning to posterity." The Abbot of Burton told of two peasants who returned from the grave with their coffins on their shoulders, roamed village and field, and spread disease everywhere they went. But once their bodies were exhumed, the heads cut off, and the hearts removed, the evil abruptly ceased.

Witty, charming Walter Map—prelate, sometime diplomat, and friend of both Henry II and Thomas Becket—wrote of a Welsh *maleficus*, or wizard, who had been reanimated by an "evil angel." The maleficus returned from the dead to sow death and destruction before a particularly heroic knight beheaded him at his tomb.

But William of Newburgh mined the richest vein of such stories. William spent most of his life as an Augustinian canon at Newburgh Abbey, which once nestled at the foot of the Yorkshire moors. It is long gone now, having been dissolved by Henry VIII and replaced by the house where, curiously enough, Oliver Cromwell's desecrated remains may have been clandestinely reburied. Newburgh Abbey was not far from the Old Northern Road that once ran from

London to Edinburgh, and along that road, William's fame as a chronicler and historian spread. His masterpiece was the *Historia rerum Anglicarum,* or *History of English Affairs,* which told of the varying fortunes of kings and nobles in the century since the Norman invasion of 1066. It also included a section entitled "Of Certain Prodigies."

"It would not be easy to believe," William wrote, "that the corpses of the dead should sally . . . from their graves, and should wander about to the terror or destruction of the living, and again return to the tomb, which of its own accord spontaneously opened to receive them, did not frequent examples, occurring in our own times, suffice to establish this fact. . . . " Ever the dutiful historian, William had combed through works of all the ancient authors known to his age but had found nothing to compare with the stories he was about to relate. "Moreover," he wrote, "were I to write down all the instances of this kind which I have ascertained to have befallen in our times, the undertaking would be beyond measure laborious and troublesome."

William heard one such instance from a "venerable archdeacon" in Buckingham, southwest of London. A certain man died and was laid in his tomb:

> On the following night, however, having entered the bed where his wife was reposing, he not only terrified her on awaking, but nearly crushed her by the insupportable weight of his body. The next night, also, he afflicted the astonished woman in the same manner,

who, frightened at the danger, as the struggle of the third night drew near, took care to remain awake herself, and surround herself with watchful companions. Still he came; but being repulsed by the shouts of the watchers, and seeing that he was prevented from doing mischief, he departed. Thus driven off from his wife, he harassed, in a similar manner, his own brothers, who were dwelling in the same street; but they, following the cautious example of the woman, passed the nights in wakefulness with their companions, ready to meet and repel the expected danger. He appeared, notwithstanding, as if with the hope of surprising them should they be overcome with drowsiness; but being repelled by the carefulness and valour of the watchers, he rioted among the animals, both in-doors and out-of-doors, as their wildness and unwonted movements testified.

Soon the entire town was alarmed, and before long, the dead man began wandering during daylight as well, though he was visible to only a few people. The terrified populace sought the protection of the church. William of Newburgh's informant then wrote for advice to the Bishop of Lincoln:

… but the bishop, being amazed at his account, held a searching investigation with his companions; and there were some who said that such things had often befallen in England, and cited frequent examples to show that tranquillity could not be restored to the people until the body of this most wretched man were dug up and burnt. This proceeding, however, appeared indecent and improper in the last degree to the reverend bishop, who shortly after addressed a letter of absolution, written with his own hand, to the archdeacon, in order that it might be demonstrated by inspection in what state the body of that man really was; and he commanded his tomb to be opened, and the letter having been laid upon his breast, to be again closed: so the sepulchre having been opened, the corpse was found as it had been placed there, and the charter of absolution having been deposited upon its breast, and the tomb once more closed, he was thenceforth never more seen to wander, nor permitted to inflict annoyance or terror upon any one.

A more dependable means for dispatching the roving dead was resorted to at Berwick, at the mouth of the river Tweed, where an "equally wonderful" event had occurred. A wealthy man died and was buried, but he soon "sallied forth (by the contrivance, as it is believed, of Satan) out of his grave by night, and was borne hither and thither, pursued by a pack of dogs with loud barkings." This struck terror into the townsfolk, and soon the leaders convened to debate the best course of action. No one wanted to be beaten senseless by this "prodigy of the grave," and the wiser among them concluded that, "were a remedy further delayed, the atmosphere, infected and corrupted by the constant whirlings through it of the pestiferous corpse, would engender disease and death."

Curiously enough, the monster, "while it was being borne about (as it is said) by Satan, had told certain persons whom it had by chance encountered, that as long as it remained unburnt the people should have no peace." So ten young men dug up the horrible carcass, and after dismembering it, they burned it. Nevertheless, a "pestilence, which arose in consequence, carried off the greater portion of them: for never did it so furiously rage elsewhere, though it was at that time general throughout all the borders of England. . . ."

Today, the ruins of Melrose Abbey loom in melancholy splendor over the hills of southern Scotland. In William of Newburgh's day, however, the abbey was a thriving Cistercian center. One of its chaplains, lamentably, was overfond of women and the chase. His weakness landed him in some metaphysical trouble, at least in William's eyes, for after the chaplain's death, Satan used his corpse as his "own chosen vessel." Thanks to the "meritorious resistance" of the monks, the vampire was barred from doing any great harm within the abbey itself, "whereupon he wandered beyond the walls, and hovered chiefly, with loud groans and horrible murmurs, round the bedchamber of his former mistress. She, after this had frequently occurred, becoming exceedingly terrified, revealed her fears or danger to one of the friars who visited her about the business of the monastery; demanding with tears that prayers more earnest than usual should be poured out to the Lord in her behalf as for one in agony."

The friar enlisted three companions. "[F]urnished with arms and animated with courage," they maintained a chilly, all-night vigil. When midnight passed with no monster, three of the quartet slipped off to the nearest warm house:

As soon as this man was left alone [William recounted], the devil, imagining that he had found the right moment for breaking his courage, incontinently roused up his own chosen vessel, who appeared to have reposed longer than usual. Having beheld this from afar, he grew stiff with terror by reason of his being alone; but soon recovering his courage, and no place of refuge being at hand, he valiantly withstood the onset of the fiend, who came rushing upon him with a terrible noise, and he struck the axe which he wielded in his hand deep into his body. On receiving this wound, the monster groaned aloud, and, turning his back, fled with a rapidity not at all inferior to that with which he had advanced, while the admirable man urged his flying foe from behind, and compelled him to seek his own tomb again; which opening of its own accord, and receiving its guest from the advance of the pursuer, immediately appeared to close again with the same facility. In the meantime, they who, impatient of the coldness of the night, had retreated to the fire ran up, though somewhat too late, and, having heard what had happened, rendered needful assistance in digging up and removing from the midst of the tomb the accursed corpse at the earliest dawn. When they had divested it of the clay cast forth with it, they found the huge wound it had received, and a great quantity of gore which had flowed from it in the sepulchre; and so having carried it away beyond the walls of the monastery and burnt it, they scattered the ashes to the winds. These things I have explained in a simple narration, as I myself heard them recounted by religious men.

Finally, there was the story William heard from "an aged monk who . . . related this event as having occurred in his own presence."

A man of "evil propensities" had fled the province of York and had found sanctuary at nearby Anantis Castle. There he married, only to become a jealous husband. Determined to catch his wife dallying with her young lover, he pretended to be away and hid on a beam overlooking his wife's chamber. Enraged at the sight of his wife lying in her lover's arms, he lost his balance and fell to the floor. Severely injured, the husband died before he had a chance to confess his numerous sins or to receive the sacrament.

That crucial omission should suffice to alert us to his fate. Although the dead husband received a Christian burial, "it did not much benefit him," wrote William archly, "for issuing, by the handiwork of Satan, from his grave at night-time, and pursued by a pack of dogs with horrible barkings, he wandered through the courts and around the houses; while all men made fast their doors, and did not dare to go abroad on any errand whatever from the beginning of the night until the sunrise, for fear of meeting and being beaten black and blue by this vagrant monster. But these precautions were of no avail; for the atmosphere, poisoned by the vagaries of this foul carcase, filled every house with disease and death by its pestiferous breath."

The once-bustling town was quickly abandoned. At that point, two brothers who had lost their father to this plague undertook a desperate mission:

Thereupon snatching up a spade of but indifferent sharpness of edge, and hastening to the cemetery, they began to dig; and whilst they were thinking that they would have to dig to a greater depth, they suddenly, before much of the earth had been removed, laid bare the corpse, swollen to an enormous corpulence, with its countenance beyond measure turgid and suffused with blood; while the napkin in which it had been wrapped appeared nearly torn to pieces. The young men, however, spurred on by wrath, feared not, and inflicted a wound upon the senseless carcase, out of which incontinently flowed such a stream of blood, that it might have been taken for a leech filled with the blood of many persons. Then, dragging it beyond the village, they speedily constructed a funeral pile; and upon one of them saying that the pestilential body would not burn unless its heart were torn out, the other laid open its side by repeated blows of the blunted spade, and, thrusting in his hand, dragged out the accursed heart.

Then came the miraculous conclusion: "When that infernal hell-hound had thus been destroyed, the pestilence which was rife among the people ceased, as if the air, which had been corrupted by the contagious motions of the dreadful corpse, were already purified by the fire which had consumed it."

EVER DEEPER

Some 500 years would pass before Henry More learned about Johannes Cuntius and the Breslau shoemaker. Yet, the same pen could have written both these accounts. There is the same emphasis on sins (of omission or commission) determining the subsequent events; the same depiction of physical brutality in the revenant; the same hysterical reaction in the various towns; and, one letter of absolution aside, the same means of destroying the pests: cutting off the heads, ripping out the hearts, and burning the carcasses.

Another pen might have written the story of Arnold Paole and that graveyard full of Serbian vampires (see Chapter 4), and a third pen still might have described those hideous undead larvae, the nachzehrer (see Chapter 5). But are these really different conceptions? Or are they rather outcroppings, each shaped by the forces of history and geography, of an even deeper, underlying layer?

CHAPTER SEVEN

THE WANDERERS

ON MARCH 6, 1710, with the Sun King, Louis XIV, still on the throne of France, a discovery was made deep in the vaults of venerable Notre Dame de Paris. While constructing a new crypt beneath the nave, workers uncovered an ancient, four-tiered stone block. Supporting part of the choir and chancel, the block had been part of a pagan temple that once stood on the site. Originally dedicated to the god Jupiter by the Nautae Parisiaci—the mariners of Parisii during the reign of the Roman emperor Tiberius—the block depicted in bas-relief a number of gods, but none so prominently as the fearsome visage bearing the antlers of a stag. The broken inscription read, "–ernunnos."

This was almost certainly Cernunnos, the ancient Celtic Lord of the Animals, the most famous horned god in

European mythology. The Christian Middle Ages, it seemed, truly rested on pagan foundations.

The image (but not the name) of Cernunnos had been known at Val Camonica in the Italian Alps, where a great antlered figure looms out from a fourth-century B.C. cave engraving, a torque necklace on his right arm and a horned serpent on his left. At Autun in France, Cernunnos bears two horned serpents. At Reims, where stags and bulls surround him, he holds a sack of coins or grain. Sometimes he appears with three faces, in the margins of illuminated manuscripts, or even, perhaps, in degraded form as Herne the Hunter, disporting with the merry wives among the oaks of Windsor Forest.

But the horned Cernunnos is most widely recognized in the features of Satan.

A once-fashionable theory suggested that the medieval witch cult was not a Satanist one—that it was not even diabolical but represented the vestiges of an old religion, displaced and driven underground by Christianity, that worshiped the horned god of European paganism. Although this thesis has come under heavy critical fire, it maintains a stubborn life, if only because it suggests that our monsters did not spring sui generis from the medieval imagination. If the demons of Christianity were perhaps the gods of a former faith—at least those not bought off with halos and sainthoods—it is to the pagan world of antiquity, and to its Indo-European underpinnings, that we now must turn.

THE HIDDEN PAST

Buried in a fourth-century Bulgarian manuscript, "Oration of St. Gregory the Theologian," is a 15th-century insertion sometimes called *The Story of How the Pagans Honored Their Idols:*

> ... to the same gods the Slavic people make fires and perform sacrifice, and to *vilas* and Mokos and the *diva* and Perun ... and Rozanica. And to vampires and *bereginas*. And dancing to Pereplut, they drink to him in horns.

This puzzling fragment has been pored over and analyzed from every possible angle. What scholars surmise is this: A vilas was a kind of demon, as was a diva. Mokos was a goddess of shearing, spinning, and weaving, while Perun was the widely worshiped Slavic god of thunder and lightning. The Rozanica were the spirits of ancestors, and Pereplut was a god revered by seafarers. As for bereginas, they are believed to be an arcane riverbank entity.

But vampires—why would *they* have once been considered fit objects for sacrifice? Even the glimmer of an answer demands a journey deep into both the historical and the mythological past.

Somewhere out on the Eurasian steppe, no one is sure exactly where, lies the homeland of the Indo-European peoples. In this prehistoric cradle, tribes that later migrated far away from one another—giving rise in the process to such related language families as the Indo-Iranian, the Italic, the

Celtic, the Germanic, and the Slavic—once shared a culture and religion. By historical times, the Greeks, Romans, and Celts, for example, had become simply local inflections of that common ancestral pattern. Their gods, too, had been customized, but in them could still be discerned the slightly distorted echoes of the distant originals.

Among all the daughters of the Indo-Europeans, the ancient Slavs have been the most challenging to trace. Think of a people about whom there are scant eyewitness accounts yet an abundance of biased, if not actively hostile, commentators. Indeed, were it not for the painstaking labors of scholars, linguists, and comparative mythologists, we would be able to glimpse today only a rustic Slavic pantheon, its idols carved from tree trunks or crudely chiseled in stone. Even so, what remains known of many Slavic gods is only their names.

One big barrier to our knowledge of Slavic deities is that the early Slavs had no alphabet. That came with the priests. Slavic tribes first came into contact with Christianity in the sixth century, when they wandered into central Europe and down into the Balkans. Not until 863, however, did Cyril and Methodius, the Slavic apostles, arrive in Moravia, the rolling region of hill and valley now part of the Czech Republic. By the time their mission was expelled for political reasons two decades later, they had created what eventually became the Cyrillic alphabet and had used it to shape what is called the Slavonic liturgy.

After 886, when Bulgaria's Khan Boris I welcomed the refugees of the Moravian mission, the Balkans, especially

Macedonia, became the true cradle of the Slavonic rite. From there, that liturgy spread to Serbia and Romania. By 988, it had reached Russia, where the statue of Perun was toppled from its site overlooking Kiev, dragged by horse to the Dnieper, given a thorough beating, and dumped into the river.

Although the church bestowed literacy, churchmen were never sympathetic to pagan "superstitions." This makes it hard to distinguish the authentic elements of medieval chronicles. The last of the Baltic Slavs were finally converted to Christianity early in the 15th century, yet the *Prussian Chronicle,* written about 1520 by a Dominican priest named Simon Grunau, gives such a fanciful account of the Slavs' chief pagan shrine that scholars still debate its veracity. According to Grunau, the idols were hung high in a sacred oak; they included a Perun-like god of thunder—all angry visage and curly beard—and a death god, all pallid countenance with green beard, a thirst for human blood, and a garland of human and animal skulls.

The Russians, for their part, were often accused of practicing a "mixed faith"—acting piously Christian in church but stubbornly pagan in woods and field. After centuries of listening to imprecations thundered down on "heretics," many Russian villagers came to clump all their suspicious dead under the single label of *eretiks.* They knew little and cared less about doctrinal disputes, and it was simpler to keep the properly Orthodox dead in hallowed ground and to consign the eretiks to the margins.

Eretiks comprised not just schismatics and Old Believers—those who objected to the 17th-century liturgical reforms—but "sorcerers" as well. A whiff of ominous familiarity shrouds those "sorcerers," especially those purported to leave their graves at night to roam the village and to eat people. A vampire, it seems, smells just as vile by any other name.

Eretiks, then, might encompass all the dangerous dead. The means of dispatching one for good likewise has a familiar cast: Open the grave, roll the corpse over, drive an aspen stake through it, and perhaps burn it as well. (In one village, it sufficed to give the body "a thorough thrashing" by horsewhip.) Beset by a prolonged drought, a village might exhume an eretik who had once been suspected of sorcery, dash the remains with water, or toss them into the Volga. During one such ritual, villagers beat the skull of a corpse while crying out, "Bring rain!"

In parts of Russia, the vampire—*upir*, in Russian—had clearly been subsumed under the broader category of spiritual outlaws dubbed heretics. Possibly that relationship began the other way around: The word *heretic*, along with *pagan*, may once have been subsumed beneath *vampire*—which may originally have had no supernatural connotations whatsoever.

Linguists seeking the origins of the word *vampire* have been shaking the etymological bushes for clues for at least a century. *Vampir, upir, upyr, upior,* and other cognate forms from around the Slavic world were long thought to have stemmed from the root word *uber*—Turkish for "witch."

That seemed logical, given the number of authorities who suspected vampires of having hatched in the Balkans, so long under the sway of the sultan. Although other linguists favored an entirely Hungarian origin or argued that the root of *vampire* was the Greek word *pi*—"to drink"—many scholars, including the influential Montague Summers, embraced the Turkish theory.

The consensus today, by contrast, is that *vampire* is almost undoubtedly Slavic. The root, as far back as it can be traced, seems to be a medieval Serbian word; when anglicized, it came to resemble something like *vampir*. Originating perhaps in the heart of the Balkans, the word gradually diffused throughout the Slavic world. Each local adaptation gave the word its own slight new twist.

The thorniest question of all, however, persists: What did *vampir* originally mean?

The earliest written evidence of *vampir*—*oupir* or *upir*, as it happens—appears in the margin of a manuscript called the *Book of the Prophets*, a copy of a work whose original dates to 1047. Its contextual significance is cryptic in the extreme; an Orthodox monk from Novgorod uses it to describe some personal shortcoming of his.

Then again, there is that mention, in *The Story of How the Pagans Honored Their Idols*, of sacrifices made to "vampires and bereginas." Since the reference is probably a 15th-century insertion, it may not shed much light on the original meaning of *vampir*. Yet the association with sacrifice, however tenuous, remains a tantalizing clue.

Its rampant polytheism aside, paganism was vilified for its blood and orgies—that is, for its public sacrifices and riotous feasting. Blood sacrifice—the cutting of an animal's throat at the altar to propitiate a divinity—was forbidden in Scripture. On the other hand, it formed a central rite in nearly every religion of pagan Europe.

On the shores of the Baltic, where paganism lingered longest, oxen and sheep were regularly sacrificed as late as the 12th century. So too were prisoners of war and (according to the Saxon priest Helmold, author of *Chronicle of the Slavs*) Christians, whose blood was said to particularly please the gods. "[A]fter the victim is felled," Helmold wrote of sacrifices in general, "the priest drinks of its blood in order to render himself more potent in the receiving of oracles. For it is the opinion of many that demons are very easily conjured with blood."

And the orgies? Pagan feast days were infamous for their licentiousness, and pagan marriage ceremonies—especially ancient fertility rituals—verged on the truly orgiastic. What's more, pagans favored barbarous initiation ceremonies, and with good reason, they were reputed to believe in reincarnation—anathema to the Church.

All of this strongly suggests that the word *vampir* arose in the crucible of the Balkans at a time when Christianity was locked in combat with paganism. If *vampir* does indeed spring from an obscure root word meaning "to drink," it's only a short logical leap to the understanding that it was likely first used as an epithet flung at those blood-drinking pagans who, tenacious of custom, refused the uncertain embrace of the Church. This may also help explain why the word lingered so long as a proper name in Russia, where an 11th-century nobleman from Novgorod went by the name Prince Upir—Prince Vampire.

By the same token, *warg*—the Nordic word for "wolf," as every Tolkien reader knows—might at one time have been used to denote outlaws. Transformed thereby from men into wolves—in the eyes of the law, at any rate—the outlaws could be killed on sight. This allegorical shape-shifting may have given rise to the "wild man of the woods" figure so common in medieval folklore, contributing to a range of myths from Robin Hood to werewolves.

Might natural outlaws, then—anathematized, excommunicated, and exiled to the forest—have metamorphosed over the centuries into supernatural ones? If so, the vampir may have been moved along that path by a heresy—one similarly centered in southern Serbia and Macedonia, where between the 10th and 14th centuries, there flourished a little-known sect called the Bogomils.

Even the Demons Fled

Arising in the highlands of Armenia, the sect of the Bogomils was one in a long line of dualist religions—faiths that condemn all matter as evil and revere all spirit as good. Named for one of their early priests, the Bogomils first entered Bulgaria, perhaps pushed west off the stark Iranian plateau by the armies of Islam, before making the Balkans their redoubt. From there they spread into Russia, central Europe, and even France, where they became known as the Albigenses.

The Bogomils, in turn, had been inspired by the Paulicians, an even more obscure Armenian sect, whose leaders the Byzantine emperors had burned at the stake for heresy. These dualistic movements threatened the Church not only because their adherents fiercely opposed anything hierarchical or liturgical, but also because they bore a disturbing resemblance to the Gnostic heresy that had split the early Christian community.

Despite being persecuted, the Bogomils exerted an insidious influence on the growing Slavic Church. After Russia embraced Orthodoxy in 988, Bulgarian priests—many of them tinged with more than a little Bogomilism—were numerous among its formative clergy. The same thing happened all over eastern Europe. Even after Bogomilism had been condemned as heresy and stamped out, the movement's dualistic imprint endured deep in the fabric of Orthodoxy, especially in its attitude toward the dead.

Bogomils had claimed that demons fled from them alone but inhabited all other men. These demons were said to instruct their hosts "in vice, lead them to wickedness and after their death dwell in their corpses." No surprise, then, that in 1143, two Orthodox bishops in Asia Minor were accused of being Bogomils after they "dug up bodies in the belief that they were possessed of demons and unfit for burial."

That belief in the demonic, married to a word associated with blood drinking and death, may have greatly propelled the transformation of *vampir* into the vampire that surfaced in the 18th century. All it needed was a corpse to wrap itself around.

Throughout this social and religious upheaval, men and women had continued dying—and their dead bodies had continued to act in strange ways, or at least were alleged to do so. A ninth-century capitulary of Charlemagne directed that "if any person, deceived by the devil, shall believe, after the manner of the Pagans, that any man or woman was a Strygis, or Stryx [night-flying bloodsucker], and was given to eat men, and for this cause should burn such person, or should give such person's flesh to be eaten, or should eat such flesh, such man or woman should be capitally punished."

And in the sixth century, just as the Slavs were beginning to infiltrate the Balkans, Clovis, king of the Franks, was inserting into the *Lex Salica*—the foundation of most European legal codes—explicit punishments for the desecration of the dead. Meanwhile, across the English Channel, Romano-British and Anglo-Saxon cemeteries of the third to seventh centuries have been discovered to contain many prone burials—that is, burials with the corpse buried facedown. Should the cadaver then choose to wander, the thinking apparently went, it would invariably head in the wrong direction.

The British graves also hold decapitated skeletons, whose severed skulls are usually lodged between the legs or feet.

Were these executions? Or were they other methods of restricting the movements of the restless dead? The bones are silent, but folklore speaks volumes. Sir James Frazer, in *The Fear of the Dead in Primitive Religion,* quotes an illuminating passage from an 1835 German source:

> In East Prussia when a person is believed to be suffering from the attacks of a vampire and suspicion falls on the ghost of somebody who died lately, the only remedy is thought to be for the family of the deceased to go to his grave, dig up his body, behead it and place the head between the legs of the corpse. If blood flows from the severed head the man was certainly a vampire, and the family must drink of the flowing blood, thus recovering the blood which had been sucked from their living bodies by the vampire. Thus the vampire is paid out in kind.

The cradle of the vampir might very well be the Balkans of the ninth and tenth centuries. And as both a word and a concept, the vampire may very well—and quite logically, in the final analysis—be rooted in the social, political, and religious realities of the day. But if we are to follow the trail of wandering corpses to its conclusion, we must now head south, to Greece.

The *Vrykolakas*

One evening in the mid-19th century, Henry Tozer, an Oxford don and authority on the geography of the far-flung Ottoman Empire, arrived in the small Greek town of Aghia. The hamlet perched on the flanks of Mount Ossa, overlooking the plains of Thessaly—fabled since classical times for the Olympics, for horses, and for superstition:

> During the night which we spent at Aghia the population were disturbed by apparitions of spirits, which they described as gliding about with large lanterns in their hands. These are called *vrykolaka* by the Greeks and *vurkolak* by the Turks, for both Christians and Mahometans believe in them; the name, however, is written and pronounced in a great variety of ways. It was curious to meet with them in this manner as soon as we descended into the plains of Thessaly, the ancient land of witches; but the belief in these appearances is widely spread, not only throughout Thessaly and Epirus, but also among the islands of the Aegean and over a great part of Turkey. The idea concerning them is, that some persons come to life again after death, sleep in their tombs with their eyes open, and wander abroad by night, especially when the moon is shining brightly.

The moon shining brightly, of course, suggests werewolves on the prowl. Vrykolakas—like the Turkish *vurkolak,*

Serbian *vukodlak*, Bulgarian *volkudlak*, Albanian *vurvolak*, and similar cognates that have burrowed deep into the linguistic map of eastern Europe—has usually been interpreted as "werewolf" because it stems from a Slavic root (probably *vârkolak*)—that presumably meant "wolf pelt." It came to be interchangeable with *vampire* the reasoning goes, only because werewolves in folklore were suspected of becoming vampires after death.

It might not be that simple, however. *Vârkolak* may indeed mean "wolf pelt," and quite literally so—denoting the wolf pelts Balkan tribesmen ritually donned during pagan times. The words it hatched then undertook a vast mythological odyssey, for when they next appear, they describe a cosmic monster that caused eclipses by eating the sun or moon before settling back on earth and taking on the additional sense of the devouring dead.

However it happened, *vârkolak* and its cognates are now thoroughly entwined with *vampir* and its derivatives. Only in Greece has *vampir* never taken root; *vrykolakas* has crowded it out.

One hundred fifty years before Tozer undertook his wanderings, the renowned French botanist Joseph Pitton de Tournefort had journeyed to the far corners of Asia Minor on a plant-collecting expedition. His three-volume *A Voyage into the Levant* is equal parts travelogue and exploration narrative, yet most modern readers ignore his rapturous descriptions of mountain forests ranging along the Black Sea coast and into the Caucasus. Instead, de Tournefort's book is best remembered for its startling description of vrykolakas hysteria on the Greek island of Mykonos, where he had stopped during the winter of 1700.

Around the time de Tournefort reached the isle, a truculent and much-disliked peasant had died. Shortly thereafter began a chain of nocturnal depredations. "[I]t was rumored," de Tournefort wrote, "that he was seen by night walking very fast; that he came into the house, overturning the furniture, extinguishing the lamps, throwing his arms round persons from behind, and playing a thousand sly tricks."

Panic quickly engulfed the island. Ten days after the body had been buried, it was dug up so the local butcher might remove its heart. "The corpse," reported the botanist, "gave out such a bad smell, that they were obliged to burn incense; but the vapour, mixed with the exhalations of that carrion, only augmented the stink, and began to heat the brain of these poor people."

De Tournefort continued his account:

> Their imagination, struck with the spectacle, was full of visions; some one thought proper to say that a thick smoke came from this body. We dared not say that it was the vapour of the incense. They only exclaimed "Vroucolacas," in the chapel, and in the square before it . . .
>
> I have no doubt that they would have maintained it did not stink, if we had not been present; so stupified were these poor people with the

circumstance, and infatuated with the idea of the return of the dead. For ourselves, who got next to the corpse in order to make our observations exactly, we were ready to die from the offensive odour which proceeded from it. When they asked us what we thought of this dead man, we replied that we believed him thoroughly dead; but as we wished to cure, or at least not to irritate their stricken fancy, we represented to them that it was not surprising if the butcher had perceived some heat in searching amidst entrails which were decaying; neither was it extraordinary that some vapour had proceeded from them; since such will issue from a dunghill that is stirred up. . . .

Despite one indignity after another being visited upon the corpse, the nightly mischief—and its attendant pandemonium—grew only worse. De Tournefort had never seen anything like it: "Every body seemed to have lost their senses. The most sensible people appeared as phrenzied as the others; it was a veritable brain fever, as dangerous as any mania or madness." Entire families fled their houses. "Every one complained of some new insult: you heard nothing but lamentations at nightfall . . . [and] every morning entertained us with the comedy of a faithful recital of all the new follies which had been committed by this bird of night. . . ."

One exorcism after another failed to rid the town of the revenant. Finally the citizens built a pyre, and de Tournefort watched from a distance as the flames consumed the meddlesome corpse. The islanders then "contented themselves with saying that the devil had been properly caught that time, and they made up a song to turn him into ridicule . . . After this, must we not own that the Greeks of to-day are not great Greeks, and that there is only ignorance and superstition among them?"

The Wanderers

Two centuries later, John Cuthbert Lawson, in *Modern Greek Folklore and Ancient Greek Religion* (1910), sought to disprove de Tournefort's final contention. Nearly half of Lawson's influential but little-known book, which Patrick Leigh Fermor called a "real triumph of scholarship and detailed reasoning," is devoted to the vrykolakas. Lawson believed that the Greeks never adopted the vampir of neighboring lands because they had their own deeply rooted ideas about the walking dead. Vrykolakas, in fact, was merely a "grafting of Slavonic branches upon an Hellenic stock."

That stock is still visible on a breathtaking Aegean island. Modern Santorini is a busy tourist resort, yet there was a time when its cliffs were famed more for their *vrykolakes* (the plural form) than for their commanding ocean views. To "send vrykolakes to Santorini" was the local equivalent of "bringing coals to Newcastle." That's because the dry, volcanic soils of Santorini are naturally preservative. Corpses buried there do not decompose as quickly as they do elsewhere.

Jesuit priest François Richard, who lived on Santorini in the 17th century, described dead bodies that "after fifteen or sixteen years—sometimes even twenty or thirty—are found inflated like balloons, and when they are thrown on the ground or rolled along, sound like drums . . ."This quality gave the cadavers the name by which they were once known in Greece: *tympaneous,* or "drumlike." That, as well as other dialectal names—*fleshy* and *gaper* among them—appear to have survived in the Aegean Islands for a time, but on the mainland—down which the Slavic tide had rolled in the sixth century—vrykolakas reigned supreme. Eventually the islands, too, gave in and adopted that term.

But why not *vampir?*

Stripping the Christian and Slavic overburdens off the original Greek idea, John Lawson concluded that the Greeks did not adopt *vampir* because of its associated savagery. In their tradition, the walking dead were not always malicious. A good example of this crops up in a well-known fragment from Phlegon's *Mirabilia,* a compendium of ghost stories written in the second century A.D. Though its beginning has been lost, the story—which Phlegon claimed to have witnessed—is set in Tralles in Asia Minor, in the house of Demostratus and Charito, whose daughter Philinnion has been dead for six months. Young Machates has been staying in their guest room, however, and he has been receiving nocturnal visits from an unknown lover, who has left her gold ring and breast band behind.

The visitor is Philinnion, of course. When her parents discover the tokens and eventually behold their dead daughter on one of her midnight manifestations, she upbraids them for spoiling her happiness—and promptly relapses into a corpse. The family vault is then opened, but Philinnion's spot is empty—save for an iron ring and gilt cup that Machates had given her. Unnerved, the townsfolk transport her corpse beyond the city limits. There, after making suitable propitiations to pagan divinities, they burn it.

Yet Philinnion is no Carmilla; there is no hint that her midnight visits are predatory. Because the despairing Machates commits suicide, the *Mirabilia* fragment strikes us as a story of star-crossed lovers, tomb and all.

Yet most ancient Greek revenants, it appears, returned from the grave to demand—or to wreak—vengeance. *Alastor* means "avenger," a kind of male version of Nemesis, the Greek goddess of retribution, and describes a supernatural figure often compared with the *Erinyes,* or furies. Greek literature and drama abound with alastors avenging such indignities as neglected burial rites, but the creatures are usually bent on blood vengeance. Nevertheless, Lawson has spied, behind the avenging fury that is the alastor, an even older figure: *Alastor,* he surmised, might originally have meant "wanderer," not "avenger."

"'To wander unburied,'" Lawson brooded, "could there be a simpler description of a revenant?":

Does not the whole misery of the unburied dead consist in this—that they must wander? It is almost inconceivable then that the name *Alastor,* "wanderer," should have been originally applied only to a single class of the wandering dead—to those whose wanderings were directed towards vengeance, and not also to those whose wanderings were more aimless, more pitiable, whose whole existence might have been summed up in that one word "wandering."

As late as the 17th century, Father Richard related the story of a Santorini shoemaker named Alexander who returned from the grave to "frequent his house, mend his children's shoes, draw water at the reservoir, and cut wood for the use of his family; but the people became frightened, exhumed him, and burned him, and he was seen no more." In one corner of the island, Father Richard continued, "these *vrykolakes* have been seen not only at night but in the open day, five or six together in a field, feeding apparently on green beans."

This touching glimpse of the vegetarian dead might strike a responsive chord in readers attuned to the more sensitive vampires of today. But in eras past, such stories, recounted at night beside a dying hearth, would have had an eerie, unsettling effect. For these figures were Lawson's "wanderers," trapped in a limbo between worlds, condemned to expiate some crime, or bound by some curse. And in the ancient way of thinking, there seemed no end of potential causes for such curses: sudden or violent death, suicide, lack of proper burial rites, unavenged murder, sorcery, or perjury. Lucian of Samosata, in the first century

A.D., mused in his *Philopseudes* that perhaps the "only souls which wander about are those of men who met with a violent death—anyone, for example, who hanged himself, or was beheaded or impaled, or departed this life in any other such way—but . . . the souls of those who died a natural death do not wander."

Such agonized figures, like tragic ones, excited pity as much as horror. Only the flame—cremation as an act of mercy—can loose the bond of suffering and bring repose.

In the thousands of years that have passed since then, this sad figure has undergone a metamorphosis. The church demonized the wanderer, thus turning the original transgression of divine law into a deadly sin—and a formula for excommunication. This ecclesiastical curse then further embraced such offenses as omission of baptism, "sorcery," apostasy, and heresy—and we have the makings of the modern vampire in Greece. When the word *vampir* first gained traction in the Balkans, the old notions surrounding the alastor were probably still entrenched, and so people resisted the new word. But those notions had considerably eroded by the time *vukodlak* and its derivatives were on the rise, and that cleared the way for the reign of *vrykolakas*.

POETIC VIEWS OF VAMPIRES

Might a notion such as the alastor lie deep in Slavic legend? We have no literature and no drama to guide us, so the road must wind through the forest of Slavic folklore. So dense are those rhetorical thickets, however—so full of thorns, so entangled with Nordic mythology—that many an expert has lost his way.

Some authorities doubt the undergrowth is more than several centuries old. Others suspect it is very deeply rooted indeed. The latter often turn to a pioneering folklorist of the 19th century, the man whose published collections of more than 600 folk- and fairy tales have earned him the sobriquet "the Russian Grimm."

Born in 1826 in a village on the edge of the steppe, Alexander Afanasiev spent most of his life plowing through Moscow's libraries before dying, penniless and racked by tuberculosis, at the age of 45. More than a mere gleaner of existing material, Afanasiev created the massive, three-volume *Poetic Views of the Slavs Toward Nature*. In this masterpiece, he traced the profusion of Slavic songs, stories, and epic tales further and further back in time until he arrived at a single, if buried, root: the nature myths of the prehistoric Indo-Europeans.

"Originally our ancestors must have understood by the name vampire," wrote Afanasiev in the 1860s, "a terrible demon who sucks storm clouds and drinks up all the moisture in them, because in the ancient myths rain was like blood flowing in the veins of cloud spirits and animals. . . . The winter cold which freezes rain-clouds plunges the creative forces of nature into sleep, death, damnation. The thunder god and lightning spirits are equated to suckers of rain who hide in cloud caves and fall asleep in cloud-graves."

If this seems fanciful, consider that poetic (or metaphorical) thought probably came more easily to steppe-dwelling people living in a prescientific age. Cloud and wind and storm; lightning, hail, and drought; sun and moon and stars might indeed have provided the cosmic patterns, the ultimate code that explained, on the principle of "as above, so below," both natural and supernatural phenomena. We know enough about Slavic mythology to recognize an attractively animistic bent in its sacred stones, trees, rivers, and lakes; its flying grass and weeping grass and dream grass.

It might be hard to grasp Afanasiev's assertion that the bellowing of the vampire upon being staked is the metaphorical echo of the thunderstorm's roar, but it is not difficult to understand how crop failures, famines, and epidemics might be ascribed to such beings. "Everywhere in the Slavic lands," Afanasiev reminds us, "the fatal activity of the plague is explained by the evil of vampires." The region also tended to identify vampires with dragons, demons, and "gluttonous Death," appearing with that grim trio in popular tales as eaters of human flesh.

And it's not that much different from the Romanian belief, in the words of one folklorist, that "*varcolaci* and *pricolici* [names of mythological monsters] are sometimes dead vampires, and sometimes animals which eat the moon."

Elusive Dragons

A century after Afanasiev coughed himself to death, respected Soviet philologists V. V. Ivanov and V. Toporov updated their

tsarist forerunner. Combing through comparative mythologies and that cornucopia of folklore, they reconstructed the
likely Slavic version of the cosmic battle between the Indo-
European gods of storm and earth. What emerged bears a
marked resemblance, with certain differences, to Afanasiev's
poetic vision.

Thousands of years ago, it seems, the Slavic tribes possessed a metaphorical understanding of the drama of storms:
Perun, the god of thunder and lightning, is chasing the drag-
onlike Volos, or Veles—deity of waters, fields, pastures, flocks,
herds, and the underworld—who has stolen the storm god's
wife (or perhaps his cattle). Lightning-shattered stumps and
splintered boulders litter the dragon's path as he tries to elude
Perun's thunderbolts: he transforms himself into now a tree,
now a rock, now a human in the course of his vain attempt.
Eventually, Volos is cornered and slain, at which point the
storm breaks and releases its torrents of fructifying rain.

Of course, because it is an eternally recurring combat, Volos never really dies. As lord of the underworld, he
is leader of all the chthonian powers; each year, as autumn
turns to winter, he allows the dead to return to the world
above for a few days, where they may visit the living, whom
they approach while singing songs about how far they have
traveled and how muddy was the way. Where Perun was the
warrior's god, Volos was that of the plowman and herdsman.
Where Perun offered an honorable death in battle, the wily
Volos offered those who broke their sacred oaths death by
pestilence or disease.

So instead of a wandering figure, we have encountered a myth. But let's return one final time to that enigmatic reference, in *The Story of How the Pagans Honored Their Idols*, about ancient sacrifices being offered to "vampires and *bereginas*."

Perhaps some grain of truth lurks behind that 15th-century emendation. The protovampire might indeed have arisen from a deep-seated ancestor cult, as that document suggests. Exactly how they might have done so we shall probably never know. Might it have something to do with a belief in reincarnation? If so, that early conception would have changed over time. Perhaps these protovampires first devolved into the mysterious bereginas, those hovering river-bank spirits—and then were generalized as *rusalki*, the "souls of the dead." That would lead, naturally enough, to the "souls of the dead who died a violent death"—and we are back on familiar ground.

Or perhaps not. Either way, for those who seek the origins of the vampire legend, one source of that stream—possibly the major contributor, possibly not—surely springs from the Balkans during the years in which they were Christianized, the years when such dualistic heresies as the Bogomils left their deep impression, and the years when religious and political struggle inflicted such lasting wounds.

Traces of that original cosmic myth have also survived. Where the Vardar River cuts through the heart of mountain-rimmed Macedonia, cradle of vampir, stands the city of Veles, surely an echo of the dragon Volos. High above it towers the peak of St. Elias the Thunderer. Not far by

eagle's wings, along the rugged Greek-Bulgarian border, vampires were once called *drakus,* or dragons. When
the Roman legions crossed the Danube to invade Dacia
(modern Romania), they encountered Dacian cavalry carrying *dracos,* or dragon standards. *Draco* became *dracul* in
Romania, where once there dwelt a folkloric dragon that,
assuming the shape of a man, seduced women and spirited
them away to its underworld lair, where only a hero could
rescue them.

All over ancient Thrace (in what is now Bulgaria) lived
a people neither Greek nor Slavic—an enigmatic people devoted to blood sacrifices and incantations; to music
and feasting and rhytons overflowing with wine, and they
were said to know the secrets of immortality. All over that
land, exquisite votive tablets once honored an unnamed figure today called simply the Thracian Hero or the Thracian
Rider. A mounted figure who might represent either a military leader or the god of thunder, he is clearly depicted as
a mighty drinker and an even mightier hunter, a lord of the
animals, and a slayer of wild boars, wolves, and dragons.
Not surprisingly, his image—horse rearing and lance (was it
once a lightning bolt, or is it a stake?) spearing the prostrate
foe—was eventually absorbed into that of St. George, whose
own cult spread as far as England and whose smoke-blackened icons are found in churches all over the Balkans and
deep into Russia. St. George himself had been assimilated to
a vegetation god, for his feast day on April 23 was celebrated
everywhere as a victory of surging spring over the forces of

winter, darkness, and death. And as every folklorist knows, vampires are said to be most active on St. George's Eve.

By the Middle Ages, the god Volos, too—at least the aspect of him that guarded flocks and herds—had acquired a halo, and became venerated everywhere in Christendom as St. Blaise, patron saint of wild animals. Yet, whereas the host of lesser deities scurried into the forest to survive as ogres and goblins, Volos's infernal face was absorbed, alongside that of his Celtic counterpart Cernunnos, into the horned figure of the devil.

Enigmatic Origins

On May 28, 1891, on Denmark's wet and windy Jutland Peninsula, peat cutters near the hamlet of Gundestrup found a great silver bowl of antique design buried in the bog. After the Gundestrup Cauldron was brought to the National Museum of Denmark in Copenhagen, it quickly became obvious that the bowl had been deposited in the bog as a votive offering or hidden there for safekeeping and never reclaimed. With its exquisite braid of mythological figures, the cauldron threw open the doors of an iconographic treasure-house.

In pride of place within the bowl sits the antlered Cernunnos, holding a torque in his right hand and a ram-headed serpent in his left. Surrounded by a stag, bulls, wolves, lions—and even a dolphin—he is the epitome of the lord of the beasts. Directly opposite is Taranis, Celtic counterpart to Perun. Taranis was a god of thunder, but also (like Volos) of the underworld. Figured elsewhere around the bowl are gods and scenes of war and sacrifice, all elegantly executed in silver.

Rising from the gloom and the muck of the Iron Age, summoning forth images of druidical sacrifices in a conjured European past, the Gundestrup Cauldron has captivated—and puzzled—generations of scholars. For one thing, the closest site of commensurate silversmithing skills lay far to the southeast, in Thrace. For another, the cauldron featured clumsily rendered elephants. They were usually explained away as a reference to the 37 elephants that Hannibal carried across the Alps with him in the summer of 218 B.C. The spectacle of those fabulous beasts tramping across southern Gaul, it was thought, would surely have fed the Celtic imagination for years.

Nobody over the past century has denied the possibility of an Eastern influence on the cauldron's iconography. Scrutinizing the figures, some scholars have pointed out that Taranis bears a striking resemblance to Vishnu. The figure bathing alongside the elephants recalls Lakshmi, a Hindu goddess of good fortune. The figure with the paired birds and nursing child suggests Hariti, Hindu protectress of children. And Cernunnos might be less and more than he appears, too: Legs folded yoga-style beneath him, he resembles not only Buddha but also the seated figure of a horned god, surrounded by a lion, an elephant, a rhinoceros, and a bull, depicted on a seal found in the Indus Valley and dating from the third or fourth millennium B.C.

Nevertheless, the cauldron was almost certainly made in Thrace, and by Thracian silversmiths. Only they could have borrowed elements from a pancultural fund of iconography, so to speak, that their imaginations could tap. Iron Age silversmiths might have been predominantly itinerant craftsmen, a valued and protected guild or caste that wandered over the ancient world, practicing an awe-inspiring and ritually sacrosanct art.

Such roving castes of craftsmen—alongside holy men, merchants, and soldiers—were the principal vehicles of cultural diffusion. They carried with them not only the germs of epidemic diseases, perhaps, but also an eclectic jumble of religious images and practices, gods and goddesses, idols and demons and rituals—and they sowed these all across Europe and the Near East. If inspiration for the decoration of a Celtic cauldron came 5,000 miles from India, might not certain attributes of the vampire have crossed those same steppes, deserts, and mountains?

CHAPTER EIGHT

TALES OF WORLDWIDE DEVILRY

DAWN ON THE RIVER GANGES—it might have been a thousand years ago, or today, or the 1890s, when American traveler Eliza Scidmore first gazed on the Hindu holy city of Benares:

> The greatest human spectacle in India, the chief inci-
> dent and motive of Benares life, and the most extraor-
> dinary manifestation of religious zeal and superstition
> in all the world, begins at sunrise by the Ganges
> bank and lasts for several hours. We started in the
> first gray light of the dawn, drove two miles across
> the city, and, descending the ghats, or broad stair-
> cases, to the water's edge, were rowed slowly up and
> down the three-mile crescent of river-front, watching
> Brahmans and humbler believers bathe and pray to

the rising sun, repeating the oldest Vedic hymns. That picturesque sweep of the city front—a high cliff with palaces, temples, and gardens clinging to its terraced embankments and long flights of steps descending to the water—is spectacle enough when lighted by the first yellow flash of sunlight, without the thousands of white-clad worshipers at the Ganges brink and far out in its turbid flood. After three sunrise visits to the river bank, the spectacle was as amazing and incomprehensible as at first, as incredible, as dreamlike, as the afternoon memory of it. I saw it with equal surprise each time, the key-note, the soul of India revealed in Benares as nowhere else—since all India flocks to Benares in sickness and health, in trouble and rejoicing, to pray and to commit crimes, the sacred city being the meeting-place and hiding-place of all criminals, the hatching-place of all conspiracies.

The thousands of worshipers might not have finished their oblations before the first white-shrouded, flower-bedecked corpse arrived. Perhaps only an hour or two had passed since the final moments when, ceremonial cow tail in hand, its spirit had loosed its hold and slipped back into the cycle of reincarnation. Brought on a bamboo bier by dirge-singing mourners, the corpse would be laid on the bottom step of the *ghats* so that its feet might be lapped by the Ganges. Only an hour or two more might pass before the body was ceremonially immersed in the river and then placed on the pyre.

The rising smoke might conceal what happened next; if not, the chief mourner might be seen prodding the burning skull with a bamboo pole and waiting for it to crack in the flames—a sign that the vital winds collected there had been released.

The scene is so spectacular that it is easy to miss the invisible. Just as all of India seems to flock to Benares, so too do its legions of devils, demons, and such terrifying figures as Kali—the bloodstained, skull-bedecked goddess of death, plague, and annihilation. The river stairways known as ghats are supernaturally charged places, as are cremation grounds all over the Indian subcontinent. In the countryside, you don't go near them unless absolutely necessary; they are always located at the margins, as far from the village as possible.

From the dying man's last moments to the ceremony of his incorporation into the ancestors 12 days later, the burial rituals serve a twofold purpose: They ease the passage of the dying and guard his soul along its way while wrapping a sheath of sanctity around the corpse, even though that won't be around for long.

According to Hindu mythology, supernatural scavengers are everywhere. Those that haunt cremation and burial grounds are loosely called Indian vampires, and they exist in bewildering varieties. Almost everywhere in India, both in villages and in the surrounding forests, stand small shrines called *bhandara*. These are for the *bhutas* (usually translated as "living beings"), and offerings of grain are made there each morning and evening to placate them.

Because the bhutas are malevolent goblins roaming the village, these offerings cannot be neglected. Otherwise, the bhutas may turn spiteful, blasting crops and livestock and visiting diseases upon the village children. Their cult is therefore observed with great ceremony: festivals, dances, and even blood sacrifices. Large temples known as *bhutastan* often house the statues of especially important bhutas.

Yet, peel back a layer, and the bhutas emerge not as gods or demons but as spirits of the dead—*bhuta* can be translated more precisely as "someone who was" or, roughly, "the departed." In some sense, then, bhutas are spirits that still cling to this world. In this aspect, they have a familiar provenance: They are the spirits of those who died untimely or violent deaths, who killed themselves, who were denied proper funeral rites, or who otherwise died unfulfilled. Meeting several such qualifications magnifies one's odds of becoming a bhuta.

More ominously, it seems that a bhuta can preempt a living body (and occasionally a dead one) to fulfill its desires. Bhutas lurk not only around cemeteries and cremation grounds but also in ruined temples and other places where owls—held in superstitious dread in India—might be found. So greatly feared are bhutas that their name encompasses a host of demonic beings, among them the *brahmaparush*, which drinks blood from its victim's skull while dancing with his intestines wrapped about its head like a turban. Like Western vampires, bhutas are said to cast no shadow, but garlic won't deter them—burning turmeric is the apotropaic ritual of choice.

Bhutas, however, have become confused and conflated with *pretas*. In one form or another, the preta has resonance all over Asia, where it often means "deceased." In China, according to Gerald Willoughby-Meade, *preta* means the "suffering soul of a suicide seeking a substitute." But *preta* implies a process more than a completion, so it might be better rendered as "one in transition." The preta is the form the soul takes on its journey to the ancestors, or *pitrs* ("protectors" or "fathers," akin to the Latin *pater,* "father"). It can take a baffling number of forms—as innumerable as seem to be the stages in Hindu soul making. The preta from a deformed child, for example, can be as small as your thumb. Yet, all pretas are potentially dangerous, and they must be propitiated by constant observation of extended funerary rites. These help them on their journey so that one day, they too can partake of the evening *bali,* or offering, which is always thrown to the south—the abode of the dead.

Another Indian embodiment of the unsatisfied dead takes a more recognizable form. *Vetalas,* which resemble giant vampire bats, were made known to the West by Sir Richard Francis Burton's *Vikram and the Vampire; or, Tales of Hindu Devilry.* This collection of stories within a story was the polyglot Burton's loose translation of the Hindu classic *Baital Pachisi,* which features an eloquent, tale-spinning vetala who greets the legendary king Vikram while hanging upside down from a tree. His fellow vetalas, however, prefer banqueting on corpses stacked at the cremation grounds or reanimating those buried in cemeteries.

On central India's broad Deccan Plateau, you commonly encounter stones (some painted a lurid red) that have been raised expressly for the use of vetalas; the vetalas serve as village guardians, and from these perches, their eerie singing may perhaps be heard.

Among the most hideous and reviled of Indian vampires are *pisachas,* or "flesh-eaters." These spirits—of criminals, liars, adulterers, or the insane—likewise loiter at cremation grounds, but they are far more insidious than bhutas or vetalas. They can enter a living person's open mouth and lodge in the intestines, where they banquet on feces—all of which sounds symbolic of disease, especially given that the great cholera, one of history's most horrible epidemics, was traced to India.

Then there are the *rakshasas,* or "destroyers." All blood and fangs, these shape-shifters might take the form of an owl, a dog, a cuckoo—or perhaps even the form of an absent lover or husband. A rakshasa has fiery red eyes and a long tongue, the better to prey on newborn infants and their mothers. They fear fire and mustard but not garlic.

Rakshasas were also once mystifyingly called "confounders of the sacrifice." Yet, peel back another layer: That epithet may be ancient indeed—dating, some experts believe, to the arrival of the Indo-Europeans in India. Coming off the dry, windswept plateaus of Iran and Afghanistan, the invaders drove away the Indian subcontinent's aboriginal inhabitants, who took to the jungles and became guerrilla fighters. Like Robin Hood and his men, the guerrillas evaded capture in their leafy new home and struck without warning—like forest demons.

In the *Rig Veda*, Indra, the thunder god, is implored to seek out and destroy these followers of an old religion, as their raids have been disrupting the elaborate sacrifices of the new one. There is some evidence that the word *pisacha* may once also have applied to tribes living in northern India. Thus, rakshasa, pisacha, and *vanara* (monkey-men), like vampir and warg-wolf, originally might have had no supernatural significance whatsoever. Perhaps they were instead ethnic epithets, once hurled in hatred.

These aboriginal tribes supposedly would have worshiped the deities of forest, mountain, stream, and hill: wolves, tigers, birds, and snakes. These deities either survived in the remoter villages, becoming protective spirits that lodged in sacred trees to which offerings were made, or were banished to the cremation grounds as cannibalistic demons.

But do these creatures correspond with European vampires? They seem to share a family tree but hang from a different branch. In India, however, you can usually find what you want if you look for it hard enough. If your pregnant wife dies during the Dewali festival or while ritually unclean, you had better bury her facedown, nail her fingers to her thumbs, and pile her grave with stones and thorns; otherwise, she will return as a churel and attack her family. That sounds more familiar.

Yet, some traces of Indian vampire lore may have been carried to Europe after all.

WANDERING VAMPIRES

Gypsies were perhaps the original bohemians. In 1423, King Sigismund of Bohemia gave a band of "outlandysshe" wanderers from "Egypt" the letter of safe conduct—and a name and reputation—that they carried all over Europe.

They had long been blacksmiths, tinkers, knife grinders, and horse traders, as well as dancers, musicians, and fortune-tellers. Black of eye and black of hair, gypsies (or Romani, as they call themselves) entered 15th-century Europe from Asia Minor just ahead of the Ottoman wave. Though they would eventually spread as far as the British Isles and then around the world, they roamed the Balkans and eastern Europe in such numbers that an 18th-century traveler to Transylvania compared them to "locusts" swarming over the land. Their clannish, secretive ways lent them an aura of superstition; they gained a reputation for being a caste apart, masters at harnessing or propitiating occult forces. And despite the widespread belief that they had come from Egypt, their original home was India.

For good reason—they once were enslaved in Romania and were nearly exterminated by the Nazis in World War II—the Romani have remained reclusive and wary. Their *kris,* or unwritten code, and their ever-changing Romani tongue have been constant bonds shared by widely dispersed bands. At the same time, their wanderings have accentuated the human tendency to diversify, making gypsies a challenge to linguists and anthropologists alike. Additionally, many of their customs are imbued with—perhaps contaminated by—those of the lands in which they sojourned.

The gypsy attitude toward the dead became less diluted than their other beliefs. They recognized two categories of dead people: *Suuntsé* were "saints" in paradise and need not be feared, whereas *mulé* died unnaturally, unexpectedly, or prematurely. In the animistic world of the gypsies, however, all death resulted from deliberate evil, so the latter category included just about everyone.

Never mind other people's ghosts or vampires; gypsies could pass untroubled nights in outsiders' graveyards. It was the *mulo* they feared. After a death in a gypsy camp, the tent where the corpse was laid would be carefully guarded so nothing untoward could affect it; meanwhile, the camp-fires outside were stoked high to scare off any ghosts. Every burial rite was observed to the letter, with the dead man's possessions—even his money—being destroyed to rob a potential ghost of any reason to pursue its former clan members and to exact its revenge for negligence or theft. The destruction extended even to the departed's home: The ritual of the burning wagon was once a spectacular gypsy custom.

Some say the mulo walks abroad by day; others that he moves only at night and must return to his grave by cock-crow. Either way, he can also be active precisely at noon, when nothing casts a shadow—a sort of witching hour in reverse. Not quite a reanimated corpse but not exactly a ghost either, the mulo is something in between—a kind of posthumous double that, though tethered to the grave, can nonetheless wander at will. Though the mulo is greatly feared for his often brutally sexual depredations, he is almost never a bloodsucker. In fact, his adventures are comically folkloric. Many aspects of his legend have been gathered from those of the vampire—the sharpened hawthorn stake, decapitation, and burning, to name just a few of the various methods used to well and truly dispatch him. This makes it likely that, as far as vampires are concerned, the gypsy got more than he gave.

On the other hand, there are those offerings. Yes, the mulo can wander, but he must always return to the grave— there to be propitiated with offerings of food and milk in a rite that might be as old as India. So, too, might be the belief in its universality. Vampirism, to the gypsy, is a principle of nature, as applicable to animals and plants as it is to humans. Pumpkins and melons, to name the two most famous examples, often turn into vampires.

All things, it seems, are full of more than just gods.

Blood and Sand

A century and more ago, when European archaeologists began excavating the earliest civilizations in the Near East, they saw in the bas-reliefs, the shattered cuneiform tablets, the broken pottery, the scattered amulets and wristbands and rings, evidence of what must have been vast pantheons of gods and demons.

According to Montague Summers, one such find—a prehistoric bowl discovered by a French archaeological mission in Persia at the turn of the 20th century—is the earliest

known representation of a vampire. It depicts a supernatural warning in the form of a man copulating with a headless
corpse (the threat of decapitation being enough to scare off a
succubus, or demon in female form said to have sexual intercourse with men while they sleep). Dr. Reginald Campbell
Thompson, author of *Semitic Magic,* is quoted as suggesting
"quite probably the man may have drunk from this bowl as
helping the magic (although this is a doubtful point)."

It might be a doubtful point; it is certainly an enigmatic
object. So is the Assyrian cylinder seal, dating to around
2000 B.C., that depicts a naked female straddling a prostrate
male while another man, wielding what looks like a stake but
could be a dagger, advances threateningly upon the woman.
This seal might have been the amulet of a man "troubled
by nightly emissions," in Campbell Thompson's decorous
phrase. It, too, would ward off a succubus by depicting the
fate that lay in store for her.

The surviving bits of literature recovered so far are full of
such warnings, spells, and exorcisms. The deserts bounding
the civilizations of Mesopotamia and Assyria were fearsome
enough places without doubling as the abodes of demons
and the dead. These included the mysterious Seven Spirits,
suckers of blood and eaters of flesh, and the dreaded *ekimmu*
or *elimmu,* ghosts of men whose bodies lay abandoned in
desert or marsh. Deprived of the proper burial rituals, they
wander between worlds, hungry and thirsty, preying on
passersby. They seem to be of ancient provenance; in Sumerian demonology, Professor Samuel Hooke noted, "the dead

who had not had funeral rites performed for them were greatly feared."

And then there was Lilith, who clawed her way up the demonological ladder until, by the Middle Ages, she was Queen of the Succubi, if not the consort of the devil himself. Lilith began inauspiciously enough, though, possibly as the Sumerian wind spirit (from *lil*, "wind"), one of the legions that arose in the solitary wastes of the desert. She got an early boost in status when she married Adam—this was before Eve, at least according to Hebrew folklore—but was eventually exiled back to the desert. There she took up residence, said the Prophet Isaiah, with jackals and ostriches and vultures. Once her name became confused with the Hebrew *layal* ("night"), Lilith became a hairy, night-flying monster—the very epitome of the female sexual predator. Solomon thought the Queen of Sheba's hairy legs betrayed her as Lilith in disguise, and indeed, in this hirsute role, she has wormed her way through poetry, drama, and fiction.

But if Lilith morphed into a literary archetype, another demonic Hebrew child killer, the *estrie*, managed to retain her original vampiric attributes. At the burial of a woman believed liable to become an estrie after death, the body was examined to see if its mouth was open. That, as we have seen, was an infallibly ominous sign—and if the mouth was in fact open, it was promptly stuffed with dirt.

Deeper in the deserts of Arabia, a demon in the shape of a beautiful enchantress was said to open graves to feed on fresh corpses. She was called the *algul*—origin, understandably, of the English word *ghoul*. Islam may have banished such monsters to the farthest liminal margins, but it could not eradicate the fear of them. An isolated grave found in an Ottoman cemetery on the Greek island of Mytilene, and dating to the late 18th or early 19th century, contained a skeleton with nails driven through its neck, pelvis, and ankles. Muslim custom calls for the imam to remain at the tomb when a funeral is over, to coach the dead man in the replies he should make to the Questioners—the angels Mounkir and Nekir—who have entered the grave to interrogate him about his faith. Even in Islam, the soul after death retains some mysterious connection with its body, and is thought to linger with it until after its burial.

No place in the ancient world, however, was more obsessed with death than Egypt. Possessing the most elaborate funerary complex of them all, as the pyramids have reminded countless generations of visitors, the Egyptians so purified, embalmed, mummified, memorialized, and mythologized their dead that surely they must have told tales of their occasional return. Yet, despite Egypt's reputation as the wellspring of all magic, all mystery, all black arts; despite its subsequent role in the literature of mystery and romance; and despite claims to the contrary, no trace of vampires has been found in the country's extensive archaeological records.

The reason: The Egyptians performed their mortuary labors too well. Many of the earliest mummies were decapitated, eviscerated, hacked into pieces, and then reassembled and wrapped in linen, rendering the body uninhabitable. Furthermore, they built for the ages. All those necropolises in the desert, all that "care that the Egyptians took to bury their dead in tombs deep in the ground and in the sides of mountains," as pioneering Egyptologist Sir Wallis Budge wrote in 1883, may have been the equivalent of constructing containment domes around some very dangerous force: "The massive stone and wooden sarcophagi, the bandages of the mummy, the double and triple coffins, the walled-up doors of the tomb, the long shaft filled with earth and stones, etc., all were devised with the idea of making it impossible for the dead to reappear upon the earth."

Níght ín the Kampongs

From Burma to the farthest-flung islands of the Malay Archipelago, in jungles where head-hunting once thrived and were-tigers and were-buffalo and even were-elephants once stalked, the rank flourish of tropical vegetation competes with a riot of supernatural bloodsucking creatures. When their tales were told at night in the scattered kampongs, or villages, protective screens of *jeruju* thorn might be drawn closer around the community's most vulnerable: pregnant women, infants, and young mothers.

In Malaysia, it is told, a mother once died of grief after giving birth to a stillborn. Her spirit flew up into a tree and became a *langsuir,* a cormorantlike vampire that eats fish and spitefully sucks the blood of other newborns through a hole in the back of her neck. By day, however, she continued to be the very picture of a beautiful Malay woman, with long, black hair and a green dress. The stillborn child, for its part, became a *pontianak*—a terrible little bloodsucking vampire that often assumes the form of an owl. Unless certain now-familiar steps are taken with their corpses, all mothers who die in childbirth, and all babies who are stillborn, are in the danger of becoming langsuir and pontianak. Needles must be jabbed in their palms, eggs lodged beneath their arms, and glass beads inserted in their mouths to block the entry or exit of spirits. Folklore being what it is, however, the roles have been reversed on crowded Java. There, the langsuir has become the stillborn child, and the pontianak the inconsolable, vengeful mother heard wailing in the night.

Stillborn children, dying newborns, mothers expiring while giving birth or before they can be ritually purified—such tragedies must have been all too common at one time, so deeply have they impressed themselves upon the folklore. Stories of dead mothers and children returning and, having been robbed of life and offspring themselves, enviously destroying those of others, convey an almost unbearable psychological truth. Yet, the local mythology saw even healthy, growing children as vulnerable, too. They might be attacked by the *bajang,* a malevolent spirit clearly based on the secretive, nocturnal civet of the jungle canopy. When captured in a hollow bamboo stalk, the bajang can become a wizard's familiar—and even his legacy, passed down from one generation to the next in a wizard family.

The most dreaded and lurid supernatural predator of mothers and infants in Malaysia is the horrible *penanggalen,* a monster reduced to its gory minimum: a fanged female head trailing only stomach and intestines. These vile viscera glow behind it at night like a macabre comet, sometimes sparkling like fireflies. Given this ghastly vision, it's easy to understand how and why only a screen of jeruju thorn might have the power to entangle and halt the demon.

When the Spanish arrived in the Philippines in the 1500s, they found a population terrified of *aswangs*—supernatural creatures that were a blend of vampire, witch, and some kind of were-animal. The aswang that flew in the night was decidedly a bloodsucker, using its long tongue to prick the jugular vein of the unwary sleeper, but during the day, it was a beautiful woman leading an ordinary village life; she achieved her supernatural powers, as did medieval witches, by rubbing herself with a special ointment.

To ward off an aswang attack—and, incidentally, to carve out more room on the communal sleeping mat—you might rub garlic in your armpits. In some places, the aswang is called *mandurugo,* or "bloodsucker." Beautiful and enticing by day, a winged monstrosity by night, the mandurugo preys on a succession of young men.

The Spanish also encountered a belief in the *danag*. Once a cultural hero as the goddess who gave humankind the gift of taro, the danag had since been demoted to a bloodsucking demon.

Such creatures both resemble the European vampire and differ from it. They suck blood. They bring death by disease. They prey upon the vulnerable. And they are often mixed up with witches and wizards. The aswang, the mandurugo, and the danag are also associated with such nocturnal aviators as the owl and the flying fox, or kalang, a fearsome-looking bat with a wingspan of six feet that Swedish botanist Carolus Linnaeus unjustifiably named *Pteropus vampyrus* in 1758, though it actually eats nothing but fruit.

And though "it is impossible," as authors Stella Martin and Denis Walls put it, "to ascertain whether *orang minyak* (oily men) were human or fictional," many women might find them creepily reminiscent of real-life vampires they have known: "These naked and reputedly handsome men molest unsuspecting women in their homes at night and if caught either slip out of their captors' hands or, according to some, turn into butterflies or rats."

Tales from China and Japan

In a land as ancient as China, where ancestor worship has been so prominent for so long, tombs and cemeteries are ubiquitous. The bodies that are laid there—or rather stood, as Chinese cadavers were often buried vertically—were also swathed in shrouds and wrapped with as many protective rituals as man was capable of inventing. For the Chinese double soul—*p'o* was earthy, made of shadowy yin, while *hun* was spirit, full of bright yang—had worked harmoniously in life but then separated at death: While the hun departed for heaven, the p'o remained with the body and ultimately returned to earth.

But leave a corpse too long exposed to sunlight (or, for the sake of ambience, to moonlight) and the p'o might absorb too much yang. The moon has always been a source of occult energy (in Europe, moonbeams were said to induce lunacy, but in China, its energy is that of yang)—thus the belief that, should moonbeams strike a fresh corpse, yang might seep into it and overwhelm the p'o. This might reawaken a need for continuing sustenance once in the grave—a need that can be met only by feeding on the corpses nearby or, failing that, by feeding on living people. In the latter case, you get a *ch'ing shih*—a Chinese vampire.

And what a vampire: With its red, staring eyes, fetid breath, talonlike fingernails, and cerements covered with the fungus of the grave, it preys on those who pass too close to graveyards at night. The only ways to stop its depredations are to be more prompt in the observances of ancestor worship (moonlight as well as neglected ritual being equally powerful progenitors of a ch'ing shih) or, as a last resort, to burn the body. It may also be the case that a demon has simply possessed a fresh cadaver; either way, as an animated corpse, it closely resembles the European vampire.

Two subtle variations: The ch'ing shih doesn't infect its victims with its own taint, and it doesn't swoop down upon them—it can only hop.

It is tempting to seek a channel of cultural transmission, perhaps back and forth along the immemorial Silk Road, where merchants might have carried legends and tales of the walking dead by telling them at night by campfire light or under the roof of caravanserais long gone to dust. But that path is probably too difficult to follow. In any event, to the west of China are those inhospitable figures: the Nepalese Lord of Death, perched on a pile of skeletons, with a crown of skulls and a necklace of severed hands; and the Mongolian Lord of Time, surrounded by bones and rotting corpses.

Tibet is no less forbidding. In 1931, French traveler Alexandra David-Neel witnessed a sort of vampire role reversal: A Tibetan shaman was wrestling with a corpse. He lay on it and, in effect, kissed it, at the same time repeating a magic formula. The corpse tried to throw him off, but the shaman clung fast and eventually succeeded in biting off the cadaver's tongue. At that, the corpse collapsed back into lifelessness and left a potent talisman—the severed tongue—in the shaman's possession. That doesn't sound very European.

Looking east from China, though, it's hard to find a vampire at all. After 1854, when Japan was first opened to the world, a flood of curious Westerners descended upon the Land of the Rising Sun and, spellbound by what they found, began interpreting this ancient culture to readers back home. Among them was Algernon B. Mitford, later Baron Redesdale, whose 1871 book, *Tales of Old Japan,* would prove to be an enduring classic. Among the stories Mitford included was one he called "The Vampire Cat of Nabeshima."

The Prince of Hizen has fallen in love with a "lady of rare beauty, called O Toyo" who, unknown to him, is throttled to death by a giant cat and buried beneath the veranda. The cat then assumes O Toyo's beautiful form and, lamia-like, begins preying on the prince while he sleeps. When eventually discovered, the beautiful woman transforms back into a cat, springs onto the roof, and gets away.

But not for long.

In classic fairy tale fashion, the cat "fled to the mountains, and did much mischief among the surrounding people, until at last the Prince of Hizen ordered a great hunt, and the beast was killed."

That is one of the few vampire stories found in the monster-rich folklore of Japan. Fragments, and occasionally entire poems, from ancient Japan mention encounters with dead people out walking, and one poem in particular somehow protects its bearer should he meet up with such a strolling corpse. Yet these are only vestiges. Sepulchers from the Jomon period (4000 to 250 B.C.) have been opened in which skeletons were curled up, stretched out, or had stones placed on chest or head. Archaeologists still puzzle over some bodies buried in fetal positions, wondering whether they signify a return to the womb or represent precautions taken against the return of dead people. Even touching a decomposing corpse demands a purification rite, and Yomi, the Japanese land of the dead, is the decomposing corpse writ large: a domain of impurity that, like most underworlds, is also the source of eventual regeneration.

Yet, the exquisite refinement that is uniquely Japanese extended even to the ancient tomb. Mitford noted how the "rich and noble are buried in several square coffins, one inside the other, in a sitting position; and their bodies are partially preserved from decay by filling the nose, ears, and mouth with vermilion. In the case of the very wealthy, the coffin is completely filled in with vermilion."

Japanese folklore had its share of demons, baby eaters, and ghouls, as Lafcadio Hearn made known in his *In Ghostly Japan*. The 19th-century literary critic and travel writer also belonged to that first generation of Westerners enraptured by Japan. Yet, he discovered something ineffably eerier in the appearance of a fleet of miniature "ghost ships." During the Bon—a three-day festival of the dead held each year in late summer—tiny ship models, each bearing their own little working lanterns, were set afloat on the sea at night. Hearn swam out into the ocean to observe the spectacle firsthand:

I watched those frail glowing shapes drifting through the night, and ever as they drifted scattering, under impulse of wind and wave, more and more widely apart. Each, with its quiver of color, seemed a life afraid,—trembling on the blind current that was bearing it into the outer blackness.... Are not we ourselves as lanterns launched upon a deeper and a dimmer sea, and ever separating further and further one from another as we drift to the inevitable dissolution? Soon the thought-light in each burns itself out: then the poor frames, and all that is left of their once fair colors, must melt forever into the colorless Void....

Even in the moment of this thought I began to doubt whether I was really alone,—to ask myself whether there might not be something more than a mere shuddering of light in the thing that rocked beside me: some presence that haunted the dying flame, and was watching the watcher. A faint cold thrill passed over me,—perhaps some chill uprising from the depths,—perhaps the creeping only of a ghostly fancy. Old superstitions of the coast recurred to me,—old vague warnings of peril in the time of the passage of Souls. I reflected that were any evil to befall me out there in the night,—meddling, or seeming to meddle, with the lights of the Dead,—I should myself furnish the subject of some future weird legend.

So he whispered a hurried Buddhist farewell, then struck out for the shore.

Rare Sightings

Voyage across the vast Pacific, and the vampire gets only more elusive. In Melanesia, where chiefs were once buried standing up with just their heads emerging from the sand, the dead are envisioned as eating lizards and excrement, among other unpleasantness. In New Caledonia, the dead are likely to return in deceptive form, like that of a living man, but they can be detected at night because they snore, or by the more reliable sign that their body disappears and leaves only the head visible. In north Malekula, the dead are ever present, their skulls arranged on a flat stone in the men's lodge, where people invoke them by spitting continuously in their direction.

Though such examples can be dug up indefinitely, few vampires are found.

Anthropologist George R. Stetson discovered evidence in Captain Cook's voyages that, as Stetson put it, the "Polynesians believed that the vampires were the departed souls, which quitted the grave . . . to creep by night into the houses and devour the heart and entrails of the sleepers, who afterward died." Other scholars, by contrast, have come up empty-handed. As in so many cultures worldwide, however, those of the South Seas warn the living that ominous occurrences should be expected when burial rituals for the dead are not observed, or if their resting places are disturbed later on.

A vampire tradition may not exist in the New World, either—but that hardly renders its every element absent. Among the Ojibwa of the Great Lakes region, for example, the soul that failed to enter the next world was doomed to return and to reanimate its body. In a Cherokee legend published in the *Journal of American Folklore* in 1892, some folklorists perceive an explanation of tuberculosis. A "Demon of Consumption," goes the tale, once lived in a cave and possessed an iron finger. At night he would steal out, impersonate a member of a given family, enter his house, "select his victim, begin fondling his head, and run his soft fingers through his hair until the unsuspecting victim would go to sleep. Then with his iron finger would he pierce the victim's side and take his liver and lungs, but without pain. The wound would immediately heal, leaving no outward mark." With no memory of the assault, the victim would go about his business, growing weaker by the day until he wasted away altogether and died.

Stetson, too, singled out a Cherokee tale. "There are in that tribe," he wrote, "quite a number of old witches and wizards who thrive and fatten upon the livers of murdered victims." Like medieval demons, they gather around those on their deathbeds, tormenting and eventually killing them. But mere death does not end the agony. After burial, the Cherokee demons dig up the body, remove the liver, and feast upon it. "They thus lengthen their own lives by as many days as they have taken from his," Stetson continued. "In this way they get to be very aged, which renders them objects of suspicion. It is not, therefore, well to grow old among the Cherokees."

Folklorist Stith Thompson includes this Abenaki tale in his *Motif-Index of Folk-Literature:* An old wizard had died and was laid in the branches of a tree in a burial grove. One evening, an Indian and his wife passed by, looking for a place to spend the night. They set up camp beneath the tree and cooked their food. Glancing up, the woman "saw long dark things hanging among the tree branches." Those were merely the dead from long ago, her husband explained. He then unaccountably fell fast asleep. But the wife, understandably, could not close an eyelid:

Soon the fire went out, and then she began to hear a gnawing sound, like an animal with a bone. She sat still, very much scared, all night long. About dawn she could stand it no longer, and reaching out, tried to wake her husband, but could not. . . . The gnawing had stopped. When daylight came she went to her husband and found him dead, with his left side gnawed away, and his heart gone.

When the body of the dead wizard was taken down and unwrapped, the "mouth and face were covered with fresh blood."

Shift that setting to Russia and exchange the grove for a graveyard, and you would have a classic folkloric vampire tale.

QUICK OR DEAD?

"Zombi!—the word is perhaps full of mystery even for those who made it," marveled Lafcadio Hearn, who washed up on Martinique after leaving Japan. Often erroneously credited with introducing the word *zombie* in its present meaning into English, in an 1889 *Harpers* article, Hearn found that in Martinique, it applied to a wide range of goblins, specters, and other monsters of the nursery, but never to the dead. It was a word, he acknowledged, that must have "special strange meanings."

Our modern word *zombie* has certainly taken a strange odyssey. It actually appeared in English 70 years earlier, in Robert Southey's 1819 *History of Brazil*. Describing an independent ex-slave republic near Pernambuco in the 1690s, Southey stated that its chief was called Zombi, which was the "name for the Deity, in the Angolan tongue." Noting that the militantly Catholic Portuguese, colonizers of both Brazil and Angola, translated *Zombi* as "devil," Southey checked certain books of religious instruction that were printed in both Portuguese and Angolan: "There I found that N'Zambi is the word for Deity."

From deity to walking corpse is a very large leap, but perhaps the devil has something to do with it after all; missionaries and colonial officials denigrated native gods everywhere as demons. Lexicographers have been combing the jungles of African etymology for decades, hunting for the origins of *zombi*. Many have sided with Southey. In Kimbundu, the language of Angola, they find the word rendered as *nzambi* ("god") or *zumi* ("ghost" or "departed spirit"). Other linguists derive greater enlightenment from Kikongo, a related language, where *zumi* means "fetish" and *nvumbi* is a body deprived of its soul. All point to the region bracketing the mouth of the Congo River, from Angola in the south to Gabon in the north.

The best-known zombie hails from a different hemisphere entirely. It is the grisliest component in the lurid assemblage of features—including pins stuck in effigy dolls, child sacrifice, and cannibalism—that for generations constituted the popular conception of Haitian voodoo. There, the zombie is a mindless if ambulatory corpse, like those spotted working in a sugarcane field by American writer William B. Seabrook. An avowed cannibal himself—he claimed to have shared with an African chief a human rump steak that was "so nearly like good, fully developed veal that I think no person with a palate of ordinary, normal sensitiveness could distinguish it from veal"—Seabrook spent months in Haiti while researching his 1929 book *The Magic Island*.

The zombies that Seabrook claimed to have encountered had "staring, unfocused, unseeing" eyes. Their faces were "not only expressionless, but incapable of expression," and they harvested the cane stalks in a kind of unconscious suspended animation, showing no response even to Seabrook's touch. Could these have been living men, put under a cataleptic spell by certain "substances," recognized by the Haitian *code pénal,* that "without causing actual death, produce a lethargic coma more or less prolonged"? Perhaps. Yet in theory, at least, they also might have been reanimated corpses, bereft of speech and free will.

In Haiti, it seems, the sorcerer can suck a man's soul out through the crack of his door and bottle it. This proves fatal; once the victim is buried, the wizard—like the resurrectionists of 18th-century England—sneaks into the graveyard and digs him up. After due propitiations to death gods, the wizard uncorks the bottle and waves it back and forth beneath the corpse's nose. This waft of his own soul reanimates the dead man, but the wizard then promptly applies some baleful herb to ensure he remains a mindless slave.

Alternatively, the wizard can simply wait until somebody dies and then, like sorcerers in Gabon, revive the body by recalling its soul—which, if not still lingering inside the cadaver, is at least hovering nearby. Either way, time is of the essence: Once decomposition sets in, the dead body is useless as a slave. It might just as well be transformed into animal meat and sold in the market. Unsurprisingly, it is reputed to spoil quickly.

Waiting to drop down upon the unwary, multitudes of bloodsucking, bloodcurdling creatures infest the forests of the African imagination—just as they do the Indian and the Malaysian. Whether or not he originated in the cult of an African snake god, the zombie is not a bloodsucker. Nor is he—despite the mindless cannibals of moviedom—a midnight predator. Rather, a zombie is simply a reanimated corpse, directed by a sorcerer. In this shaman-centered world of divisible souls and of cadavers restored to dimly fluttering life, we can glimpse yet another clue to the origins of the primitive vampire.

The deeper in time we venture—and the farther from Eurasia—the more elusive the vampire grows. He may not appear at all times and in all places. One element, though, seems universal: The dead body must undergo a fixed sequence of changes before being reduced to its fundamental form, the skeleton. That transition, from demise to dissolution, is everywhere deemed a dangerous interlude for both the quick and the dead.

CHAPTER NINE

THE LARVAE

IN 1784, IN THE CAUCASUS MOUNTAINS near what is now North Ossetia, Russia, a traveler named Stöder witnessed a gripping and no doubt ancient ceremony. A young woman had just been struck and killed by lightning. Immediately afterward, the residents of her village, heedless of the storm, rushed to her body, crying joyously and dancing in a circle around her corpse while singing a song to Elias, or Elijah the Thunderer—the ancient Indo-European god of storms and lightning, draped in the more acceptable garments of an Old Testament prophet.

The dead girl was dressed in new clothes and placed in a coffin atop a platform. For eight days, everyone—including the girl's parents, sisters, and husband—celebrated. A fire was kept burning, and all work was suspended. Any expression of grief was thought to be a sin against Elijah. Present at the ritual was a youth who had himself survived a lightning strike, which gave him special status as a servant and messenger of Elijah. He sang and danced, then fell into convulsions; when he opened his eyes, he told what he had seen in the heavenly company of Elijah, naming previous lightning victims who were standing at Elijah's side.

On the eighth day, the dead girl was laid on a new cart, pulled by a pair of oxen with white spots, and paraded through the neighboring villages, accompanied by singing youths and relatives who collected gifts of livestock and food. Then the oxen were turned loose; the patch of grass on which they stopped nearby was designated the burial spot. The coffin was placed on a rectangle of stones several feet high; next to it villagers erected a pole, on which they stretched the skin and head of a goat. Here, everyone feasted.

Remarkably similar ceremonies were once reported all over the Caucasus—among the few commonalities in a fragmented region where each valley otherwise seemed to be its own tribal enclave, speaking its own language and practicing its own traditions. In some places, the lightning-seared body was left on the platform until it decomposed. In others, the body might be hung from a tree for three days while dances and sacrifices took place. Sometimes a "banquet of the thunderstruck" was held on the anniversary of the unfortunate soul's death. And always the victim's livestock were released into pastures, specially marked to warn the shepherds away.

Most important, a nimbus of the holy surrounded the lightning's victim. The survivor was endowed with prophetic powers, to be sure, but the dead were assumed to be sitting among the heavenly elite. Whether quick or dead, these people were charged with a divine energy; they were *tabu, hieros, sacer,* all meaning "consecrated, holy, untouchable"—and "terrifying." For it's not the lightning, but what it illuminates: The joy evident in the community often hid a deeper fear, because the newly dead were believed to enjoy sudden access to supernatural powers. And "primitive man," as anthropologist Sir James Frazer put it in 1933, saw the handiwork of the dead everywhere, particularly "in earthquakes, thunderstorms, drought, famine, disease and death. No wonder that he regards the supposed authors of such evils with awe and fear, and seeks to guard himself against them by all the means at his command."

The Power of the Perished

In *Curiosities of Olden Times* (1895), the English reverend Sabine Baring-Gould, best known for penning the hymn "Onward, Christian Soldiers," quotes two lines from the priest officiating at the funeral of *Hamlet*'s Ophelia, who has drowned herself in a brook: "For charitable prayers / Shards, flints, and pebbles should be thrown on her."

"Unquestionably it must have been customary in England," Reverend Baring-Gould observes, "thus to pelt a ghost that was suspected of the intention to wander. The stake driven through the suicide's body was a summary and complete way of ensuring that the ghost would not be troublesome."

Fear of the dead: Just as it has cast its dank shadow over myth and legend worldwide, so too is it apparent in the tangible artifacts of funerary practices. In graves thousands of years old, skeletons have been found staked, tied up, buried facedown, decapitated, pinned with arrows, crushed by boulders, partially cremated, or exhumed and then reburied—all well-attested ways of preempting the depredations of wandering corpses.

The ancestors are the apotheosized dead. Having been gathered unto their forefathers, they now dwell in an idealized, timeless realm. The recently dead are another story: No matter who they are—parents, siblings, children, friends—they are often conceived as resentful, aggressive, and willing to use their newly enhanced powers against the living. As anthropologists Peter Metcalf and Richard Huntington wrote in 1991, "[t]he corpse is feared because, until its reconstruction in the beyond is complete, part of its spiritual essence remains behind, where it menaces the living with the threat of further death." So mortuary rites were devised primarily to help the spirit adjust to its new status during this perilous period, to push it on down the line, and to isolate it from the living.

Among the forest tribes of South America, dead bodies were often buried in a fetal position somewhere out in the woods. There were no cemeteries, because cemeteries "incorporate" the dead into the larger community. These tribes wished to do the opposite: They wanted to exclude the deceased, and even banish their memory. Nevertheless, the spirits of the recently dead were believed to wander about at night, sowing illness in their wake.

Occasionally, after a member of the community died, people simply abandoned their village altogether. Sometimes they indulged in a bit of preliminary flattery instead, as among the Bororo of Mato Grosso in Brazil: A death would be followed by an elaborate, two-stage burial. First, the body was interred, and it was permitted to remain for several weeks while ritual hunts and dances took place to honor the spirit. Next, the body was exhumed and defleshed. The skeleton was then painted with *urucu*—a red dye from a local shrub—and plastered with feathers. In a final indignity, it was placed in a basket and cast into the river.

"There is almost no end to the expedients adopted for getting rid of the dead," marveled Reverend Baring-Gould:

> Piles of stones are heaped over them, they are buried deep in the earth, they are walled up in natural caves, they are enclosed in megalithic structures, they are burned, they are sunk in the sea. They are threatened, they are cajoled, they are hoodwinked. Every sort of trickery is had recourse to, to throw them off the scent of home and of their living relations.
>
> The wives, horses, dogs slain and buried with them, the copious supplies of food and drink laid on their graves, are bribes to induce them to be content with their situation. Nay, further—in very many

places no food may be eaten in the house of mourning for many days after an interment. The object of course is to disappoint the returning spirit, which comes seeking a meal, finds none, comes again next day, finds none again, and after a while desists from returning out of sheer disgust.

The primary defense against such malevolent spirits was a good offense—that is, the proper care of their dead bodies. "It is affirmed that persons who have been struck dead by lightning do not decay, and for that reason the ancients neither burnt them nor buried them," wrote Benedictine exegetist Dom Augustin Calmet in the 18th century. The "reason they are not subject to corruption is because they are as it were embalmed by the sulphur of the thunder-bolt, which serves them instead of salt."

But "unenlightninged" bodies *are* subject to corruption, and the history of disposing of such noxious corpses is novel indeed. It has ranged from exposing them to scavengers, to burning them to cinders, to burying them in the ground, to simply eating them. The sequence has varied from place to place; most cultures have had recourse to some mixture of all these elements.

Not that it has helped them understand one another. Two and a half millennia ago, the Greek historian Herodotus told how King Darius of Persia once gathered some Greeks who practiced cremation of their dead and asked what it would take to eat them instead:

They said that no price in the world would make them do so. After that, Darius summoned those of the Indians who are called Callatians . . . [who did practice funerary cannibalism] and . . . asked them what price would make them burn their dead fathers with fire. They shouted aloud, "Don't mention such horrors!" These are matters of settled custom, and I think Pindar was right when he says, "Custom is king of all."

Death Lifts Us Up Where We Belong

Several centuries ago, when travelers returned from the Caucasus Mountains and reported having seen dead bodies carefully laid in tree branches, they were describing a tradition that was already venerable when the kings of ancient Colchis—keepers of the Golden Fleece—ruled the area. Deliberate exposure is perhaps humankind's oldest way of disposing of cadavers.

Chimpanzees, when faced with the corpse of a fellow chimp, prod it gingerly a bit and then take to their heels, abandoning it to forest scavengers. Early hominids probably fared no better. "When they died," archaeologist Timothy Taylor wrote in 2002, "there was little to stop ape-men, ape-women, and ape-children from being torn to pieces. The dead were edible. Vultures, hyenas, crocodiles, rodents, insects, fish and bacteria each took the meat, blood, and fat they wanted. What remained was scattered and trampled, then shattered and powdered by wind and rain."

At some point in the distant past, our forebears made a virtue—or something like it—of necessity deliberately by exposing human bodies to scavengers. Not just any scavengers, however. Nearly everywhere there was a decided preference for birds of prey, no doubt because they descend from the heavens. Whether standing in the desiccating wind of the Dakota prairie or hanging from the branches of an Australian eucalyptus, exposure platforms therefore served a dual purpose: They kept terrestrial scavengers at bay and brought the body nearer to heaven, where the vultures wheeled.

At Çatal Hüyük, a Neolithic village excavated in southern Turkey, 8,000-year-old wall paintings seem to depict vultures alighting on headless corpses. The "birds" might instead represent women dressed as vultures, however, engaging in some long-forgotten funerary rite. If so, they may be prototypes of the classical harpies (called snatchers in Greek)—ravenous, loathsome mythological birds with the faces of women. Certainly vultures carried an association with the divine into historical times. The Vaccaei, for example, who inhabited parts of Spain and Portugal during the third century B.C.E., sneered at those who succumbed to disease; let them be cremated. Death in battle was the nobler quietus; the bodies of those so righteously slain should be entrusted to nothing less than vultures.

For more than 300 years, the Parsees of Mumbai have been famous for their Towers of Silence: Atop these circular stone platforms, they expose their dead for vultures to devour. Earth, fire, and water are all sacred elements, the

Parsees believe, and are essential for life; they must therefore not be polluted by exposure to death. This rules out disposing of corpses by burial, burning, or consignment to a river. Instead, they are carefully laid out on these stone floors—men here, women there, children in another place—for the circling birds to feast upon. "One afternoon," wrote Edward Ives in the 1750s, "I resolved to satisfy my curiosity so far as to peep into one of these edifices. I perceived several dead bodies, but there was little flesh left upon the bones; and that little was so parched up by the excessive heat of the sun, that it did not emit those stinking effluvia which there was reason to expect."

In fact, until quite recently, when India's vulture population crashed after widespread poisoning, this method of disposing of the dead was both highly organized and extremely hygienic: Nobody was allowed to touch the bodies, lest they spread contagion around the city. The corpses were instead maneuvered by means of metal hooks. Vultures, moreover, worked "more expeditiously than millions of insects would do, if dead bodies were buried in the ground," as the Parsee Sir Ervad Jivanji Jamshedji Modi (1854–1933) explained. "By this rapid process, putrefaction with all its concomitant evils, is most effectually prevented."

On the treeless Tibetan Plateau, where the soil is thin, rocky, and often frozen, the Buddhists don't worry about even the leftover bones. In their traditional "sky burials," the corpse is first defleshed by ritual specialists. Its skeleton is then pounded into fragments with hammers. Within an hour of the first vulture's arrival, not a scrap is left, making this perhaps the most ecologically pure of all methods for the disposal of human remains.

Elsewhere, carcasses were often left exposed on platforms for months on end. Some Australian tribes occasionally gathered beneath such podia, which had been suspended from trees, to anoint themselves with the fluids dripping down from their decomposing cargoes. Eventually, whatever bones remained would be collected and buried. Funerary groves such as these—be they in Australia or the Caucasus or North America—were sites both holy and dreadful. Nevertheless, as a Goulburn Island Aboriginal woman once commented matter-of-factly, "It's cleaner on a tree than under the ground—and we can go back and look at them sometimes."

It's a Man-Eat-Man World

Exposure is often associated with excarnation—deliberately stripping the flesh from a corpse to turn it into a skeleton as quickly as possible. Sometimes the reason has to do with ritual, as in Tibetan sky burials. At other times, the goal is the brutally immediate—and nutritive—one of the human flesh itself. "All the vampire stories have developed out of facts concerning primitive cannibalism," declared MacLeod Yearsley in *The Folklore of Fairy-Tale* (1924). His facts may be suspect—anthropologists have debated the scope and extent of human cannibalism for decades—but how much does the grisly practice pertain to the origin of vampire stories?

Deep in Spain's wooded Atapuerca Mountains is a cluster of caves that have long provided a wealth of ancient human remains. In one cave, Gran Dolina, bone fragments recovered in the mid-1990s show clear evidence of having been butchered with stone tools. Dating from 780,000 years ago, they represent the oldest archaeological evidence of cannibalism ever discovered.

In 1976, a nearly complete hominid skull was unearthed near Bodo in Ethiopia. Dated to 600,000 years before the present, it bears cut marks indicating it was deliberately defleshed—yet another sign suggesting cannibalism. Judging from the number of later Paleolithic bones displaying similar expertly placed incisions, cannibalism may have been a common practice. The uncertainties of Stone Age hunting and gathering, after all, placed a premium on protein gathered from whatever sources were available.

Travelers' tales describing smoked flesh hanging in huts, or prisoners being fattened in wooden cages, or "long pig" gracing chiefly tables were once routine from Africa to the South Pacific. The conquistadors brought back their own lurid tales of the supposed Aztec and Mayan predilection for human meat. As 19th-century Chicago anthropologist Rushton M. Dorman noted,

> The Mayas also ate the flesh of human victims sacrificed to the gods. In Nicaragua, the high-priest received the heart, the king the feet and hands, the captors took the thighs, and the tripe was given to the

trumpeters. The natives of Honduras said the Spaniards were too tough and bitter to be eaten.

That was exo-cannibalism, or the eating of people from outside one's own community. Endo-cannibalism, on the other hand, is typically practiced as a reverential funerary rite, and it may have once been widespread. Among the Tapuyas of Brazil, for example, Dorman claimed that, "when an infant died it was eaten by the parents. Adults were eaten by the kindred, and their bones were pounded and reserved for marriage-feasts, as being the most precious thing that could be offered. When they became old they offered themselves to their children, who devoured them after putting them to death. They thought their spiritual substance became incorporated."

However exaggerated these reports might be, the idea of incorporation was the motive behind all funerary cannibalism—which did not necessarily entail a feast of flesh. One way of incorporating the dead was "to grind their bones to powder or to burn them to ashes," according to Frazer, "and then to swallow the powder or the ashes mixed with food or drink." The Yanomamo, an Amazonian tribe, mixed the ashes of their dead into plantain soup, which they drank from gourd bowls. That way, in Dorman's words, they "received into their bodies the spirits of their deceased friends."

The most heart-wrenching cannibal accounts must surely be those of mothers eating their dead children. Among certain Australian tribes, in which infant mortality was high, the bereaved mother might partake of her departed child in a bid to facilitate its rebirth. If such practices were widespread in prehistoric times, their dim memories could conceivably underlie the legends of child-eating lamias, witches, and ogres, as such archaic practices might have become (understandably) demonized over time.

Perhaps ceremonial endo-cannibalism, misremembered and reembroidered over countless generations, is the vestigial fact underpinning many folk- and fairy tales. Certainly the pagans accused the earliest Christians of eating flesh and drinking blood in a deliberately calculated insult to the Eucharist. Hurling their own charges in return, the Christians accused pagans of blood sacrifices. And because it was under Christianity that the vampire evolved into the refined bloodsucker we know today, his buried links to cannibalism may not be all that far-fetched.

Voltaire, wouldn't you know it, had his own take on cannibalism. "The body of a man, reduced to ashes, scattered in the air, and falling on the surface of the earth, becomes corn or vegetable," the French philosopher and dramatist wrote in his *Dictionnaire philosophique* in 1764. "So Cain ate a part of Adam; Enoch fed on Cain; Irad on Enoch; Mahalaleel on Irad; Methuselah on Mahalaleel; and thus we find that there is not one among us who has not swallowed some portion of our first parent. Hence it has been said, that we have all been cannibals."

CONSIGNED TO THE FLAMES

In 1658, when Sir Thomas Browne published his *Hydriot-aphia,* or *Urn Burial,* he had been reflecting on some ancient funerary urns—containing the ashes of men and women deceased for untold centuries—that had recently emerged from the muddy Norfolk flats that were his English home. "To be knav'd out of our graves," Browne mused, "to have our sculs made drinking-bowls, and our bones turned into Pipes, to delight and sport our Enemies, are Tragicall abominations, escaped in burning burials."

Judging from the remains of "Mungo Lady"—discovered in 1969 at Mungo Lake in Australia, and marking the earliest-known cremation—burning burials have been around for at least 40,000 years. Mungo Lady's skeleton appears to have been deliberately shattered after she had been burned, but *before* she was put to the torch a second time. What apocalyptic deeds she may have committed in life to deserve this treatment after death, we shall never know.

Deliberately putting the fleshly tabernacle to the flame, reducing it to sifting ash and crumbled bits of bone, seems to be a late addition to the panoply of funerary options—possibly because cremation, as we have seen, is trickier than it appears. Because of the high water content in fresh bodies— the intestines and heart being notoriously incombustible, as in the cases of Joan of Arc and Percy Bysshe Shelley— proper cremation demands an intensely hot and enduring flame. Nevertheless, it seems to have been widely adopted in the prehistoric period—part of a confusing flip-flop from

burial to cremation and back that continues to puzzle archaeologists today. Not until the Bronze Age, with its improved
high-temperature fire technology, did the pyre replace the
grave—but even then only for a while. The so-called "Urn-
field culture" dominated the death rituals of heavily forested
central Europe for about half a millennium, from roughly
1300 to 750 B.C.E.

Cremation made short work of many a troublesome
corpse problem, yet it tended to release the soul with a roar,
before it was ready, thus magnifying its maleficence. In the
Balkans and parts of eastern Europe, there persists a deep
tradition, touched on in Chapter 6, that the soul requires 40
days before it is ready to leave its former lodgings and push
on. The arrival of Christianity and its emphasis on the resurrection of the body extinguished pyres all across Europe.

Cremation is a rapid and violent desiccation. Deliberate smoke drying is a statelier one. On the Lower Murray
River, the Aborigines often smoked their dead, by placing
them in a sitting position (but with arms outstretched) on a
bier above an outdoor fire. Once the skin blistered, the body
was removed, its hair was scraped off, and its apertures were
all sewn tight. The smoke-dried corpse was then smeared
with red ochre—a naturally antibacterial iron-oxide pigment derived from tinted clay. Placed above a second fire, this
one contained within a special hut, the dead person would
smoke away while wailers brushed off the flies. After being
removed, wrapped, and carried about with the tribe for several months, the body might at long last be cremated, after

which a kinsman would retrieve the skull and—yes—fashion it into a drinking bowl.

THE BEGINNING OF THE END

And that leaves burial. Using high-tech methods to fix the date of remains found in Israel's Skhul Cave, anthropologists have concluded that modern *Homo sapiens* were being deliberately interred by at least 120,000 years ago. Yet, intentional burial may be far older than that. Nearly 30 skeletons have been recovered from the thousands of hominid bones filling the Sima de los Huesos (Pit of Bones) in Spain's Atapuerca Mountains. They had been lying there for at least 350,000 years, and some—but not all—archaeologists believe they represent a ritual deposit.

Burial was certainly a feature of human societies by the later Stone Age, or Upper Paleolithic (between about 40,000 and 10,000 years ago), given that 150 or so examples from that period have been discovered. The triple inhumation at Dolní Věstonice, in today's Czech Republic, has elicited much comment. Two male bodies were placed flanking a female body in sexually suggestive poses, as if the trio had been killed for some sexual transgression around 26,000 years ago.

Burial became common after the establishment of settled agricultural communities in the Neolithic. At Çatal Hüyük in Turkey, dead ancestors were sometimes deliberately incorporated into living households—for example, some were buried beneath sleeping platforms. At British hill forts, slain warriors were interred behind the battlements, thus inviting their supernaturally empowered spirits to help protect the ramparts from assault. There are even cases where the living agreed to be buried alive so that their spirits might guard the community. Spanish conquistadors recorded an episode in which an Inca girl volunteered to be interred on a remote Andean peak as an offering to the sun god, so that she would be revered forever after as a goddess of healing and abundance. And some priest-kings of the Dinka in southern Sudan chose to be inhumed while still alive, convinced that their spirits would eternally hover above their villages.

Live burial also has a rich if macabre history as an enforced punishment. In ancient Rome, for example, four (and later six) virgins were charged with tending the sacred fire kept burning on the altar of Vesta, goddess of the hearth. If any one of them was discovered to have broken her vow of chastity, she was led down a ladder to a small underground cell, supplied with a little food and water, and covered up with earth. A citizen passing by would thus be reminded that *here* is where it happened, that beneath *this spot* still lie the scandalous bones. It all points up a central fact about burial: Graves are specially charged places, and as such can readily come to be haunted.

Even in today's secular world, few would care to spend an entire night in a cemetery. The ancient tombs of forgotten peoples can be even spookier. In parts of North America, each new spring plowing once turned up bones from old Indian mounds. These are deposits of the dead that tribes such as the Hurons and the Iroquois gathered annually from scaffolds, trees, houses, temples, and rock shelters for burial in an ancestral ossuary. Scattered across western Europe and the British Isles, meanwhile, large communal graves—among them bank barrows, long barrows, round barrows, passage graves, and megalithic tombs—were serving as bone repositories long before the time of Christ. Subsequent generations viewed such places as haunted. A century ago, historian John Arnott MacCulloch, having studied Norse sagas, claimed that in "ancient Scandinavia the idea that the dead were alive in their barrows gave rise to the belief that they might become unhallowed monsters of the vampire kind.... Parallels occur in Saxon England and among the early Teutons and Celts."

In agricultural societies, in which the underworld was seen as both the abode of death and the seat of fertility, the buried body, like the buried seed, gave rise to new life. In Egypt, the billowing grain flanking the Nile rose annually from the buried god Osiris. In Scottish balladry, Sweet William becomes a green-red rose and Barbara Allen a briar. And in Slavic folklore, claimed Sir James Frazer, a "tree that grows on a grave is regarded by the South Slavonian peasant as a sort of fetish. Whoever breaks a twig from it hurts the soul of the dead, but gains thereby a magic wand, since the soul embodied in the twig will be at his service."

Yet, the dark side of burial may have been uppermost in the minds of its earliest practitioners. Archaeologist Timothy Taylor suspects that burial might originally have been conceived as a form of punishment—a kind of ostracism for the community's scapegoats. Those bodies being laid in the backs of caves (or sunk deep in lakes, or interred in earth whose chemical properties deterred decomposition) could never be physically reincorporated into the community; instead, they were exiled to its cold, dark margins.

Over the past few centuries, for example, hundreds of remarkably well-preserved bodies have been recovered from the bogs of Denmark's Jutland Peninsula (the same general area where the Gundestrup Cauldron was found). Mostly dating from 100 B.C.E. to about 400 C.E., these finds include many—Tollund Man, Grauballe Man, Windeby Girl, Yde Girl—who have won a peaty immortality because the stubble on their chins or the plaits in their hair look nowhere near the several thousand years old that scientists have determined them to be. The bodies were buried in these bogs for a reason. And because their Iron Age communities overwhelmingly cremated their dead, that reason must have something to do with sacrifice or punishment.

Forensic anthropologists have figured out that many of those buried here were victims: They had been hanged, garroted, or otherwise strangled. In addition, many had been beaten and broken—perhaps after death, perhaps before. It is therefore likely that they had violated some taboo. Taylor believes they were buried in bogs in order to "vex the ghost and prevent the progress of the soul." Pinned down by preservative peat, their bodies could not decay—and release their souls in the process.

It's easy to see how a superstitious community might come to believe that its scapegoats, its sacrificed outcasts, the sick, lame, or deformed lying out there in those lonely graves might resent their fate and—especially if their corpses weren't decomposing—might return one night to seek revenge.

LIFEBLOOD

Dead bodies may have been charged with supernatural power, but so were living ones—if it resided in their blood.

Those stately columns and orders—Doric, Ionic, Corinthian—that grace our courts, capitols, and schools are rooted in the traditions of Greek temple architecture. But that means they are also steeped in blood: The pillars evolved from the posts to which sacrifices were once tied, creating scenes that second-century Christian theologian Clement of Alexandria called "disgusting murders and burials." In a Greek temple, the holiest of altars was also the most sanguinary, distinguishing the structures as places where, in the words of Nietzsche, the "beauty tempered the dread, but this dread was the prerequisite everywhere."

Sacrifice enshrined the most ancient of bargains. The gods might hurl their thunderbolts, but men propitiated (and even manipulated) them with offerings of life and its vehicle, blood. Pagans did not need to read in Deuteronomy that "the blood is the life" to realize the essential truth of that statement. Blood—lose enough of it and you die. That was as obvious to the primitive as it is to the

21st-century physician. Blood, served by the heart, must be the seat of vitality.

Roman gladiators gulped the blood of fallen opponents, thereby doubling their strength. Ancient Europeans poured blood into graves to slake the thirst of the dead. In the *Odyssey*, Odysseus placates those in Hades by slitting the throats of sheep and letting the blood soak into the earth. The blood of martyrs, of patriots, of innocents and kings— all had magical healing powers. In some places, a single drop of blood is believed to possess power enough to reanimate old bones. The sacred smolders in bone, too—but not like it does in blood.

The fierce Botocudos of Brazil were said to open wounds in their victims and drink their blood before killing them. The Tongaranka of New South Wales would not bury a body without arranging for a male relative to stand over the grave and submit to a beating with the sharp edge of a boomerang; his blood then flowed over the corpse. Zapotec priests in Mexico sacrificed their blood by cutting themselves with stingray spines or blades of obsidian; they believed that blood, like wind or lightning, had *peè*—a life force that manifests itself in flowing movement.

Blood consecrated in ritual sacrifice—whether that of a human or an animal—was deemed to be doubly charged with the sacred. By consecrating the bread and wine, the Catholic priest transubstantiates it to the body and blood of Christ. But in earlier centuries, the consumption of consecrated blood, like lightning strikes in the Caucasus, led to prophecy. "In the temple of Apollo Diradiotes at Argos," Sir James Frazer wrote in *The Golden Bough*, "a lamb was sacrificed by night once a month; a woman . . . tasted the blood of the lamb, and thus being inspired by the god she prophesied or divined. At Aegira in Achaia the priestess of the earth drank the fresh blood of a bull before she descended into the cave to prophesy." And among the Achomawi Indians of California, the shamans would drink the blood of the sick; not only did it contain the seeds of the malady, but the shaman's attendant spirits were thirsty and he needed their help.

Before there were priests, there were shamans—the name, derived from a Siberian Tungusic word, now generally applies to folk healers and religious specialists in tribal cultures worldwide. Whether man or woman, the shaman is a prophet, a seer, and a metaphysical traveler, able to speak the language of animals, turn into a bird, become invisible, enter other people's dreams, and—able to manipulate the cyclical process of death and rebirth—visit the land of the dead.

The English astronomer and mathematician Thomas Harriot, in the 1580s, might almost have been describing just such an eerie visit when he related what he had been told by a Native American residing near Roanoke Island in eastern North Carolina:

> [I]t was told me for strange news that one being dead, buried, and taken up again . . . showed that although his body had laid dead in the grave, yet his soul was alive, and had travelled far in the long, broad way, on

both sides whereof grew most delicate and pleasant trees, bearing more rare and excellent fruits than ever he had seen before. He at length came to most fair houses, near which he met his father that had been dead before, who gave him great charge to go back again and show his friends what good they were to do to enjoy the pleasures of that place.

If not a journey and return, it might be a symbolic death and resurrection: "Among the Eskimos," Rushton Dorman wrote, "if a man wished to become of the highest order of priests, it was requisite that he should be drowned and eaten by sea-monsters; then, when his bones were washed ashore, his spirit, which had spent all this time gathering information about the secrets of the invisible world, would return to them, and he would rejoin his tribe."

Such journeys and rejuvenations empowered the shaman to battle demons, witches, and vampires on an equal footing. For in his concomitant role of medicine man or witch doctor, the shaman was also charged with protecting the community from death and disease.

One field of battle was the human body—dead, alive, or somewhere in between. The shaman would exorcise whatever unclean spirits were parasitically consuming the flesh and blood of a person from within. He would also contest the possession of fresh corpses. Among the Karens of Burma, an enemy shaman might steal the soul of a sleeper—much as the African shaman does to obtain a zombie—and then slip it into a corpse. The dead body returns to life, while the living one perishes without awakening.

In the Torres Strait between Australia and New Guinea, a wizard of the Banks Islands might project his soul into a fresh cadaver and then consume whatever traces of life he finds lingering there. Batak witch doctors in the highlands of Sumatra lock horns with evil spirits for possession of a corpse. Among their principal weapons in the struggle: garlic.

In the Balkans, there were once several classes of shamanic figures—if, that is, the dead could be enlisted in that role. The *kresnik* was a reanimated corpse who rose from the grave not to prey on the living, but to help fight evil forces. His clashes with the Serbian vukodlak, for example, might reflect a buried memory of ancient battles between enemy shamans. "Quite similar beliefs and practices," writes Slavic scholar Bruce McClelland of the University of Virginia, "surround a broadly dispersed group of folkloric figures in southern and central parts of Europe who all functioned on the positive side of the village social ledger yet nevertheless were themselves associated, in the Christianizing mind, with their very enemies—witches, sorcerers, vampires."

Such shamans or seers of the Slavic world might have played an important if now buried role in the evolution of the vampire legend. Because the shaman could project his soul on visits to the underworld, revive the dead, enter other people's dreams, steal their souls, raise storms, promote fertility, rout famine and disease, and slay monsters, he was a type of St. George, the protector of so many rural communities. But after Christianity deprived this village defender of his arsenal and cast him in the role of witch or wizard, his adversaries—the bringers of pestilence, plague, and death—were left holding the field, so to speak, free to stalk the European imagination. This guardian figure, though, has occasionally been resurrected in such figures as Abraham van Helsing of Stoker's *Dracula*—to say nothing of that stalwart defender of Sunnydale, California, Buffy the Vampire Slayer.

Forever Undead

By 1913, even Sigmund Freud was speculating about why there had once been such a widespread fear of the dead. In *Totem and Taboo,* the Austrian founder of psychoanalysis took up the ideas of a German classicist named Rudolf Kleinpaul, who maintained that primitive people believed the dead—even deceased loved ones—sought to drag the living to the grave. Perhaps this is why the emblem of death has always been a skeleton; it symbolizes the departed's double status as both slain and slayer. Over time, that conception narrowed until the hostile dead were restricted to souls entitled to feel resentment: murder victims, young brides, and others cut off in their prime or living unfulfilled lives.

"But originally," Freud reported Kleinpaul as stating, "all of the dead were vampires, all of them had a grudge against the living and sought to injure them and rob them of their lives. It was from corpses that the concept of evil spirits first arose."

If so, that concept would have traveled a very long way before leaving its first tracks in the historical record.

Humankind's transition from hunting and gathering to agriculture some 8,000 years ago gave rise to settlements, and with settlements came epidemics. As Edward Jenner, the "father of immunology," wrote in 1798, "The deviation of man from the state in which he was originally placed by nature seems to have proved to him a prolific source of diseases." Even the earliest sedentary communities were more infested with intestinal worms and parasites than were nomadic bands. The arrival of an unknown microbe could easily destabilize whatever tenuous equilibrium had been established between a community and its parasites.

In a world where supernatural agency ruled everything, where the dead played a pivotal role, such invisible parasitism demanded a scapegoat—and what better figure could early cultures imagine than a walking corpse, death literally stalking the land? From an epidemiological point of view, then, the vampire—so long twinned with epidemic disease—is a pathology of civilization: Both require settled communities, where humans dwell cheek by jowl and a cemetery is always conveniently nearby.

Yet, an incommensurably long time had passed before agriculture arose. Whenever and wherever symbolic meaning evolved in our life as a species, monsters hatched alongside it. Whether the sense of an all-encompassing supernatural is a hominid inheritance or was born with *Homo sapiens*, it was operative by the time of the "creative explosion"

30,000 years ago, when the figures of bison and aurochs were being painted on cave walls in Spain and France. After all, "[t]here were shamans before there were gods," as American anthropologist Weston La Barre declared in 1970. These shamans were the "masters of animals" during the long eons of the Paleolithic hunt, and quite likely, they were the first to consecrate beasts with the energy of *tabu*. Animals would therefore have readily provided the forms and figures of our earliest monsters. Dread of the ominous night-flying owl, for example, apparently helped engender the ancient Greek *Strix*, a mythic death-bird that became, in turn, a nocturnal devouring monster to the Romans—and, along the way, likely contributed to the evolving vampire legend, too.

Demons long associated with such common physiological episodes as night terrors or sleep paralysis probably have an equally ancient lineage. Occurring just on the verge of slumber, night terrors manifest themselves as a suffocating pressure on the chest—with the result that the sleeper erupts in panicked wakefulness. In Germanic folklore, they have long been attributed to the Old Hag who sits on sleepers' chests. In other places, the perpetrator is the original "night mare" (from *mer-*, a reconstructed Indo-European root meaning "to harm") or the female succubus and the male incubus—demons said to have sexual intercourse with sleepers. Such fiends no doubt contributed their share to what became the vampire as well.

We have seen how the roots of the Slavic vampire—the most important and influential member of his species—might lie in obscure ancestor worship, quite likely involving fear and propitiation of the dead. We have also glimpsed, in the wandering figure of the alastor, the possible precursor of the Greek vrykolakas. But far older conceptions might lie beneath even these archaic notions, obscured by layers too deep for us to discern.

Nevertheless, if there is such a thing as an archetype of the vampire, it may resemble the Larvae of ancient Rome. These terrifying specters of the hungry dead haunted and injured their living relations—and appeared in the form of horribly decaying corpses. (*Larva* means "mask," which is why Linnaeus adopted it in 1691, to describe the juvenile stage of insects that "mask" the adult form, as the caterpillar does the butterfly.) The same figure surfaces half a world away, in Australia's Arnhem Land, where the dead of the Gunwinggu people are said to undertake a long journey to reach their tribal waterhole, or Dreaming Center. Most of them eventually arrive, but the *mam* are malevolent spirits that have strayed off the path. Dangerously unpredictable because their brains have rotted away, they too appear as skeletal corpses, hung with strips of decaying flesh and announced by a putrid stench.

In Sulawesi, one of the large islands of Indonesia, the dead of the Toradja people are greatly feared. "They persistently return from the underworld in all manner of fearful guises," reported anthropologists Peter Metcalf and Richard Huntington, "and their presence can be detected by smells of decomposition or low grumbling sounds. Their touch burns the skin, their breath causes dizziness, and they frequently frighten people at night."

The Larvae, the mam, and the phantoms of the Tor-adja—these are but three examples of what seems to be a very ancient conception of the walking dead. Quite likely we have wended our way about as far beneath the trampled clay as we are ever likely to get. Yeats's vampires, with their wet mouths and bloody shrouds, are securely in their coffins. Yet the fig-ure that haunted the imagination of poet Charles Baudelaire (1821–1867) might still be out and about. Baudelaire's dis-quieting "Metamorphosis of the Vampire" aptly recapitulates our journey in this book, beginning with the night world's demon lover, "expert in voluptuous charms," and ending with dawn's revelation that she is, after all, but a corpse, a "slimy rotten wineskin, full of pus." As Kleinpaul and Freud sus-pected—and as the evidence from archaeology, folklore, and forensics strongly suggests—the corpse is the larva, spawned in the grave and nourished on bodily corruption, from which the figure of the vampire most likely hatched, before meta-morphosing over the centuries into that caped and fanged figure found waiting expectantly on your doorstep.

Yet, something more fearful still may lurk behind, or within, the decaying corpse. The most abiding emblem of that corruption is not the skeleton but the worm—that squirming, wriggling, vermiform voluptuary that in reality is the maggot but in symbol is the seed of all-devouring death.

English poet William Blake understood this dynamic all too well when he wrote "The Sick Rose" in 1798. Vampires may have come out of the coffin, but in Blake's lament, disease remains as insidious as ever:

> *O Rose, thou art sick!*
> *The invisible worm*
> *That flies in the night,*
> *In the howling storm,*
>
> *Has found out thy bed*
> *Of crimson joy:*
> *And his dark secret love*
> *Does thy life destroy.*

ACKNOWLEDGMENTS

YOU WOULD NOT have this book in which to sink your teeth were it not for the efforts of those individuals who pulled together and produced it under very challenging circumstances. Its attractive design is due to the talents of Cameron Zotter and the magic wand of Melissa Farris. If it reads well it is thanks to the exacting labors of copy editor Heather McElwain—not much escapes her eye—and the ability (as well as acuity) of text editor Allan Fallow to plane rough lumber to a smooth luster. To Bridget English and especially to managing editor Jennifer Thornton, I apologize for wheezing into the station so far behind schedule. By sleight of hand they somehow kept things moving.

Nor could this book have been written without the input of the staff and collections of the National Geographic Society Library. Alyson Foster handled all those tiresome requests for books and articles while covering my occasional derelictions of duty. Suz Eaton, who not only has a complete set of Dark Shadows novels but also has read every subsequent vampire tale ever penned, provided me with newspaper clippings. Maggie Turqman always had a cup of coffee or glass of wine to offer. Alison Ince's thoughtful suggestions on books to read and places to go were and are always welcome. Thanks especially to Cathy Hunter for occasionally lifting the lid to see how I was faring, and to Renee Braden, who dragged me out from time to time for a little fresh moonlight.

A study of vampires is a fascinating but also a grim business. I am grateful to Jim and Elise Blair for providing such a comfortable haven for me to cogitate on such dreary matters as death and burial. The way, of course, had been dug for me by generations of vampire scholars, and I did but follow their burrowings into the dark. To some who have emerged hale and hearty I owe a special obligation: Dr. Mark Yoffe introduced me to Afanasiev and opened a curtain on the hinterlands of Slavic mythology; Paul Sledzik took time during his vacation to chat about his pioneering work on JB-55; and Matteo Borrini not only reviewed Chapter 5—all remaining errors being mine—he also stands at the beginning of the beginning, for it was his work that inspired our efforts.

Finally, my thanks to Lisa Thomas, longtime editor and friend: I met with things dying; you with things newborn. And on that note this book should end.

Notes

Full bibliographic citations may be found in the Selected Bibliography. Readers, of course, will already be aware that many print resources are now available on the Web.

Chapter One: Twilight Zone

7   See Thomas, *The Lives of a Cell*, 77.

8   See Ruth La Ferla, "A Trend With Teeth," *New York Times*, July 2, 2009; Bell, *Food for the Dead*, 295; and Stephen Dixon, "Why Dracula Never Loses His Bite," *Irish Times*, March 28, 2009.

10   See Clute and Nicholls, *The Encyclopedia of Science Fiction*, 1186. The Yarbro quotes are from *Hotel Transylvania*, 278.

14   On *nosophorus* as "plague carrier," see for instance Mamunes, *"So Has a Daisy Vanished": Emily Dickinson and Tuberculosis*, 131.

15   For rabies, see Juan Gomez-Alonso, "Rabies: A Possible Explanation for the Vampire Legend."

16   For porphyria, see "Rare Disease Proposed as Cause for 'Vampires,'" *New York Times*, May 31, 1985.

17   For pellagra, see Hampl and Hampl, "Pellagra and the Origin of a Myth," 636–38.

19   Summers, *The Vampire: His Kith and Kin*, vii. For Canon Paul Fenneau, see D'Arch Smith, *The Books of the Beast*, 84.

20   For the black mass and "strange bat-like figure," see D'Arch Smith, *The Books of the Beast*, 40–42.

21   For Father Brocard's remembrance, see Summers, *The Vampire in Europe*, xvi.

22   Ibid., xvii–xviii, for Summers's quotes.

23   Though information, or at least opinion, on the Highgate Vampire is abundant on the Web, I have generally relied on Matthew Beresford's account in *From Demons to Dracula*, 175–92. See also Melton, *The Vampire Book*, 333–36. Don't miss the hilarious few paragraphs that Eric Nuzum devotes to it in *The Dead Travel Fast*, 122–27.

26   For the vampire "gorged and stinking," see Manchester, *The Highgate Vampire*, 86.

28   For more on Agron, see George Spiegler, "The Capeman Murders" (http://www.homicides quad.com/images/capeman_murders.htm). For more on Ferrell and Menzies, see the profiles by Katherine Ramsland at http://www.trutv.com/library/crime/serial_killers/weird/vam pires/8.html and http://www.trutv.com/library/crime/serial_killers/weird/vampires/13.html.

29   For Krafft-Ebing, see *Psychopathia Sexualis*, 113, 129.

30–31   For more on Haarmann, Haigh, and Kürten, see Melton, *The Vampire Book*, 317–319 and 400–401; there are also many Web resources. For Kürten's quote, see http://www.trutv.com/library/crime/serial_killers/history/kurten/trial_5.html.

32   For more on Kuno Hoffman, see Perkowski's *Vampire Lore*, 63–64. For more on Chase, see Katherine Ramsland, "The Making of a Vampire" (http://www.trutv.com/library/crime/serial_killers/weird/chase/index_1.html). For the information on Riva, see Jennifer Mann, "Marshfield's 'Vampire Killer' Up for Parole."

33   Concise overviews of Báthory are legion; see, for example, Melton, *The Vampire Book*, 34–39. For arguments that political motives *may* have played a role in her trial, see McClelland,

VAMPIRE FORENSICS

Slayers and Their Vampires, 150–51. For other treatments, see Valentine Penrose's *The Bloody Countess* and novelist Marguerite Yourcenar's *That Mighty Sculptor, Time*, 100–101.

34 For Jaffé and DiCataldo's quote, see their essay, "Clinical Vampirism: Blending Myth and Reality," in Dundes, *The Vampire: A Casebook*, 143.

CHAPTER TWO: "THE VERY BEST STORY OF DIABLERIE"

37 On Stoker's note to Gladstone, see Miller, *Bram Stoker's Dracula*, 274.

38 Ibid., 267, for Conan Doyle's note.

39 For the 1831–32 cholera epidemic, see Belford's *Bram Stoker and the Man Who Was Dracula*, 18–19.

41 On the literary background, see Twitchell, *The Living Dead: A Study of the Vampire in Romantic Literature*, 32–38. For Croglin Grange, see Summers, *The Vampire in Europe*, 111–15.

42 Emily Gerard's article is excerpted in the Norton Critical Edition of *Dracula*, 332–33.

43 All quotes are from Klinger, *The New Annotated Dracula*.

51 For Hamilton Deane, see David J. Skal, "'His Hour Upon the Stage': Theatrical Adaptations of Dracula," in Miller, *Bram Stoker's Dracula*, 300–308.

52 For a concise look at Florence Stoker versus *Nosferatu*, see Miller, *Bram Stoker's Dracula*, 299.

53 Ibid., 304–05, for the reference to the cape.

54 For Béla Lugosi, see Miller, *Bram Stoker's Dracula*, 319–20, and Klinger, *The New Annotated Dracula*, 556–59. For his effectiveness in the role, see Douglas, *Horrors!*, 66–67. For a humorous look at Lugosi's funereal cape, see Nuzum, *The Dead Travel Fast*, 204.

54 Zoologist David E. Brown has collected fascinating facts and anecdotes in Brown's *Vampiro: The Vampire Bat in Fact and Fantasy*. See also Ditmars and Greenhall, "The Vampire Bat," 295–310 in Perkowski's *Vampire Lore*.

57 On "Vlad the Impaler," the standard biography is still Florescu and McNally, *Dracula, Prince of Many Faces*. A concise sketch is Elizabeth Miller's essay, on pages 209–17 of her sourcebook, *Bram Stoker's Dracula*. Another paper of note is Grigore Nandris, "The Historical Dracula: The Theme of His Legend."

58 For a Romanian perspective during the Ceauşescu dictatorship, see Nicolae Stoicescu, *Vlad Tepes: Prince of Walachia*.

60 For stories of Vlad's atrocities, see the comprehensive list neatly tabulated in McNally and Florescu, *In Search of Dracula*, 193–219.

61 On the "art" of impalement, see the *Tyndale Bible Dictionary*, 269. Although hardly objective, "Turkish Culture: The Art of Impalement" (http://www.e-grammes.gr/2004/11/souvlisma_en.htm) is worth a glance. See also http://www.angelfire.com/darkside/forgottendreams/Impalement.html.

62 On Dracula's campaign, see Florescu and McNally, *Dracula: Prince of Many Faces*, 125–52.

63 For the Snagov tomb, see Florescu and McNally, *Dracula: Prince of Many Faces*, 179–83.

CHAPTER THREE: GATHERINGS FROM GRAVEYARDS

67 For more on the summer of 1816 at the Villa Diodati, see Hoobler and Hoobler, *The Monsters: Mary Shelley and the Curse of Frankenstein*, 127–50. Details of the conversations—including vampires, galvanism, and of course, the famous ghost story contest—are related there.

278

69 On the Byron-Polidori split, see Hoobler and Hoobler, *The Monsters*, 219–30. On Byron's description and character, see Trelawny, *Recollections of the Last Days of Shelley and Byron*, 33–34, 53, 225.

70 For Charlotte Brontë and the "corsair," see Heather Glen, *Charlotte Bronte: The Imagination in History*, 109. Quotations from Polidori's "The Vampyre" came from Morrison and Baldick, eds., *The Vampyre and Other Tales of the Macabre*.

71 On Byron being credited with "The Vampyre," see Hoobler and Hoobler, *The Monsters*, 227. For more on Bérard and Nodier, see Melton, *The Vampire Book*, 223. On the success of "The Vampyre," especially in Paris, see Senf, *The Vampire in Nineteenth Century English Literature*, 40–42; Twitchell, *The Living Dead: A Study of the Vampire in Romantic Literature*, 104–16; and an unsigned article, "On Vampirism," 140–49.

72 For more on Planché, see Senf, *The Vampire in Nineteenth Century English Literature*, 42. On Polidori's suicide, see Hoobler and Hoobler, *The Monsters*, 233–35.

73 On Shelley's pyre, see Trelawny, *Recollections*, 135–37. On the desiccated heart, see Sunstein, *Mary Shelley: Romance and Reality*, 384-385.

74 On the "restless graveyard," see Newcomb, *The Imagined World of Charles Dickens*, 166–69.

75 For premature burial in general, see Bondeson's fascinating *Buried Alive: The Terrifying History of Our Most Primal Fear*. On "Bateson's Belfry," see http://www.members.tripod.com/DespiteThis/death/prebur.htm.

76 On Chopin's heart, see "Home Is Where the Heart'll Stay" (http://www.news24.com/Content/SciTech/News/1132/d9a2b6c0e9a241b392fe947c69380a7a/26-07-2008-10-51/Home_is_where_the_heartll_stay). The *Blackwoods* article is mentioned in Senf, *The Vampire in Nineteenth Century English Literature*, 23.

77 For "burking" in general, see Thomas Frost, "Burkers and Body-Snatchers" in Andrews's *The Doctor in History*, 167–80. On grave robbing methods, see "The Resurrectionists" in Chambers's *Book of Days*, 251–52.

78 On William Burke's remains, see http://www.webcitation.org/5bUW8rrX2. For the "snatching" of John Harrison and the quote from the Zanesville paper, see Schultz, *Body Snatching*, 85–90.

79 The ghoulish Wendish superstition is quoted in Bell's *Food for the Dead*, 213.

80 The authorship of *Varney the Vampyre* was once ascribed to Thomas Peckett Prest but is now largely credited to James Malcolm Rymer. Twitchell's quote is found in Twitchell, *The Living Dead*, 123. Anyone not wishing to wade into the daunting original should not miss Twitchell's hilarious plot synopsis (207–14).

83 On the "trashy" quote, see Skal, *Vampires: Encounters with the Undead*, 48.

84 For insightful readings of *Wuthering Heights* and the vampire, see Senf, *The Vampire in Nineteenth Century English Literature*, 75–93, and Twitchell, *The Living Dead*, 116–22.

85 For the wider significance of Dickens's graveyard scenes, see Trevor Blount's "The Graveyard Satire of *Bleak House* in the context of 1850," 370–78. For the "two million" London dead, see Dr. George Walker, *Gatherings from Grave Yards*, 196.

86 The Spa Fields gravedigger's testimony originally appeared in March 5, 1845 edition of *The Times;* it is reprinted in the Norton edition of *Bleak House*, 906–09. The "body bugs" are described in Walker, *Gatherings from Grave Yards*, 155.

87   For "mephitic vapors" and their deleterious impact, see Walker, *Gatherings from Grave Yards*, 114–44. On the smallpox killing Lady Dedlock, see John Sutherland's *Who Betrays Elizabeth Bennet? Further Puzzles in Classic Fiction*, 115–27.

88   See McNeill, *Plagues and Peoples*, 231. James Hogg's "Some Terrible Letters from Scotland" is found in *The Vampyre and Other Tales of the Macabre*, edited by Morrison and Baldick, 99–112.

89   See "John Snow and the Broad Street Pump," Ockham's Razor, September 5, 2004 (http://www.abc.net.au/rn/science/ockham/stories/s1190540.htm). For the "witch-ridden" quote, see Bell, *Food for the Dead*, 246.

90   The 1799 description is from Dubos and Dubos, *The White Plague: Tuberculosis, Man and Society*, 118.

91   For the information on Lucy Westenra fitting a tuberculosis diagnosis as much as an anemia one, I am indebted to Paul Sledzik, who first pointed that out in his paper, "Vampires, the Dead, and Tuberculosis: Folk Interpretations." He also pointed out the *Nicholas Nickleby* quote.

92   For Sheridan Le Fanu, see Alfred Perceval Graves, "A Memoir of Joseph Sheridan Le Fanu" (http://ebooks.adelaide.edu.au/l/lefanu/graves/), and M. R. James, "The Novels and Stories of J. Sheridan Le Fanu," *Ghosts & Scholars Newsletter* 7 (http://www.users.globalnet.co.uk/~pardos/ArchiveLeFanu.html).

95   On the original Styrian locale, see Miller, *Bram Stoker's Dracula*, 171–73.

96   The anonymous "Travels of Three English Gentlemen," originally written in 1734, was not published until 1810, when it appeared in the *Harleian Miscellany*, 218–319. Lord Byron's quote can be found in Hoobler and Hoobler, *The Monsters*, 228.

CHAPTER FOUR: THE VAMPIRE EPIDEMICS

99   For the Browne quote, see Jill Steward, "Central Europe," *Literature of Travel and Exploration: An Encyclopedia*, 220–24. For the distribution of the "Turkey Oak" (*Quercus cerris*) in southeastern Europe, see Polunin and Walters, *A Guide to the Vegetation of Britain and Europe*, 143–55.

100 For the "orientalizing" of eastern Europe, and for Mozart, see Steward, "Central Europe."

101 For landscapes, agriculture, and the shifting zone of desolation, see Thomas Kabdebo, "Pre-World War II Eastern Europe," in *Literature of Travel and Exploration*, 368–373, and Kann and David, *The Peoples of the Eastern Hapsburg Lands 1526-1918*, 10, 78, and 97. For the Durham quote, see Omer Hadziselimovic, "Pre-1914 Balkans," 67–71. For the establishment of *lazzaretti*, see Steward, "Central Europe."

102 For Balkan travel, see Hadziselimovic, "Pre-1914 Balkans." For the colorful details—the slivovitz, the mosques, the churches, the garb—see De Windt, *Through Savage Europe*, 167–90. On the *zapis* tree, carved with a cross outside Balkan churches, see Traian Stoianovich, *Balkan Worlds: The First and Last Europe*, 38.

103 For the Balkan forests and the lyrical paean to them, see Stoianovich, *Balkan Worlds*, 24–29. For the Belgrade details and for the warning not to be caught out at night, see De Windt, *Through Savage Europe*, 114–20, 192.

104 For the impenetrable Serbian forests, see Stoianovich, *Balkan Worlds*, 26. For Mary Wortley Montague's experiences in them, see her letter of April 1, 1717, to the Princess of Wales in *The Letters of M.W. Montague 1716-18*. For the Janissaries' treatment of villagers, see the same letter, and Wolff, *Inventing Eastern Europe*, 71–72.

105   On the hajduks, see Stu Burns, "'And With All That, Who Believes in Vampires?': Undead Legends and Enlightenment Culture." For events in Medvegia, I have followed the version of Lieutenant Flückinger's report, *Visum et Repertum,* found in Barber, *Vampires, Burial, and Death,* 16–18.

106   For more on Peter Plogojowitz, see Barber, Ibid., 3–9, and Beresford, *From Demons to Dracula,* 110.

111   For the impact of *Visum et Repertum,* and for the flood of dissertations it inspired, see Senf, *The Vampire in Nineteenth Century English Literature,* 23; and Massimo Introvigne, "Antoine Faivre: Father of Contemporary Vampire Studies," 602.

112   For the debate between the doctor and the lady, and for Walpole and King George II, see Clery and Miles, *Gothic Documents: A Sourcebook 1700-1820,* 24–25. For the word *vampire* entering western European languages, see Katharina M. Wilson, "The History of the Word *Vampire*" in Dundes, *The Vampire: A Casebook,* 3–11. For the *Lettres Juives,* see D'Argens, *The Jewish Spy,* 122–32. For the Grimaldi quote, see Introvigne, 609.

113   I have drawn from the Reverend Henry Christmas's translation of Calmet's *Traite,* published as *The Phantom World* in 1850.

116   For Davanzati, Pope Benedict, and the "fallacious fictions of human fantasy," see Introvigne, 608–09.

117   For Empress Maria Theresa and her physician Gerhard Van Swieten, see McClelland, *Slayers and Their Vampires,* 126–46. For the vampire decrees, see Ankarloo and Clark, *Witchcraft and Magic in Europe: The Eighteenth and Nineteenth Centuries,* 71–72; and Bostridge, *Witchcraft and Its Transformation,* 220.

118   Voltaire's entry on vampires in the *Dictionnaire Philosophique* can be found in Volume 14 of his *Works,* 143–49.

119   For Rousseau's "Letter," see Kelly and Grace, *The Collected Writings of Jean-Jacques Rousseau,* 68. It is widely quoted elsewhere, and much of the letter is in Morley, *Rousseau,* 284–87.

120   On the Pantheon tombs, see "Voltaire and Rousseau: Their Tombs in the Pantheon Opened and Their Bones Exposed," *New York Times,* January 8, 1898 (http://query.nytimes.com/mem/archive/).

122   For the Thoreau quote, see Bell, *Food for the Dead,* 225. For the Walton Cemetery and JB-55, see Sledzik and Bellantoni, "Bioarcheological and Biocultural Evidence for the New England Vampire Folk Belief"; Bellantoni, Sledzik, and Poirier, "Rescue, Research, and Reburial: Walton Family Cemetery, Griswold, Connecticut," in Bellantoni and Poirier, *In Remembrance: Archaeology and Death,* 131–54; and Bell, 167–76.

125   For stories of various New England "vampires," see Bell, especially 7–12, 18–22, 140–43, and 283–89. On the relation of tuberculosis to the vampire belief, I found Paul Sledzik's unpublished "Vampires, the Dead, and Tuberculosis: Folk Interpretations" to be illuminating.

CHAPTER FIVE: CORPI MORTI

131   On the "macabre" in medieval art, see Elina Gertsman, "Visualizing Death: Medieval Plagues and the Macabre" in Mormando and Worcester, *Piety and Plague: From Byzantium to the Baroque,* 64–85. For the spear-wielding angel and winged devil, see Snodgrass, *World Epidemics,* 48. For the Black Death's toll, see McNeill, *Plagues and Peoples,* 168.

132   For the Kaffa story, see Sherman, *Twelve Diseases That Changed Our World,* 79; McNeill, *Plagues and Peoples,* 166; and Snodgrass, *World Epidemics,* 33–34. For plague symptoms and

Paris diet, see Snodgrass, 34; for killing dogs and cats, see Kohn, *Encyclopedia of Plague and Pestilence*, 374.

133   For more on rats and fleas, see McNeill, *Plagues and Peoples*, 172; and Kohn, *Encyclopedia of Plague and Pestilence*, 172 and 374. On the three forms of plague, see Sherman, *Twelve Diseases That Changed Our World*, 76. For events in Pistoia, see Snodgrass, *World Epidemics*, 37.

134   For the plague in Avignon, the Sienese chronicler, the Muslim reaction, the loss of villages, the heroic Scotswoman, and Les Innocents, see Snodgrass, 37–42. On the Vienna grave, see Kohn, *Encyclopedia of Plague and Pestilence*, 375.

135   For Venetian measures and wolves in Ragusa, see Snodgrass, 35. For "corpi morti," see Longworth, *The Rise and Fall of Venice*, 106. For the 1423 lazzaretto, Matteo Borrini references Nelli-Elena Vanzan Marchini, "Il Lazaretto Nuovo fra Venezia e il Mediterraneo." See also Matteo Borrini, "Il Lazzaretto Nuovo, l'Isola dei Morti," 10–11.

136   For Venetian preparations, and for Titian's *St. Mark Triumphant*, see Kohn, *Encyclopedia of Plague and Pestilence*, 374. For the 1576–77 epidemic, see Snodgrass, *World Epidemics*, 67, and Kohn, 34.

137   For doctors' garb, see Sherman, *Twelve Diseases That Changed Our World*, 69. The image of the encircled islands comes from Matteo Borrini. For the Benedetti quote, see Maria Cristina Valsecchi, "Mass Plague Graves Found on Venice 'Quarantine' Island."

138   For the 2006 dig details, I am indebted to conversations with Dr. Borrini, though any errors are mine.

140   For Philip Rohr's *De Masticatione Mortuorum*, see Summers, *The Vampire in Europe*, 178–206.

141   Ibid.

142   For the Rohr quote, see Ibid. On Salem, see Bell, *Food for the Dead*, 257. For the "Pest Jungfrau," see Kohn, *Encyclopedia of Plague and Pestilence*, 375. For Philip V, see Snodgrass, *World Epidemics*, 32–62.

143   For these examples, see Snodgrass, 32–62.

144   For the malign conjunction, see Snodgrass, *World Epidemics*, 32, and Donald G. McNeil, Jr., "Finding a Scapegoat When Epidemics Strike." On ID6, I again thank Dr. Matteo Borrini. See also his paper, "An Exorcism Against a Vampire in Venice: An Anthropological and Forensic Study on a Burial of the XVI Century."

146   For the London Bills of Mortality, see Wills, *Yellow Fever, Black Goddess*, 37–39. The quote is from John Graunt, 1662.

147   On bloodsucking and folklore, see Barber, *Vampires, Burial, and Death*, 100.

148   For Gettysburg, see Stiles, *Four Years Under Marse Robert*, 219–20.

149   For Elwood Trigg's quote, see Barber, *Vampires, Burial, and Death*, 112. On telltale signs, see Barber, 106.

150   On skin slippage, saponification, and rigor mortis, see Barber, 161, 108, 117.

151   On the chromatic stages of decomposition, my thanks to Dr. Borrini.

152   On explosive gas, see Walker, *Gatherings from Grave Yards*, 204. On the "corpse light," see Bell, *Food for the Dead*, 150–52.

153   On "purge fluid," my thanks to Dr. Borrini.

154   On the groaning Paole, see Barber, 161. For the hole in the shroud, my thanks to Dr. Borrini.

155 For Defoe's *A Journal of the Plague Year*, see the Wellcome Library (http://library.wellcome.ac.uk/doc_wtx049939.html).

156 For the epidemic stomach rumbling, see Barber, 128.

157 For plague casualties and Il Redentore, see Snodgrass, *World Epidemics*, 67. See also McNeill, *Plagues and Peoples*, 171. See also Barber, 25, and Tylor, *Primitive Culture*, 192.

158 See Barber, 18, and Borrini, "An Exorcism Against a Vampire in Venice."

CHAPTER SIX: TERRA DAMNATA

159 For More's spiritualist proclivities, including his ventures into haunted vaults, see Rupert Hall, *Henry More and the Scientific Revolution*, 128–45. On "objective ghost stories" in general, see Clery, *The Rise of Supernatural Fiction 1762–1800*, 19–21.

160 For quotations from More's *An Antidote Against Atheism*, see Summers, *The Vampire in Europe*, 133–43.

164 On the *Ars moriendi*, see Duffy, *The Stripping of the Altars*, 313–36, and Ariès, *The Hour of Our Death*, 95–106.

165 For the rabble of demons and infernal dukes, see Paine, *The Hierarchy of Hell*, 59–67. For last rites and "stinking Lazarus," see Duffy, 310 and 313.

167 The "cult of the living in the service of the dead" is attributed to A. Galpern and cited in Duffy, 301. For Eastern Orthodox last rites, see Andrew Louth, "Eastern Orthodox Eschatology" in Walls, *The Oxford Handbook of Eschatology*, 233–47, and Garnett, *Balkan Home-Life*, 119–53.

168 For leaping cats and excommunication, see Lawson, *Modern Greek Folklore and Ancient Greek Religion*, 396–99, 410; and Bunson, *The Vampire Encyclopedia*, 88.

169 For the witch and vampire, see Perkowski, *Vampire Lore*, 195–211. For the papal bull against witchcraft, see Hughes, *Witchcraft*, 178.

170 On werewolves and Peter Stubbe, see Hill and Williams, *The Supernatural*, 185–94.

171 For "disenchantment by decapitation," see Kittredge, *A Study of Gawain and the Green Knight*, 200–17.

172 For King Charles I's tomb, see Halford, *An Account of What Appeared on Opening the Coffin of King Charles the First*, 1–15.

174 For the burial of the damned, see Ariès, *The Hour of Our Death*, 42–45.

175 For Cromwell's head, see Wilkinson, "A Narrative of the Circumstances Concerning the Head of Oliver Cromwell," and Howarth, "The Head of Oliver Cromwell." The head seems to have blown to the ground anywhere from 1672 to the turn of the 18th century; I followed Mould, *Mould's Medical Anecdotes*, 16–17.

176 For Joan of Arc's purported remains, see Butler, "Joan of Arc's Relics Exposed as Forgery."

177 For the mummy trade, see Roach, *Stiff: The Curious Lives of Human Cadavers*, 221–26. For the Dutch apothecary's quote, see Van der Sanden, *Through Nature to Eternity*, 43.

179 The standard English translation of William of Newburgh's *Historia Rerum Anglicarum* still remains Stevenson's of *The Church Historians of England*, from which I have drawn. For William's intellectual context, see Watkins, *History and the Supernatural in Medieval England*, 33–35.

CHAPTER SEVEN: THE WANDERERS

187 For Cernunnos, see "Cernunnos, the God with the Horns of a Stag," in *Mythologies*, ed. Yves Bonnefoy, 268–70, and R. Lowe Thompson, *The History of the Devil: Or the Horned*

God of the West, 63–64. See also "Cernwn" on the site Nemeton: The Sacred Grove (http://www.celtnet.org.uk/gods_c/cernwn.html).

188   On the witch cult as old religion, see Thompson, *The History of the Devil,* and Hughes, *Witchcraft*, 16–18. See also Stephen Hayes, "Christian Responses to Witchcraft and Sorcery" (http://hayesfam.bravehost.com/WITCH1.HTM).

189   For *The Story of How the Pagans Honored the Idols,* see "Slavic Myths, Rites, and Gods" in Bonnefoy's *Mythologies,* 295–302. See also, however, McClelland, *Slayers and their Vampires,* 39–42—origin of the translation I have used—and his further note on page 203.

190   For the Slavs, see Roman Jakobson, "Slavic Mythology," in Leach, *Funk & Wagnalls Standard Dictionary of Folklore, Mythology, and Legend,* 1025–28. For the enigma of the Indo-European heartland, see Mallory, *In Search of the Indo-Europeans,* and Renfrew, *Archaeology and Language,* both of which are devoted to examining it.

191   For Simon Grunau and the Baltic gods, see Puhvel, *Comparative Mythology,* 224–26 and Harris, *The Cult of the Heavenly Twins,* 47–50.

192   On *eretiks* in Russia, see Oinas's "Heretics as Vampires and Demons in Russia."

193   For the etymology of *vampir,* see Katharina M. Wilson, "The History of the Word *Vampire,*" in Dundes, *The Vampire: A Casebook,* 3–11. See also Peter Mario Kreuter, "The Name of the Vampire: Some Reflections on Current Linguistic Theories on the Etymology of the Word Vampir," in Day, *Vampires: Myths and Metaphors of Enduring Evil,* 57–63.

194   For the idea that *vampir* might have originally been applied to pagans and not reanimated corpses, see McClelland, *Slayers and Their Vampires,* 31–48.

195   For the legally dead status of certain outlaws, see Lincoln, "The Living Dead: Of Outlaws and Others." For *warg,* see Alby Stone, "Hellhounds, Werewolves and the Germanic Underworld" (http://www.primitivism.com/hellhounds.htm). For Helmold's quote, see his *Chronicle of the Slavs,* 159.

196   For the Bogomils and quotations, see Perkowski, *Vampire Lore,* 339–44.

197   For the capitulary of Charlemagne, see "On Vampirism," 140–49. For the *Lex Salica,* see Bunson, *The Vampire Encyclopedia,* 231. On Anglo-Saxon cemeteries and the quote from Frazer, see Bell, *Food for the Dead,* 168–70.

199   For Tozer's recollections, see Perkowski, *Vampire Lore,* 354.

200   For the derivation of vrykolakas, see Perkowski, 351–68.

201   For de Tournefort, see the Reverend Christmas's translation in Calmet, *The Phantom World,* 113–19.

203   For much of what follows, see Lawson, *Modern Greek Folklore and Ancient Greek Religion,* 361–484.

204   For the story of Philinnion, see Lawson, 412–15.

205   For the "misery of the unburied dead," see Lawson, 475.

206   For the vegetarian dead, see Lawson, 368.

207   For more on Afanasiev, see "Poetic Views of the Slavs Regarding Nature" in Perkowski, *Vampire Lore,* 195–211.

209   For weeping grass and dream grass, see Yoffe and Krafczik, *Perun, the God of Thunder,* 43–48.

210   For Toporov and Ivanov, see Alex Fantalov, "Mythological Images of the Balts" (http://greek-gods.tripod.com/Baltic.htm) and "Veles" (http://www.statemaster.com/encyclopedia/Veles/).

211 On the protovampire, see "Slavic Myths, Rites, and Gods" in Bonnefoy's *Mythologies,* 295–302.

212 On the Thracian Hero, see Hoddinott, *The Thracians,* 169–75. On St. George as a vegetation god, see Varner, *The Mythic Forest, the Green Man and the Spirit of Nature,* 124–28.

213 On the Gundestrup Cauldron, see Green, *Dictionary of Celtic Myth and Legend,* 100–108, and especially Taylor, "The Gundestrup Cauldron," 84–89.

Chapter Eight: Tales of Worldwide Devilry

217 For dawn on the Ganges, see Scidmore, *Winter India,* 152.

218 For Hindu mortuary customs, see "Deathbed Rites" and "Antyeshti Samskara" in Lochtefeld, *The Illustrated Encyclopedia of Hinduism,* 44 and 180. See also "Popular Hinduism" in Bonnefoy, *Mythologies,* 842–49.

220 For bhutas, pretas, vetalas, pisachas, and the rest of the Hindu bloodsuckers, see relevant entries in Lochtefeld's *Illustrated Encyclopedia of Hinduism,* Dallapiccola's *Dictionary of Hindu Lore and Legend,* Stutley and Stutley's *Harper's Dictionary of Hinduism,* and Bunson's *The Vampire Encyclopedia.*

222 For *rakshasas* as "confounders of the sacrifice," see Stutley and Stutley, *Harper's Dictionary of Hinduism,* 245.

224 For gypsies and vampires, see Melton, *The Vampire Book,* 310–15; Fraser, *The Gypsies,* 243–45; and Clébert, *The Gypsies,* 150–51; Perkowski, *Vampire Lore,* 230–59; and McDowell, *Gypsies: Wanderers of the World.*

227 For Assyrian and Babylonian demons, and the early vampire representations and quotes, see Summers, *The Vampire: His Kith and Kin,* 217–28.

228 For the Hooke quote, see Stutley and Stutley, *Harper's Dictionary of Hinduism,* 233. For Lilith, see "Lilith" in Leach, *Funk & Wagnalls Standard Dictionary of Folklore, Mythology, and Legend,* 622–23. For the Queen of Sheba's hairy legs, see Graves and Patai, *Hebrew Myths,* 68.

229 For the Mytilene vampire, see Hector Williams, "The Vampire of Lesbos," 22. For the questioning Imam, see Garnett, *Balkan Home-Life,* 281. For Egyptian mortuary practices, see "Death in Egyptian Religion," in Bonnefoy, *Mythologies,* 111–15.

230 For the Budge quote, see Varner, *Creatures in the Mist,* 93. For various Malaysian vampires, see Melton, *The Vampire Book,* 441–44; Summers, *The Vampire: His Kith and Kin,* 251–56; and Bunson, *The Vampire Encyclopedia,* 167.

232 For Philippine vampires, see Melton, *The Vampire Book,* 520–22.

233 For the *orang minyak,* or "oily men," see Martin and Walls, *In Malaysia,* 59.

234 For Chinese customs, see "Chinese Demons," in Bonnefoy, *Mythologies,* 1028–31. For the *ch'ing shih,* see Summers, *The Vampire: His Kith and Kin,* 237–49; Melton, *The Vampire Book,* 114–15; and Bunson, *The Vampire Encyclopedia,* 46.

235 For Lords of Death and Time, see Bunson, *The Vampire Encyclopedia,* 177, 188. For a transmission between east and west, see Perkowski, *Vampire Lore,* 348–50. For Alexandra David-Neel, see Hill and Williams, *The Supernatural,* 205. For "The Vampire Cat of Nabeshima," see Freeman-Mitford (Lord Redesdale), *Tales of Old Japan,* 245–52.

236 For Jomon burials and Japanese ghosts, see "The Vital Spirit and the Soul in Japan" and "Japanese Conceptions of the Afterlife," both in Bonnefoy, *Mythologies,* 1041–47.

237 For more on the Bon, see Hearn, *In Ghostly Japan*, 230–33.

238 For the New Caledonia sleepers and the Malekula ceremony, see "Religions and Mythologies of Oceania" in Bonnefoy, *Mythologies*, 1214–15.

239 For the Cook quote and the Polynesians, see Stetson, "The Animistic Vampire in New England," 2. For the Ojibwa, see Bunson, *The Vampire Encyclopedia*, 186. For the Stith Thompson, Stetson, and the Cherokee and Abenaki tales, see Bell, *Food for the Dead*, 237–40.

241 For the Hearn quotes, see Hearn, *Two Years in the French West Indies*, 188, 369. For Southey's quote, see Ellis, *The History of Gothic Fiction*, 212.

242 For the etymology of the word *zombie,* see those given in the *Oxford English Dictionary*, the *Oxford American Dictionary*, the *New Shorter Oxford Dictionary*, *Webster's Ninth Collegiate Dictionary*, and the *American Heritage Dictionary of the English Language*. For Seabrook's cannibalism, see Cummins, *Cannibals*, 267.

243 For Seabrook in Haiti, see Hill and Williams, *The Supernatural*, 204, and for Haitian and Gabonese sorcerers, 203–05.

Chapter Nine: The Larvae

245 See Kevin Tuite, "The Choppa ritual in the traditional religions of the Caucasus" (http://www.mapageweb.umontreal.ca/tuitekj/caucasus/Choppa.htm). See also the articles "The Religions and Myths of the Georgians of the Mountains" and "The Religions and Myths of the Ossets" in Bonnefoy, *Mythologies*, 308–19.

247 For Frazer's quote, see *The Fear of the Dead in Primitive Religion*, 167. See also Baring-Gould, *Curiosities of Olden Times*, 8–14.

248 For the corpse being feared, see Metcalf and Huntingdon, *Celebrations of Death*, 81. For the Amazonian practices, see "Indians of the South American Forest," Bonnefoy, *Mythologies*, 1194–99.

249 See Baring-Gould, 8–14.

250 For Calmet's quote, see *The Phantom World*, 107.

251 For Herodotus, see David Grene, *Herodotus: The History*, 228. For the death of chimpanzees and hominids, see Taylor, *The Buried Soul*, 29–31.

252 For Çatal Hüyük paintings and the harpies, see Barber, *Vampires, Burial, and Death*, 172–74. For the Vaccaei, see Green, *Dying for the Gods*, 46.

253 For the Ives quotation, see Kaul, *Travellers' India: An Anthology*, 87–88. For Sir Jivanji's comments, see Modi, "The Funeral Ceremonies of the Parsees."

254 For "Sky Burial," see Seth Faison, "Tibetans and Vultures Keep Ancient Burial Rite." For the Australian practices and the Goulburn Island quote, see Berndt and Berndt, *The World of the First Australians*, 396–99, 410.

255 For early traces of cannibalism, from Gran Dolina onward, see Taylor, *The Buried Soul*, 77–85; and Green, *Dying for the Gods*, 56–61. Dorman's examples are from *The Origin of Primitive Superstitions*, 150–52.

256 For drinking powdered ash, see Frazer, *The Golden Bough*, 519.

257 For infant cannibalism, see Berndt and Berndt, *The World of the First Australians*, 403.

258 For the Mungo Lake cremation, see "New Age for Mungo Man."

259 For Bronze Age cremations, see Beresford, *From Demons to Dracula*, 33. For Australian smoke-drying, see Berndt and Berndt, *The World of the First Australians*, 392–93.

260   For Paleolithic and Neolithic burials, see Taylor, *The Buried Soul*, especially 1–38 and 223–50.

261   For human sacrifice and burial alive, see Green, *Dying for the Gods*, 111–35.

262   See MacCulloch's article, "Vampire," in Hastings, *Encyclopedia of Religion and Ethics*, Volume 12, 589–91. For the Frazer quote, see Bell, *Food for the Dead*, 222.

263   For "vexing the ghost" and the bog bodies, see Taylor, *The Buried Soul*, 144–69.

264   For Greek sacrifice and the quotes from Clement and Nietzsche, see Hersey, *The Lost Meaning of Classical Architecture*, especially 11–46.

265   For blood rituals, see Bell, *Food for the Dead*, 211–13; Berndt and Berndt, *The World of the First Australians*, 394–95; and Green, *Dying for the Gods*, 79–91.

266   For the Greek rites, see Frazer, *The Golden Bough*, 63. For the Harriot quote and Eskimo story, see Dorman, *The Origin of Primitive Superstitions*, 197–99.

267   For the Karens, see Bunson, *The Vampire Encyclopedia*, 141.

268   On the Banks Island and Batak shamans, see Bunson, *The Vampire Encyclopedia*, 17, 251. For the *kresnik*, see McClelland, *Slayers and Their Vampires*, 120–25. See also Liam Rogers, "Exhuming the Vampire."

269   See Freud, *Totem and Taboo*, 51–63.

270   For the Jenner quote, see Clendening, *Source Book of Medical History*, 294. See also McNeill, *Plagues and Peoples*, especially 4–25.

271   For early shamans, see La Barre, *The Ghost Dance*, 161. For the old hag, nightmare, incubus, and so on, see relevant entries in Leach, *Funk & Wagnalls Standard Dictionary of Folklore, Mythology, and Legend*.

272   On the Larvae, see Fowler, *The Roman Festivals of the Period of the Republic*, 106–11. See also Steuding, Harrington, and Tolman, *Greek and Roman Mythology*, 165–66. On the *mam*, see Berndt and Berndt, *The World of the First Australians*, 415. On the Toradja, see Metcalf and Huntington, *Celebrations of Death*, 100.

Adams, Arthur E., Ian M. Matley, and William O. McCagg. *An Atlas of Russian and East European History*. New York: Frederick A. Praeger, 1966.

Andrews, William, ed. *The Doctor in History, Literature, Folklore, etc.* Hull, England: The Hull Press, 1896.

Ankarloo, Bengt, and Stuart Clark. *Witchcraft and Magic in Europe: The Eighteenth and Nineteenth Centuries*. Philadelphia: University of Pennsylvania Press, 1999.

Ariès, Philippe. *The Hour of Our Death*. New York: Alfred A. Knopf, Inc., 1981.

———. *Western Attitudes Toward Death*. Baltimore: The Johns Hopkins University Press, 1974.

Barber, Paul. *Vampires, Burial, and Death*. New Haven: Yale University Press, 1988.

Baring-Gould, Sabine. *Curiosities of Olden Times*. Edinburgh: John Grant, 1896.

Bartlett, Wayne, and Flavia Idriceanu. *Legends of Blood: The Vampire in History and Myth*. Gloucestershire, England: Sutton Publishing, 2005.

Bass, Bill, Dr., and Jon Jefferson. *Beyond the Body Farm*. New York: HarperCollins, 2007.

Belford, Barbara. *Bram Stoker and the Man Who Was Dracula*. Cambridge, MA: Da Capo Press, 1996.

Bell, Michael E. *Food for the Dead: On the Trail of New England's Vampires*. New York: Carroll and Graf, 2001.

Bellantoni, Nicholas F., and David A. Poirier, eds. *In Remembrance: Archaeology and Death*. New York: Bergin & Garvey, 1997.

Beresford, Matthew. *From Demons to Dracula: The Creation of the Modern Vampire Myth*. London: Reaktion Books, 2008.

Berndt, Ronald M., and Catherine H. Berndt. *The World of the First Australians*. Chicago: University of Chicago Press, 1964.

Bernheimer, Richard. *Wild Men in the Middle Ages*. Cambridge, MA: Harvard University Press, 1952.

Blount, Trevor. "The Graveyard Satire of *Bleak House* in the context of 1850." *The Review of English Studies* XIV 56 (1963).

Bondeson, Jan. *Buried Alive: The Terrifying History of Our Most Primal Fear*. New York: W.W. Norton, 2001.

Bonnefoy, Yves, ed. *Mythologies*. Translated under the direction of Wendy Doniger. Chicago: University of Chicago Press, 1991.

Borrini, Matteo. "An Exorcism Against a Vampire in Venice: An Anthropological and Forensic Study on a Burial of the XVI Century," 2008. Societé d'Anthropologie de Paris.

———. "Il Lazzaretto Nuovo, l'Isola dei Morti." *Archeologia e Beni Culturali IV*, April-December, 2008.

Bostridge, Ian. *Witchcraft and Its Transformation*. New York: Oxford Historical Monographs, Oxford University Press, 1997.

British Admiralty. *Handbook of Bulgaria*. H.M. Stationery Office, 1916.

Brown, David E. *Vampiro: The Vampire Bat in Fact and Fantasy*. Salt Lake City: University of Utah Press, 1999.

Browne, Thomas Sir. "Hydriotaphia, or Urne-Buriall." In *The Major Works*, edited by C. A. Patrides. London: Penguin Books, 1977.

Bryant, Clifton D., ed. *Handbook of Death and Dying*. Los Angeles: SAGE Publications, 2003.

Budge, E. A. Wallis. *Babylonian Life and History*. London: Religious Tract Society, 1884.

Bunson, Matthew. *The Vampire Encyclopedia*. New York: Crown Publishers, 1993.

Burkert, Walter. *Creation of the Sacred: Tracks of Biology in Early Religions*. Cambridge, MA: Harvard University Press, 1996.

———. *Homo Necans: The Anthropology of Ancient Greek Sacrificial Ritual and Myth.* Trans. by Peter Bing. Berkeley: University of California Press, 1983.

Burns, Stu. "'And With All That, Who Believes in Vampires?': Undead Legends and Enlightenment Culture." 33rd Annual European Studies Conference, October 2008.

Burton, Richard F. *Vikram and the Vampyre, or Tales of Hindu Devilry.* London: Longman Green, 1870.

Butler, Declan. "Joan of Arc's Relics Exposed as Forgery." *Nature,* April 5, 2007. http://www.nature.com/nature/journal/v446/n7136/full/446593a.html.

Byrd, Brian F., and Christopher M. Monahan. "Death, Mortuary Ritual, and Natufian Social Structure." *Journal of Anthropological Archaeology* 14 (1995).

Calmet, Augustin Dom. *The Phantom World.* Vol. II. Trans. Henry Christmas. London: Richard Bentley, 1850.

Caron, Richard, Joscelyn Godin, and Wouter J. Hanegraaf, eds. *Esoterisme, Gnoses & Imaginaire Symboliques.* Leuven, The Netherlands: Peeters Publishing, 2001.

Chambers, Robert. *The Book of Days.* Vol. I. London: W & R Chambers, 1883.

Chapman, John. "The Living, the Dead and the Ancestors: Time, Life Cycles and the Mortuary Domain in Later European Prehistory." In *Ritual and Remembrance: Responses to Death in Human Societies,* edited by Jon Davies. England: Sheffield Academic Press, 1994.

Chapman, Robert, Ian Kinnes, and Klaus Randsborg. *The Archaeology of Death.* Cambridge: Cambridge University Press, 1981.

Clausen, J. Earl. "These Plantations." *Greater Providence Evening Bulletin,* December 23, 1936, 21.

Clébert, Jean-Paul. *The Gypsies.* London: Vista Books, 1963.

Clendening, Logan. *Source Book of Medical History.* New York: Dover Publications, 1960.

Clery, E. J. *The Rise of Supernatural Fiction 1762–1800.* Cambridge: Cambridge University Press, 1999.

Clery, E. J., and Robert Miles. *Gothic Documents: A Sourcebook 1700-1820.* Manchester: Manchester University Press, 2000.

Clute, John, and Nicholls, Peter. *The Encyclopedia of Science Fiction.* New York: St. Martin's Griffin, 1993.

Cummins, Joseph. *Cannibals: Shocking True Tales of the Last Taboo on Land and at Sea.* Guildford, CT: Lyons Press, 2005.

Dallapiccola, Anna L. *Dictionary of Hindu Lore and Legend.* London: Thames and Hudson, 2002.

D'Arch Smith, Timothy. *The Books of the Beast: Essays on Aleister Crowley, Montague Summers, and Others.* Oxford: Mandrake, 1987.

D'Argens, Marquis. *The Jewish Spy.* Vol. IV. London: A. Millar; J. Rivington; R. Baldwin; W. Johnston; A. Shuckburgh, 1746.

Darling, J. Andrew. "Mass Inhumation and the Execution of Witches in the American Southwest." *American Anthropologist* 100, no. 3 (1999).

Davenport, R. A. *Sketches of Imposture, Deception, and Credulity.* Philadelphia: G. B. Zieber, 1845.

Dawkins, J. M. "The Modern Carnival in Thrace and the Cult of Dionysus." *The Journal of Hellenic Studies,* Vol. 26, (1906).

Day, Peter, ed. *Vampires: Myths and Metaphors of Enduring Evil.* New York: Rodopi Press, 2006.

De Windt, Harry. *Through Savage Europe.* Philadelphia: J.P. Lippincott, 1907.

Dickens, Charles. *Bleak House.* A Norton Critical Edition, edited by George Ford and Sylvère Monod. New York: W.W. Norton, 1977.

Dorman, Rushton M. *The Origin of Primitive Superstitions: And Their Development into the Worship of Spirits and the Doctrine of Spiritual Agency among the Aborigines of America.* Philadelphia: J.B. Lippincott, 1881.

Douglas, Drake. *Horrors!* Woodstock, NY: Overlook Press, 1989.

Dubos, Rene, and Jean Dubos. *The White Plague: Tuberculosis, Man and Society*. Boston: Little, Brown, 1952.

Duffy, Eamon. *The Stripping of the Altars: Traditional Religion in England, 1400–1580*. New Haven: Yale University Press, 1992.

Dundes, Alan, ed. *The Vampire: A Casebook*. Madison: University of Wisconsin Press, 1998.

Echenberg, Myron J. *Plague Ports*. New York: NYU Press, 2007.

Eliade, Mircea. *Zalmoxis: The Vanishing God*, translated by Willard R. Trask. Chicago: University of Chicago Press, 1972.

Ellis, Markman. *The History of Gothic Fiction*. Edinburgh: Edinburgh University Press, 2000.

Elwell, Walter A., and Philip Wesley Comfort. *The Tyndale Bible Dictionary*. Carol Stream, IL: Tyndale House Publishers, 2001.

Emmons, Charles F. "Ghosts: the Dead Among Us." In *Handbook of Death and Dying*, edited by Clifton D. Bryant, 98–100. Los Angeles: SAGE Publications, 2003.

Enright, D. J. *The Oxford Book of Death*. Oxford: Oxford University Press, 1983.

Faison, Seth. "Tibetans and Vultures Keep Ancient Burial Rite." *New York Times*, July 3, 1999. http://www.nytimes.com/1999/07/03/world/lirong-journal-tibetans-and-vultures-keep-ancient-burial-rite.html?sec=&spon=&pagewanted=all.

Fernandez-Jalvo, Yolanda, J. Carlos Diez, Isabel Caceres, and Jordi Rosell. "Human Cannibalism in the Early Pleistocene of Europe." *Journal of Human Evolution* 37 (1999).

Florescu, Radu R., and Raymond, T. McNally. *Dracula: Prince of Many Faces*. New York: Little, Brown, 1989.

Fol, Alexander, and Ivan Marazov. *Thrace and the Thracians*. New York: St. Martin's Press, 1977.

Fowler, William Warde. *The Roman Festivals of the Period of the Republic*. London: Macmillan, 1899.

Fraser, Angus. *The Gypsies (The Peoples of Europe)*. London: Wiley-Blackwell, 1995.

Frazer, James George, Sir. *The Fear of the Dead in Primitive Religion*. Cambridge: Cambridge University Press, 1933.

———. *Folklore in the Old Testament*. New York: MacMillan, 1923.

———. *The Golden Bough: A New Abridgement*, ed. Robert Fraser. Oxford: Oxford University Press, 1994.

Freeman-Mitford, Algernon Bertram (Lord Redesdale). *Tales of Old Japan*. London: MacMillan, 1908.

French, Christopher C. "Factors Underlying Belief in the Paranormal: Do Sheep and Goats Think Differently?" *The Psychologist*, July 1992.

Freud, Sigmund. *Totem and Taboo*. New York: W.W. Norton, 1950.

Frye, Northrop. *Fearful Symmetry: A Study of William Blake*. Princeton: Princeton University Press, 1947.

Gamble, Clive. *The Palaeolithic Societies of Europe*. Cambridge: Cambridge University Press, 1999.

Gargett, Robert H. "Grave Shortcomings: The Evidence for Neandertal Burial." *Current Anthropology* 30, no. 2 (April 1989).

———. "Middle Paleolithic Burial Is Not a Dead Issue." *Journal of Human Evolution* 37 (1999).

Garnett, Lucy M. J. *Balkan Home-Life*, London: Methuen, 1917.

Gavazzi, Milovan. "The Dug-Out Coffin in Central Bosnia." *Man* 53 (September 1953).

Gimbutas, Marija. *The Slavs*. New York: Praeger Publishers, 1971.

Glen, Heather. *Charlotte Bronte: The Imagination in History*. Oxford: Oxford University Press, 2004.

Gogol, Nikolai. *Collected Tales*, trans. by Richard Pevear and Larissa Volokhonsky. New York: Vintage, 1999.

Gomez-Alonso, Juan. "Rabies: A Possible Explanation for the Vampire Legend." *Neurology* 51, American Academy of Neurology, September 1998.

Graves, Robert, and Raphael Patai. *The Hebrew Myths: The Book of Genesis.* Manchester, England: Carcanet Press Ltd, 2004.

Green, Miranda. "Humans as Ritual Victims in the Later Prehistory of Western Europe." *Oxford Journal of Archaeology* 17, no. 2 (1998).

Green, Miranda Aldhouse. *Dying for the Gods: Human Sacrifice in Iron Age and Roman Europe.* Gloucestershire, England: Tempus Publishing, 2001.

Green, Miranda J. *Dictionary of Celtic Myth and Legend.* New York: Thames and Hudson, 1992.

Grene, David, trans. *Herodotus: The History.* Chicago: University of Chicago Press, 2001.

Grimm, Jacob. *Teutonic Mythology,* trans. by James Steven Stallybrass. New York: Dover Publications, 1966.

Hadziselimovic, Omer. "Pre-1914 Balkans." In *Literature of Travel and Exploration: An Encyclopedia.* London: Routledge, 2003.

Halford, Henry Sir. *An Account of What Appeared on Opening the Coffin of King Charles the First.* London: Nichols, Son, 1813.

Hall, A. Rupert. *Henry More and the Scientific Revolution.* Cambridge: Cambridge University Press, 1990.

Hallcox, Jarrett, and Amy Welch. *Bodies We've Buried: Inside the National Forensic Academy.* New York: Berkley Books, 2006.

Hampl, Jeffery S., Dr., and William S. Hampel. "Pellagra and the Origin of a Myth." *Journal of the Royal Society of Medicine* 90 (November 1997): 636–38.

Harleian Miscellany. Volume XI. London: Robert Dutton, 1810.

Harris, James Rendel. *The Cult of the Heavenly Twins.* Cambridge: Cambridge University Press, 1906.

Hastings, James A. *Encyclopedia of Religion and Ethics.* Vol. 12. New York: Charles Scribner's Sons, 1922.

Hayes, Stephen. "Christian Responses to Witchcraft and Sorcery." *Missionalia* 23, no. 3 (November 1995): 339–54.

Hearn, Lafcadio. *In Ghostly Japan.* Boston: Little, Brown, 1899.

———. *Two Years in the French West Indies.* New York: Harper and Brothers, 1890.

Heiland, Donna. *Gothic and Gender: An Introduction.* London: Wiley-Blackwell, 2004.

Helmold of Bosau. *Chronicle of the Slavs.* New York: Octagon Books, 1966.

Hersey, George. *The Lost Meaning of Classical Architecture: Speculations on Ornament from Vitruvius to Venturi.* Cambridge: MIT Press, 1988.

Hill, Douglas, and Pat Williams. *The Supernatural.* London: Aldus Books, 1965.

Hoddinott, Ralph F. *The Thracians.* London: Thames and Hudson, 1981.

Hoobler, Dorothy, and Thomas Hoobler. *The Monsters: Mary Shelley and the Curse of Frankenstein.* New York: Little, Brown, 2006.

Howarth, Sir Henry H. "The Head of Oliver Cromwell." *The Archaeological Journal* 68 (1911): 233–57.

Hughes, James Pennethorne. *Witchcraft.* London: Pelican Books, 1965.

Hupchick, Dennis P., and Harold E. Cox. *The Palgrave Concise Historical Atlas of the Balkans.* New York: Palgrave, 2001.

———. *The Palgrave Concise Historical Atlas of Eastern Europe.* New York: Palgrave, 2001.

Ince, Alison J. "Sexual Aberrations in *Dracula.*" Unpublished paper, University of North Carolina, 1996.

Introvigne, Massimo. "Antoine Faivre: Father of Contemporary Vampire Studies." In *Esoterisme, Gnoses & Imaginaire Symboliques,* edited by Caron et al. Leuven, The Netherlands: Peeters Publishing, 2001.

James, M. R. *Collected Ghost Stories.* Hertfordshire, England: Wordsworth Editions, 1992.

Janusosis, Michael. "Our Own Vampire, Exeter's Mercy Brown, Gets Her Revenge in New Film." *Providence Journal,* July 17, 2009.

Jevons, Frank Byron. *An Introduction to the History of Religion.* London: Methuen, 1902.

Kabdebo, Thomas. "Pre-World War II Eastern Europe." In *Literature of Travel and Exploration: An Encyclopedia.* London: Routledge, 2003.

Kaltenmark, Maxime. "Chinese Demons." In *Mythologies,* edited by Yves Bonnefoy. Translated under the direction of Wendy Doniger. Chicago: University of Chicago Press, 1991.

Kann, Robert A., and Zdenek V. David. *The Peoples of the Eastern Hapsburg Lands 1526-1918.* Vol. VI: *A History of East Central Europe,* edited by Peter F. Sugar and Donald W. Treadgold. Seattle: University of Washington Press, 1984.

Kaul, H. K. *Travellers' India: An Anthology.* Delhi: Oxford University Press, 1979.

Kelly, Christopher, and Eve Grace, eds. *The Collected Writings of Jean-Jacques Rousseau,* Hanover, NH: University Press of New England, 2001.

Keyworth, G. David. "Was the Vampire of the Eighteenth Century a Unique Type of Undead-corpse?" *Folklore* (December 2006).

Kingslake, A. W. *Eothen: Traces of Travel Brought Home from the East,* 1844.

Kittredge, George Lyman. *A Study of Gawain and the Green Knight.* Cambridge: Harvard University Press, 1916.

Klinger, Leslie S. *The New Annotated Dracula.* New York: W.W. Norton, 2008.

Kohn, George C. *Encyclopedia of Plague and Pestilence,* New York: Facts on File, 1995.

Kostova, Elizabeth. *The Historian.* New York: Little, Brown, 2005.

Krafft-Ebing, Richard von. *Psychopathia Sexualis,* trans. by F. J. Rebman. New York: Rebman, 1903.

La Barre, Weston. *The Ghost Dance: Origins of Religion.* New York: Dell, 1978.

Lawson, John Cuthbert. *Modern Greek Folklore and Ancient Greek Religion: A Study in Survivals.* Cambridge: Cambridge University Press, 1910.

Leach, Maria, ed. *Funk & Wagnalls Standard Dictionary of Folklore, Mythology, and Legend.* New York: Harper and Row, 1949.

Leatherdale, Clive. *The Origins of Dracula: The Background to Bram Stoker's Gothic Masterpiece.* London: William Kimber, 1987.

Lincoln, Bruce. "Death and Resurrection in Indo-European Thought." *Journal of Indo-European Studies* 5 (1977).

———. "The Living Dead: Of Outlaws and Others." Review of Hans-Peter Hasenfratz's *Die Toten Lebenden.* In *History of Religions* 23, no. 4 (May 1984).

Lochtefeld, James G., Dr. *The Illustrated Encyclopedia of Hinduism.* Vol. 1. New York: Rosen Publishing Group, 2002.

Longworth, Philip. *The Rise and Fall of Venice.* London: Constable, 1974.

Lukacs, John. *Budapest 1900.* New York: Grove Press, 1988.

Mallory, J. P. *In Search of the Indo-Europeans: Language, Archaeology, and Myth.* London: Thames and Hudson, 1989.

Mamunes, George. "*So Has a Daisy Vanished": Emily Dickinson and Tuberculosis.* Jefferson, NC: McFarland, 2007.

Manchester, Sean. *The Highgate Vampire.* London: Gothic Press, 1991.

Mann, Jennifer. "Marshfield's 'Vampire Killer' Up for Parole," *MetroWest Daily News*, August 3, 2009. http://www.metrowestdailynews.com/state/x1911311076/Marshfields-vampire-killer-up-for-parole.

Marchini, Nelli-Elena Vanzan. "Il Lazaretto Nuovo fra Venezia e il Mediterraneo." In *Isola del Lazaretto Nuovo*, ed. Gerolamo Fazzini, 2004.

Marigny, Jean. *Vampires: The World of the Undead.* London: Thames and Hudson, 1994.

Marks, Geoffrey, and William K. Beatty. *Epidemics.* New York: Charles Scribner's Sons, 1976.

Martin, Stella, and Denis Walls. *In Malaysia.* Buckinghamshire, England: Bradt Publications, 1986.

McClelland, Bruce A. *Slayers and Their Vampires.* Ann Arbor: University of Michigan Press, 2006.

McDowell, Bart. *Gypsies: Wanderers of the World.* Washington, D.C.: National Geographic Society, 1970.

McNally, Raymond T., and Radu Florescu. *In Search of Dracula: The History of Dracula and Vampires.* Boston: Houghton Mifflin, 1994.

McNeil, Donald G., Jr. "Finding a Scapegoat When Epidemics Strike." *New York Times*, August 31, 2009.

McNeill, William H. *Plagues and Peoples.* New York: Anchor Press/Doubleday, 1976.

———. *Venice: The Hinge of Europe 1081–1797.* Chicago: University of Chicago Press, 1974.

Melton, J. Gordon. *The Vampire Book.* Canton, MI: Visible Ink Press, 1999.

Metcalf, Peter, and Richard Huntington. *Celebrations of Death: The Anthropology of Mortuary Ritual.* Cambridge: Cambridge University Press, 1991.

Miller, Elizabeth, ed. *Bram Stoker's Dracula: A Documentary Journey into Vampire Country and the Dracula Phenomenon.* New York: Pegasus Books, 2009.

Minta, Stephen. "Albania." In *Literature of Travel and Exploration: An Encylcopedia.* London: Routledge, 2003.

The Mirror of Literature, Amusement, and Instruction. Vol. 42 (1843).

Modi, Jivanji Jamshedji. "The Funeral Ceremonies of the Parsees." *Journal of the Anthropological Society of Bombay,* 1928. http://www.avesta.org/ritual/funeral.htm.

Montague, Mary Wortley. *The Letters of M.W. Montague 1716-18.* Vol. I. London: John Sharpe, 1820.

More, Henry. *An Antidote Against Atheism: An Appeal to the Naturall Faculties of the Minde of Man, Whether There Be Not a God.* London: J. Flesher, 1655.

Morley, John. *Rousseau.* London: Chapman and Hall, 1873.

Mormando, Franco, and Thomas Worcester, eds. *Piety and Plague: From Byzantium to the Baroque.* Kirksville, MO: Truman State University Press, 2007.

Morris, Jan. *The Venetian Empire.* New York: Harcourt Brace Jovanovich, 1980.

Morrison, Robert, and Chris Baldick, eds. *The Vampyre and Other Tales of the Macabre,* Oxford: Oxford University Press, 1997.

Mould, Richard F. *Mould's Medical Anecdotes,* Omnibus Edition. London: Taylor and Francis, 1996.

Murray, Margaret A. *The God of the Witches.* Oxford: Oxford University Press, 1952.

Nandris, Grigore. "The Historical Dracula: The Theme of His Legend." *Comparative Literature Studies* 3, no. 4 (1966).

"New Age for Mungo Man." University of Melbourne News, 2003 (February 19). http://uninews.unimelb.edu.au/news/352/.

Newcomb, Mildred. *The Imagined World of Charles Dickens.* Columbus: Ohio State University Press, 1989.

Newton, Michael. "Written in Blood: A History of Human Sacrifice." *Journal of Psychohistory* 24, no. 2 (Fall 1996).

New York Times. "Voltaire and Rousseau: Their Tombs in the Pantheon Opened and Their Bones Exposed," January 8, 1898. http://query.nytimes.com/mem/archive-free/pdf?_r=1&res=9F02 E3DD1638E433A2575BC0A9679C94699ED7CF.

Norwich, John Julius. *A Traveller's Companion to Venice.* London: Constable, 1990.

Nuzum, Eric. *The Dead Travel Fast: Stalking Vampires from Nosferatu to Count Chocula.* New York: St. Martin's Griffin, 2007.

Oinas, Felix J. "East European Vampires and Dracula." *Journal of Popular Culture* 16 (1982).

———. "Heretics as Vampires and Demons in Russia." *The Slavic and East European Journal* 22, no. 4 (1978).

"On Vampirism." *New Monthly Magazine and Literary Journal* 5 (January–June 1823).

Paine, Lauran. *The Hierarchy of Hell.* New York: Robert Hale, 1972.

Patrides, C. A. *The Cambridge Platonists.* Cambridge: Cambridge University Press, 1980.

Pearson, Mike Parker. "The Powerful Dead: Archaeological Relationships between the Living and the Dead." *Cambridge Archaeological Journal* 3, no. 2 (1993).

Penrose, Valentine. *The Bloody Countess.* London: New English Library, 1972.

Perkowski, Jan Louis. *Vampire Lore: From the Writings of Jan Louis Perkowski.* Bloomington, Indiana: Slavica Publishers, 2006.

Poe, Edgar Allan. *Selected Poetry and Prose,* edited by T. O. Mabbitt. New York: Random House, 1951.

Polunin, Oleg, and Martin Walters. *A Guide to the Vegetation of Britain and Europe.* Oxford: Oxford University Press, 1985.

Pounds, Norman J. G. *Eastern Europe.* Chicago: Aldine Publishing, 1969.

Propp, V. *Morphology of the Folktale,* trans. by Laurence Scott. Austin: University of Texas Press, 1968.

Puhvel, Jaan. *Comparative Mythology.* Baltimore: Johns Hopkins University Press, 1987.

Ramsland, Katherine. *The Science of Vampires.* New York: Berkely Boulevard Books, 2002.

Rees, Brinley. "Cernunnos, the God with the Horns of a Stag." In *Mythologies,* edited by Yves Bonnefoy. Translated under the direction of Wendy Doniger. Chicago: University of Chicago Press, 1991.

Renfrew, Colin. *Archaeology and Language: The Puzzle of Indo-European Origins.* Cambridge: Cambridge University Press, 1987.

Rickels, Laurence A. *The Vampire Lectures.* Minneapolis: University of Minnesota Press, 1999.

Roach, Mary. *Stiff: The Curious Lives of Human Cadavers.* New York: W.W. Norton, 2003.

Rogers, Liam. "Exhuming the Vampire." Originally published in *Samhain,* 1997. http: //www .whitedragon.org.uk/articles/vampire.htm.

Rowdon, Maurice. *The Silver Age of Venice.* New York: Praeger Publishers, 1970.

Ryan, Alan, ed. *The Penguin Book of Vampire Stories.* New York: Penguin Books, 1987.

Schultz, Suzanne M. *Body Snatching: The Robbing of Graves for the Education of Physicians.* Jefferson, NC: McFarland, 1992.

Scidmore, Eliza. *Winter India.* New York: Century, 1903.

Senf, Carol A. *The Vampire in Nineteenth Century English Literature.* Bowling Green, OH: Bowling Green State University Popular Press, 1988.

Sherman, Irwin W. *Twelve Diseases That Changed Our World.* Washington, D.C.: ASM Press, 2007.

Sherratt, Andrew. "Sacred and Profane Substances: The Ritual Use of Narcotics in Later Neolithic Europe." In Sherratt, *Economy and Society in Prehistoric Europe.* Princeton: Princeton University Press, 1997.

Simpson, Jacqueline. *European Mythology.* Library of the World's Myths and Legends, New York: Peter Bedrick Books, 1987.

Skal, David J. *Vampires: Encounters with the Undead*. New York: Black Dog and Leventhal, 2006.

Sledzik, Paul S. "Vampires, the Dead, and Tuberculosis: Folk Interpretations." Manuscript copy.

Sledzik, Paul, and Nicholas Bellatoni. "Bioarcheological and Biocultural Evidence for the New England Vampire Folk Belief." *American Journal of Physical Anthropology* 94 (1994).

Smirnov, Yuri. "Intentional Human Burial: Middle Paleolithic (Last Glaciation) Beginnings." *Journal of World Prehistory* 3, no. 2 (1989).

Snodgrass, Mary Ellen. *World Epidemics*: A Cultural Chronology of Disease from Prehistory to the Era of Sars. Jefferson, North Carolina: McFarland Press, 2003.

Sorensen, Eric. *Possession and Exorcism in the New Testament and Early Christianity*. Tübingen, Germany: Paul Mohr Verlag, 2002.

Speake, Jennifer. *Literature of Travel and Exploration: An Encyclopedia*. London: Routledge, 2003.

Stetson, George R. "The Animistic Vampire in New England." *The American Anthropologist* IX, no. 1 (January 1896).

Steuding, Hermann, Harrington, Karl Pomeroy, and Herbert Cushing Tolman. *Greek and Roman Mythology*. Boston: Leach, Shewell, and Sanborn, 1897.

Stevenson, Joseph. *The Church Historians of England*, Volume IV, Part II. London: Seeleys, 1861.

Steward, Jill. "Central Europe." In *Literature of Travel and Exploration: An Encyclopedia*. London: Routledge, 2003.

Stiles, Robert. *Four Years Under Marse Robert*. New York: Neale Publishing, 1903.

Stoianovich, Traian. *Balkan Worlds: The First and Last Europe*. New York: M.E. Sharp, 1994.

Stoicescu, Nicolae. *Vlad Tepes: Prince of Walachia*. Bucharest: Editura Adademie Republicii Social-iste Romania, 1978.

Stoker, Bram. *Dracula*, edited by Nina Auerbach and David J. Skal. Norton Critical Edition. New York: W.W. Norton, 1997.

Stutley, Margaret, and James Stutley. *Harper's Dictionary of Hinduism: Its Mythology, Folklore, Philosophy, Literature, and History*. New York: Harper and Row, 1977.

Summers, Montague. *The Vampire: His Kith and Kin*. New York: E. P. Dutton, 1929.

————. *The Vampire in Europe*. New York: E.P. Dutton, 1929.

Sunstein, Emily W. *Mary Shelley: Romance and Reality*. Baltimore: Johns Hopkins Press, 1989.

Sutherland, John. *Who Betrays Elizabeth Bennet? Further Puzzles in Classic Fiction*. Oxford: Oxford University Press, 1999.

Taylor, Timothy. *The Buried Soul: How Humans Invented Death*. Boston: Beacon Press, 2002.

————. "The Edible Dead." *British Archaeology* 59 (June 2001).

————. "The Gundestrup Cauldron." *Scientific American* (March 1992).

Thomas, Lewis. *The Lives of a Cell: Notes of a Biology-Watcher*. New York: Viking Press, 1974.

Thompson, R. Lowe. *The History of the Devil: Or the Horned God of the West*. London: Keegan, Paul, Trench, Trubener, 1929.

Trelawny, Edward John. *Recollections of the Last Days of Shelley and Byron*. Boston: Ticknor and Fields, 1858.

Tsaliki, Anastasia. "Vampires Beyond Legend: A Bioarchaeological Approach." In *Proceedings of the XIII European Meeting of the Paleopathology Association, Chieti, Italy, 18-23 Sept. 2000*, edited by M. La Verghetta and L. Capasso, 295–300. Teramo-Italy: Edigrafital S.P.A.

Twitchell, James B. *The Living Dead: A Study of the Vampire in Romantic Literature*. Durham: Duke University Press, 1981.

Tylor, Edward Burnett. *Primitive Culture*: Researches into the Development of Mythology, Philosophy, Religion, Art, and Custom. Volume II. Gordon Press, 1974.

Valkenburg, Samuel Van, and Ellsworth Huntington. *Europe*. New York: John Wiley and Sons, 1935.

Valsecchi, Maria Cristina. "Mass Plague Graves Found on Venice 'Quarantine' Island." National Geographic News, August 29, 2007. http://news.nationalgeographic.com/news/2007/08/070829-venice-plague.html.

Van der Sanden, W.A.B. *Through Nature to Eternity: The Bog Bodies of Northwest Europe,* trans. S. J. Mellor. Amsterdam: Batavian Lion International, 1996.

Varner, Gary R. *Creatures in the Mist.* New York: Algora Publishing, 2007.

———. *The Mythic Forest, the Green Man and the Spirit of Nature: The Re-emergence of the Spirit of Nature from Ancient Times into Modern Society.* New York: Algora Publishing, 2006.

Villa, Paola. "Cannibalism in Prehistoric Europe." *Evolutionary Anthropology* 1, no. 3 (1992).

Voltaire. "Philosophical Dictionary: Vampires." Vol. 14: *Works,* edited by Tobias Smollett. Paris: E. R. Du Mont, 1901.

Voous, Karel H. *Owls of the Northern Hemisphere.* Cambridge: MIT Press, 1988.

Walker, George, Dr. *Gatherings from Grave Yards, Particularly Those of London.* London: Longman, 1839.

Walls, Jerry L. *The Oxford Handbook of Eschatology.* Oxford: Oxford University Press, 2007.

Ware, Timothy. *The Orthodox Church.* London: Penguin Books, 1963.

Watkins, Carl S. *History and the Supernatural in Medieval England.* Cambridge: Cambridge University Press, 2008.

White, Tim D., and Nicholas Toth. "The Question of Ritual Cannibalism at Grotta Guattari." *Current Anthropology* 32, no. 2 (April 1991).

Wilkinson, Josiah Henry. "A Narrative of the Circumstances Concerning the Head of Oliver Cromwell." *The Archaeological Journal* 68 (1911): 233–57.

Williams, Hector. "The Vampire of Lesbos." *Archaeology* (March/April 1994): 22.

Wills, Christopher. *Yellow Fever, Black Goddess: The Coevolution of People and Plagues.* New York: Basic Books, 1997.

Wolff, Larry. *Inventing Eastern Europe: The Map of Civilization on the Mind of the Enlightenment.* Stanford: Stanford University Press, 1994.

Yarbro, Chelsea Quinn. *Hotel Transylvania,* New York: St. Martin's Press, 1978.

Yoffe, Mark Dr., and Joseph Krafczik. *Perun, the God of Thunder.* New York: Peter Lang, 2003.

Yourcenar, Marguerite. *That Mighty Sculptor, Time.* New York: Farrar, Straus and Giroux, 1993.

INDEX